China Briefing, 1992

中國

China Briefing, 1992

edited by
William A. Joseph

Published in cooperation with
The Asia Society

Deborah Field Washburn
Series Editor

中國

Routledge
Taylor & Francis Group
LONDON AND NEW YORK

Cover characters designed by Willow Chang

First publishing 1993 by Westview Press, Inc.

Published 2018 by Routledge
52 Vanderbilt Avenue, New York, NY 10017
2 Park Square, Milton Park, Abingdon, Oxon OX14 4RN

Routledge is an imprint of the Taylor & Francis Group, an informa business

Library of Congress ISSN: 0740-8005

ISBN 13: 978-0-3670-0388-3 (hbk)

ISBN 13: 978-0-367-15375-5 (pbk)

Contents

Preface

Since its inception in the late 1970s, *China Briefing* has earned a deserved reputation as the best in-depth annual review of China, Taiwan, and Hong Kong. As director of The Asia Society's China Council when this publication was launched, I am especially proud to see its growing and enduring impact.

China Briefing, 1992 is one of the very best volumes in this distinguished history. Its authors have written in a crisp, substantive, and engaging style. As a result, this book is an important starting point for anyone, including specialists, seeking a capsule presentation of recent developments in China.

Such a review is especially needed in the early 1990s, now 20 years after the Sino-American detente, when American outlooks on China are deeply interlaced with suspicion. Tiananmen continues to cast a long shadow, though one now sees somewhat heightened U.S. interest in China's continued and renewed economic momentum. How we assess—and how we engage—the leaders of the one-quarter of humankind in China is central to the future stability and dynamism of the Asia-Pacific region.

Many of this year's authors reflect a rising, though still cautious, optimism about the People's Republic of China and its relations with Hong Kong and Taiwan. Nineteen ninety-two has been a year of powerful recommitment to economic modernization, spearheaded by China's paramount octogenarian, Deng Xiaoping. The surge of growth in coastal South China, the rapid increase in foreign investment, and the recently unleashed capital markets are at the heart of this story.

The interweave of politics and economics is a subject of serious analysis and conjecture in *China Briefing, 1992,* published on the eve of the 14th Congress of the Chinese Communist Party. Who succeeds and what policies dominate are linked issues that will shape China's future for the rest of the century. Who dies, and in what order deaths occur, is important to the succession process now unfolding in Beijing. No one, not even those in the Forbidden City, knows precisely how these events will play out, but our authors offer a well-articulated array of scenarios.

But what are the broader ripple effects of succession politics and modernization economics? How does China cope with a post–cold war era in which the Soviet Union, which evolved from heroic to demonic proportions during the history of the PRC, no longer exists? How will China manage its prickly relationships with Japan (which now seem to be improving), with the United States (which have descended to an all-time low over the past two decades), and with the rest of Asia (where much hatchet-burying has occurred)? And what will be the impact of this evolution on China itself—on the arts and film, on health care, on the environment?

All these issues will unfold over many years ahead. *China Briefing, 1992* does not seek to provide long-term, conclusive answers, but we think that—thanks to editor William A. Joseph and the fine team of authors he has assembled—it addresses questions over the short and medium term in a timely, informative, and useful way.

Robert B. Oxnam
President
The Asia Society

September 21, 1992

CHINA
National capital
0 100 200 300 400 Miles
RUSSIA
KAZAKHSTAN
MONGOLIA
UZBEKISTAN
KYRGYZSTAN
TAJIKISTAN
AFGHANISTAN
PAKISTAN
INDIA
NEPAL
BHUTAN
BANGLADESH
MYANMAR
THAILAND
LAOS
VIETNAM
NORTH KOREA
SOUTH KOREA
JAPAN
TAIWAN
PHILIPPINES
Xinjiang Uygur
Tibet
Qinghai
Gansu
Inner Mongolia
Ningxia Hui
Shaanxi
Shanxi
Sichuan
Yunnan
Guizhou
Guangxi Zhuang
Guangdong
Hunan
Hubei
Henan
Hebei
Beijing Municipality
Beijing
Tianjin Municipality
Shandong
Jiangsu
Anhui
Shanghai Municipality
Zhejiang
Jiangxi
Fujian
Liaoning
Jilin
Heilongjiang
Hainan
Hong Kong (UK)
Macao (Portugal)
Zhu (Pearl)
Huang
(Yellow)
Chang Jiang
(Yangtze)
Sea of Japan
Yellow Sea
East China Sea
Philippine Sea

Introduction: Deng's Gamble

William A. Joseph

The 1992 Summer Olympics in Barcelona were a time of international triumph and national pride for the People's Republic of China (PRC). China won a total of 54 medals—16 gold, 22 silver, and 16 bronze—to finish fourth in the overall medal count, a remarkable improvement over the 28 medals (including only 5 gold) captured in the 1988 Seoul Olympics. However, the athletic achievements at Barcelona and the accolades accorded the PRC's medal winners on their return to Beijing could not dispel the clouds of uncertainty that hang over China's future. A seemingly calm political exterior is enforced by an only slightly relaxed post-Tiananmen repression, and a recent resurgence of economic reform is threatened by deep factional divisions and a looming succession crisis. As China approaches a watershed generational change in political leadership, seething tensions and unresolved contradictions are likely to be the most telling legacies bequeathed by the last of the veteran revolutionaries to their immediate successors.

China Briefing, 1992 surveys recent developments in China's politics, economics, and foreign relations and provides longer-term analyses of the legal system, public health, and filmmaking in the PRC. The chapters in this volume help to further understanding of what has happened in China in the recent past; and by probing some of the most trenchant contradictions now present in Chinese society, they also serve as a guide to making sense of future events in China as they unfold.

One future that the leadership of the Chinese Communist Party (CCP) certainly hopes to avoid is the fate that befell the Soviet Union in late 1991. Tony Saich's chapter examines the impact of the Soviet collapse on the PRC's domestic politics and policies, while John Garver appraises the implications for China's international relations of the disintegration of Moscow's empire.

Although there were sharply differing perspectives within the CCP on how to interpret events in the Soviet Union, Deng Xiaoping seems to have concluded that Mikhail Gorbachev failed on both the economic and political fronts: the Soviet leader moved too slowly in implementing fundamental changes in the economy and too quickly in liberalizing the political system. This perspective on the Soviet collapse has reassured Deng and other top leaders that they did the right thing in suppressing the pro-democracy demonstrations in June 1989, but it has also propelled Deng to undertake a political offensive to maintain the economic vibrancy that is one of the central reasons the CCP has been able to weather the global storm that has swept away most other Marxist-Leninist regimes in the last three years. Deng's big gamble is that continued economic growth will not only restore the Tiananmen-tarnished legitimacy of the CCP, but also siphon off political discontent as the nation and its people go about the business of getting rich.

Tony Saich details the stunning revival of the momentum toward economic reform that began with Deng Xiaoping's inspection tour in early 1992 of the boom areas of southern China, including the free-wheeling Shenzhen Special Economic Zone that has often been the target of hard-line critics of market-oriented development policies. Deng's speeches during the tour, and the party documents and media commentaries that subsequently publicized his remarks throughout the country, put the senior leader squarely on the side of faster and bolder reforms and presented a challenge to those in the leadership who have serious misgivings about the ideological and economic effects of continued rapid changes in the direction of a market economy.

The impetus given to reform by Deng's travels has exacerbated the factionalism Saich says has sundered the coalition of elderly party leaders and their minions that formed around common opposition to the 1989 democracy movement. Factional maneuvering was intensified by efforts to influence policy directives and personnel changes to be adopted at the 14th Party Congress scheduled for October 1992; Deng and the other leaders realized that the party congress would set the tone for the next stage of China's development and would very likely be the last national party gathering dominated by the behind-the-scenes power of the aged patriarchs. Their anxiety to put their stamp on China's future could only have been heightened by the deaths in 1992 of a number of senior figures, most notably former PRC president Li Xiannian. The momentum had clearly shifted towards reenergized reform in mid-1992; but any excess—be it a return of hyperinflation or public displays of citizen discontent—produced by the robust growth or new policy initiatives could be seized upon as reasons to slow the pace of change by factions skeptical of Deng's plan to use capitalism to save socialism in China.

Deng's call for a renewed commitment to reform and for opening the PRC to the outside world will likely dominate the party's priorities after the 14th Congress and bodes well for China's economic prospects; but, as Saich points out, Deng "has drawn the line at political reform" and made it abundantly clear that there will be no meaningful steps in the direction of democratization. Indeed, the factional divisions that pervade the party leadership revolve primarily around *economic* issues such as the speed and extent of market reform and the terms of China's participation in the international economy. For the current leadership, political change is a nonissue: whatever principles and policy preferences may separate market reformers, orthodox planners, neoconservatives, and proto-Maoists, all CCP factions agree that the party's "leading role" (i. e., its dictatorship over state and society) is not to be questioned.

Saich highlights the numerous problems that reflect the CCP's intractable refusal to acknowledge the need for fundamental political change: the continued domination of individuals and personal relationships over stable institutions and regularized procedures; the inability to find less conflictual means for handling policy disputes within the leadership; the denial of a legitimate public voice to the very social forces created by the country's new prosperity; and the growing assertiveness of provinces and localities against what they see as the heavy hand of the central government.

These political problems—particularly their implications for the succession sweepstakes that will inevitably follow from the deaths of Deng Xiaoping and the other octogenarian leaders—cast a pall of potential political instability over what Gary Jefferson portrays in his chapter as "a rosy picture of the current state of the Chinese economy and the prospects for continued reform." Jefferson analyzes the impressive recent growth rates in various sectors of China's economy and spotlights the wide gamut of renewed reform initiatives that range from price rationalization to trade liberalization. He examines in some detail the economic effects of industrial reforms in the state sector and the spread of financial markets in the form of stock exchanges, foreign currency trading centers, and commodities futures.

While China is castigated for lack of progress in political reform, its record of economic development in the 1980s is being cited as a model for the transition from central planning to market economy in Eastern Europe and the former Soviet Union, as well as for the deregulation of state-dominated economies of the Third World. Jefferson draws on three recent papers by economists to discuss some of the key "lessons from China's reform experience." Some of these lessons are positive, such as the importance of establishing a fast-growth "leading sector" (e.g., China's household-based agriculture), while others are negative, such as the observation that "flawed institutions and bad policy" impede reform (e.g., the PRC's ineffective fiscal system); all are seen as applicable to other countries that face similar challenges in de-Stalinizing or modernizing their economies.

It is rather ironic that Deng's capitalist-like reform policies are now being hailed as a model for other nations to emulate, much as were the very contrary radical Maoist developmental policies of the 1960s. It is also ironic that for all their differences, Deng Xiaoping and Mao Zedong seem to have made many of the same mistakes in undermining their nation's political development. Mao's political errors did much to nullify China's economic progress during his reign. Deng's reforms could also falter if he and his successors continue to insist that economic revitalization can be separated from political change. As Jefferson notes, problems such as inflation, labor-force growth and restiveness, and ecological quandaries may disrupt the path of economic reform in China, but overshadowing all these concerns is the mounting contradiction between "China's inexorable drive toward economic modernization and the hesitant reform of its political system."

John Garver's chapter on the PRC's foreign relations looks at the impact of the collapse of the Soviet Union on China's view of the world and its international behavior. The CCP certainly felt no ideological affinity with Mikhail Gorbachev, and it blames his "betrayal of the proletariat" for fatally weakening communism in Eastern Europe and the Soviet Union. But the emergence of a noncommunist, Western-oriented Russia under Boris Yeltsin was an even more unpalatable turn of events in the eyes of Chinese leaders. As Garver points out, the decline of Soviet power as a counterweight to the United States in world affairs that began under Gorbachev was a serious disruption of what China saw as a favorable trend toward a multipolar global order. Beijing's "strategic nightmare" is that an anti-China alliance composed of the West, Russia, and Japan will form to isolate the PRC in an attempt to exterminate one of the few remaining bastions of Marxism-Leninism.

Much of China's recent foreign policy as described by Garver has been geared to responding to the new realities of the post–cold war international situation and has been largely motivated by efforts to counter what Beijing sees as the potential dangers of U.S. global dominance. Chinese policy in the Persian Gulf War of 1991 was "reasonably cooperative" with the United States and the United Nations in order to gain some post-Tiananmen international legitimacy; but the PRC's leaders were also concerned that the defeat of Iraq by an overwhelming display of U.S. military prowess would further the movement toward a "Pax Americana" in which Washington would be able to impose its will on the world. China acted quickly to make the best of the "fundamental geopolitical gain" it derived from the disintegration of the Soviet empire in Central Asia. The PRC has also sought to develop an "*entente cordiale*" with Japan that would promote cooperation between the two nations on "peace, stability, and economic development in Asia"; the effort to promote the special relationship between China and Japan is based in part on Beijing's perceptions of growing tensions between Japan and the United States. China has also been supportive of Western European integration, again because of the tempering effect a strong "European pole" would have on the extension of American power.

Chinese foreign policy in the early 1990s manifests a fundamental contradiction similar to that which plagues the country's domestic reform initiatives: the desire to reap the benefits of change and openness, together with fear of the consequences of change and openness. Deng Xiaoping has again proclaimed the necessity for China to open its doors even wider to the outside world if it is to achieve its development objectives; and recent steps toward trade liberalization and the expansion of foreign investment opportunities attest to the fact that China's open policy is being reinvigorated. But China's worldview is still animated by pervasive fears of subversion from foreign influences and almost paranoid apprehensions about anti-China plots and coalitions. As Garver demonstrates, talk of intrigues by the United States to subvert communism in China by gradual cultural and economic infiltration (so-called peaceful evolution) may have subsided as Deng seeks to enlist international support for China's modernization; but Chinese foreign policy retains a "fundamentally anti-U.S. orientation" that is part of a deep ambivalence about the potential impact that fuller involvement in the global community may have on China.

Changes in China's legal system, as described in the chapter by Margaret Woo, have reflected the ebb and flow of reform in post-Mao China. Following the disruptions of the Cultural Revolution, a major revamping of the judiciary was launched, primarily owing to the leadership's "recognition that a coherent legal system was critical for economic development" and the desire to provide some institutional safeguards against the political excesses of the Maoist era. Limited, though still significant, progress in that direction was short-circuited by the emphasis on order and stability that followed the June 1989 crackdown. The subsequent use of Chinese courts to punish political activists led to an outpouring of international criticism of China's human rights record. Most recently, there have been signs of a "renewed interest in legal reform" that are obviously an outgrowth of Deng's push for faster economic change and represent what Woo describes as "the latest turn in the winding road of legal reform" in China.

Woo's description of the workings of the legal system of the PRC presents a bifurcated picture of the role of law in contemporary China. On the one hand, the courts often provide effective redress for the grievances of ordinary citizens and sometimes do work to check abuses of power by officials; in such cases, there is, indeed, "a convergence of goals between the state and the Chinese people." On the other hand, judicial autonomy is clearly circumscribed by party policy and "political cases . . . remain beyond the protection of due process." Woo's conclusion that the "law and legal institutions are still primarily an instrument of the Chinese Communist Party state" is yet another indication that reform—be it economic, political, or legal—will be pursued only on terms defined by the CCP and will be sanctioned only if it is judged to present no threat to party control.

Public health in China has long been a subject of considerable international interest. As Gail Henderson's chapter illustrates, for the first half of this century attention was focused on the deplorable health conditions for the vast majority of Chinese; in the 1960s and 1970s the world marveled at the advances made in improving health care, while more recently, questions have been raised about the impact of economic reform on China's public health system.

Henderson's discussion of the tremendous gains made in health care in China during Mao's rule reminds us that the record of that time—at least in terms of social welfare—is not as unrelievedly bleak as some Chinese and Western commentators would suggest. The fact that the PRC was able to attain health standards (e.g., higher life expectancy, lower infant mortality) well above those of countries at similar levels of economic development was the result of "a series of economic, educational, and organizational policies which created a system that defined health as part of the broader economic and social objectives of the regime." And though much of Deng Xiaoping's reform program has been directed at negating the collectivist institutions and mindset of the Maoist era, China's prospects for modernization are immensely improved by "the rural health-care infrastructure that was the foundation of the Maoist model of primary care [and] is still functioning."

China's health care in the reform period presents "complex, contradictory images," according to Henderson. There have been some worrisome trends, such as increasing inequalities in access to health care, attributable to the marketization and privatization of some aspects of medical services. However, China "continues to produce impressive results in public health." Rather than the necessity to cope with the afflictions of poverty that characterize most of the Third World, China's greatest health challenges are to confront the diseases of prosperity (such as the consequences of a high-fat diet) and "to avoid the health-care dilemmas experienced by more-developed nations," including cost-control of an increasingly capital-intensive medical profession. These are serious challenges for any country, and China's ability to deal with them successfully will depend in large measure on whether its leadership continues to accord a high priority to public health or lets it slip off the national agenda in favor of more materially profitable pursuits.

The shifting fortunes of the Chinese film industry are, according to Paul Clark's analysis, a barometer for gauging "the cultural climate, political control, and level of economic development" in China. From its emergence as a modern art form in the 1920s, Chinese cinema has often been a medium for political statements and social commentary by filmmakers, either on their own behalf or as an instrument of state indoctrination. The height of the politicization of Chinese film came during the Cultural Revolution, when the radical culture czars under Jiang Qing initially limited cinematic fare to a literal handful of ideologically correct productions. The post-Mao reforms ushered in a period of innovation and experimentation in Chinese film as directors found themselves much freer to explore new artistic styles and probe previously forbidden subjects such as rural "backwardness." The Tiananmen crackdown led to renewed controls on filmmakers as the party leadership once again became sensitive to the potential of cultural media to be used in various ways to question the status quo. Nevertheless, PRC filmmakers are managing "to produce works of considerable merit, despite tight ideological oversight," as witnessed by the international acclaim accorded Chinese films such as *Ju Dou* and *Raise the Red Lantern*. The current situation in Chinese cinema reflects an uneasy tension between a growing core of dynamic directors, producers, and actors and the dogma-bound bureaucrats who watch their every move.

Clark's chapter points once again to one of the most troubling aspects of the current situation in China: like Chinese rulers through the ages—from the emperors and the mandarins, through Sun Yatsen and Chiang Kai-shek, to Mao Zedong—the party leadership in the early 1990s still conceives of its relationship to the Chinese people as a paternalistic one. True, far more scope is now permitted for artistic creativity than during the Maoist years, and audiences can choose from a much richer repertoire of cultural diversions. But the CCP holds fast to its claim to be the ultimate arbiter of what the "masses" need in terms of culture and to have the right to dictate to intellectuals and artists how that need should be met.

Will Deng's gamble pay off? Will the CCP be able to use prosperity as a substitute for democracy? In the short run, perhaps: if economic reform proceeds with no catastrophic setbacks, it may well mitigate some of the pressure for political change. But, in the longer run, this kind of trade-off is unlikely to prove tenable.

The Chinese Communist Party likes to tout the example of the Newly Industrializing Countries of East Asia to bolster the argument that economic progress requires political stability that can only be assured by authoritarian rule. But the recent experiences of South Korea and Taiwan also suggest that modernization breeds increasing and irresistible pressures for democratization. Thus far, China's leaders have shown that their only response to such pressures is repression. It remains to be seen whether the next generation of powerholders in Beijing will have a different and more productive perspective on how to manage the complex relationship between economic development and political change that lies at the heart of China's contemporary dilemma.

1
Peaceful Evolution with Chinese Characteristics

Tony Saich

The year 1992 witnessed yet another dramatic shift in the publicly stated policy of the Chinese Communist Party (CCP). This shift followed a trip to South China early in the year by China's senior patriarch, Deng Xiaoping. What he observed there convinced him that the only way for the People's Republic of China (PRC) to move forward was to push ahead rapidly with economic reform. Furthermore, he concluded that "leftist" opposition to market reforms was a greater danger to China's development than the formerly denounced "rightist" dangers like "bourgeois liberalization." In the Shenzhen Special Economic Zone (SEZ), Deng called for bold experimentation in the economic sphere and even suggested that those who stood in the way of reform be asked to step down.

This shift in public policy did not go uncontested, and influential opposition remains, led by a decreasing band of Deng's octogenarian colleagues and their younger clients. In particular, Chen Yun, head of the Central Advisory Commission, and Li Xiannian, head of the Chinese People's Political Consultative Conference, tried their best to prevent Deng's ideas from being transmitted through the party and governmental apparatus. When Deng's policy directive could no longer be ignored, his opponents resorted to a second tactic—paying lip service to it while seeking to water down the content or deflect the main thrust of the policy.

If Deng Xiaoping is successful in keeping his reform wagon on the road, the next stage will certainly prove more difficult than the first phase of reform, which was completed during the 1980s. Those who suffer as factories close and housing rents rise will need a clear explanation of why today's suffering will offer a better opportunity for sound economic health over the long term. Unfortunately, this message is one that China's population has listened to frequently over the last 40 years, and the credibility gap is growing. China will have to find a new, skillful leadership with sufficient imagination to guide it through the next phase of political and economic development. At present, it is difficult to see who those leaders might be. Most of the successor generation has to keep a constant eye on its elderly puppet masters and thus finds it difficult to develop an independent policy position and power base.

The gap between party rhetoric and economic policy on the one hand and social practice on the other has grown greatly since the events of 1989. To a large degree, Deng's recent comments merely reflect the current situation in China, where realities in many regions have begun to diverge substantially from policy statements at the center. Deng seems to have recognized the danger that the impressive economic developments in many provinces and localities could leave the center behind while it engages in increasingly irrelevant ideological polemics.

The campaigns to study the selfless and self-sacrificing soldier of Maoist lore, Lei Feng, and to be on guard against the "spiritual pollution" said to come from the West have little effect on an urban population that is busy making money and listening to the phenomenally popular mainland rock singer Cui Jian and to Hong Kong and Taiwanese pop songs. The gap between government statement and public perception is reflected in the increase of black humor and the rise in nostalgia (the "Mao Zedong craze"). As in the former East European countries, many ordinary citizens find comfort in poking fun at official rhetoric. This has the effect of undermining confidence in the regime; as a Chinese intellectual commented, "It's the only weapon we have." In summer 1991 the Beijing authorities were moved to ban a series of T-shirts that expressed youthful resentment and *ennui*; for the June 4 anniversary of the Tiananmen crackdown, they banned laughter in Tiananmen Square.[1] This is a credibility gap that any future leadership will need to close.

Deng's renewed stress on faster and bolder economic reform will constitute the basis of the policy agenda for the 14th Party Congress scheduled for late 1992. Yet Deng's calls for experimentation with economic reform are balanced by his continuing wariness of genuine political reform. Thus the second plank of the party congress's platform will be continued commitment to tough party rule enshrined in the "four cardinal principles" (keep to the socialist road, uphold the dictatorship of the proletariat, uphold the leadership of the Communist

---

[1] Beijing citizens referred to these T-shirts as "cultural shirts," claiming that this was the only culture they had.

Party, and uphold Marxism-Leninism-Mao Zedong Thought). However, as in other periods during the last decade when economic reform has been speeded up, the political consequences remain unpredictable. The leaders appointed to run China after the party congress will need to show more imagination than in the past in dealing with the social and political consequences of their quest for fast-track economic growth.

When the CCP celebrated its 70th anniversary on July 1, 1991, the chances for a dramatic change of course looked slim. The party remained defensive in the aftermath of Tiananmen and felt threatened by enemies both from within and from without. Yet the CCP prided itself on the fact that it had ridden out the storm of protest in 1989 and been spared the consequences of the dramatic collapse of the communist regimes in Eastern Europe and the profound changes then taking place in Gorbachev's Soviet Union. Open dissent had been quashed, and inner-party battles were kept within acceptable limits. General Secretary Jiang Zemin, in his speech commemorating the party's founding, reaffirmed the hard line by claiming that "class struggle" would continue for a considerable period within "certain parts" of China. This contrasted markedly with the party line that had dominated since the late 1970s, when Deng Xiaoping and his supporters claimed that class struggle was dying and that henceforth the main focus would be on economic development. Social harmony was to replace class warfare. In response to the situation in Eastern Europe, Jiang claimed: "We Chinese communists are convinced the temporary difficulties and setbacks recently experienced by socialism in its march forward cannot and will not ever prevent us from continuing to develop." As far as the West was concerned, CCP policy was still to focus on resisting the capitalists' presumed attempts to transform China through "peaceful evolution" (*heping yanbian*).[2]

Three factors combined to convince Deng Xiaoping and his allies that it was necessary to reassess the hard-line policy and to push China once more along the road to reform. The first was the fallout from the failed August 1991 coup in the Soviet Union. The second was the need to come to grips with the deep-seated structural prob-

[2] Jiang Zemin, "Building Socialism the Chinese Way," July 1, 1991, in *Beijing Review*, July 8–14, 1991, pp. 14–31. See also "Firmly Follow Our Own Road—Celebrating the 70th Anniversary of the Founding of the Chinese Communist Party," *Renmin ribao* (People's Daily), July 1, 1991. "Peaceful evolution" is the term used by the CCP to refer to what it sees as the West's attempts to subvert the socialist system in China. The party believes that the Western powers are pursuing a deliberate policy of promoting "capitalism" in China in order to change the nature of the regime.

lems in the Chinese economy. And the third was the task of laying down a clear agenda for the upcoming 14th Party Congress.

The Soviet Coup: Lessons for China

The failed Soviet coup, the subsequent disintegration of the USSR, and the collapse of the Communist Party of the Soviet Union (CPSU) disturbed the air of complacency and the notion that everything was under control that Jiang Zemin had expressed on July 1, 1991. While publicly the CCP claimed that the coup and its failure were an "internal matter" for the Soviet people and that China had no desire to interfere, internal publications displayed alarm and fear about the possible consequences for China. Even before the coup, internal reports for senior CCP members had been harshly critical of Gorbachev, blaming him for the collapse of communism in Eastern Europe and on occasion even calling him a traitor. Internal reports had been still more critical of Boris Yeltsin, and in May 1991 Jiang Zemin, visiting Moscow, declined to meet him. Yeltsin's assumption of power in Russia realized one of the worst nightmares of the orthodox leaders in Beijing.[3]

Circumstantial evidence suggests that China's leaders knew about the possibility of a backlash against Gorbachev and were in favor of action being taken to remove him and to moderate his policies. For some time China's more orthodox leaders had been cultivating contacts with conservative elements in the Soviet military. Indeed Soviet Defense Minister Yazov had been warmly received in Beijing in May 1991.[4] On the day of Gorbachev's arrest, a document was circulated to middle-level and senior party officials, titled "A Victory for the Soviet People Is a Victory for the Chinese People." It roundly condemned Gorbachev, while praising the coup leaders for returning the Soviet Union to the path of socialism.[5] That this document was in the hands of officials within a day of the coup, when such a sensitive paper would normally take at least three days to produce and disseminate, strengthens the notion that at least some in Beijing were in the know.

The initial impact of the coup's failure was to strengthen the hand of the orthodox faction in the CCP. However, each faction within the

[3] The Chinese news agency, Xinhua, reported the unfolding of the coup quickly and accurately, and the first official reaction on August 20 was extremely bland. The term "orthodox" is used in this chapter to refer to those opposed to Deng's policy of economic reform. "Conservative" and "liberal," "moderate" and "radical" tend to confuse by creating false assumptions for Western audiences.

[4] Yazov was one of the eight leaders of the failed coup.

[5] Information from an informed source in Beijing.

party leadership used the coup to push its own case: for tighter political control, for limited economic reform, or for rapid economic reform. Initially the failed coup was used to justify the CCP's tough stance in 1989, and a call was made to tighten up ideological work. At a Politburo meeting convened to discuss the implications of the coup, the orthodox ideologue Deng Liqun advocated beefing up the campaign against "bourgeois liberalization," and many intellectuals in Beijing were gearing themselves for a harsh autumn and winter. However, their fears were unfounded.

The best example of this tough reaction to the Soviet coup is provided by Gao Di, the editor of the *People's Daily*, in a speech to senior staff members.[6] Gao claimed that Gorbachev's decision to dissolve the CPSU amounted to the most traitorous act in the history of world communism. He blamed Gorbachev for having sown confusion in the minds of the Soviet people and traced his mistakes back to his criticism of Stalin. This had led Gorbachev down the slippery slope to criticism of the party, of socialism, and ultimately of Marxism and Leninism. Linking his critique to recent domestic concerns, Gao claimed that Gorbachev's greatest mistake was to dispense with class struggle and to adopt a social-democratic rather than a communist viewpoint. Nor did Gao have much time for the plotters. He claimed that they should have taken a leaf from China's book by copying the arrest of the Gang of Four in 1976, when there was no advance warning, no escape, and no communications with the outside world. The general incompetence of the Soviet coup makers and their failure to grab Yeltsin revealed them to be "immature proletarian politicians" who did not understand the basics of proletarian warfare. Ominously, Gao declared that in a life-and-death situation such as this one, law and the constitution mean nothing.

Gao felt that socialism could continue in China without the Soviet Union and that economic growth had brought a stability to China that had been lacking in the USSR. For Gao, the coup's failure demonstrated the correctness of China's chosen path. He called for support for the party and rejected ideas of a multiparty system. Proletarian dictatorship was to be strengthened to prevent the emergence of a "capitalist democratic system," and ideological pluralism was also to be prevented; the state-run economy was to dominate over the private. Summing up, Gao called for a policy of "observing soberly" (*lengjing guancha*), "holding one's ground" (*wenzhu zhenjiao*), "hiding

---

[6] Gao Di, "The Question of the Soviet Coup," August 30, 1991. Gao was assigned to run the *People's Daily* after June 4, 1989.

one's capacities and biding one's time" (*taoguang yanghui*), and "not taking the lead" (*bu shi daitou*).

While Gao's "sit-tight, do-nothing" approach dominated for a time, others recognized that some change was necessary to prevent Soviet-like problems from arising in China. This was the point of breakdown in the post-Tiananmen coalition of those who favored ideological *and* economic orthodoxy and those who were moving toward acceptance of authoritarian political rule but preferred a more deregulated, market-oriented economy. The children of a number of orthodox veterans, such as Chen Yuan, the son of Chen Yun, argued that a positive, measured response rather than a hard-line one was needed. However, this group, who referred to themselves as neoconservatives (*xin baoshou*), still wanted the state sector to predominate within the economy and the party to use its monopoly of political power to become the leading force in economic activity. This line of reasoning would be acceptable to many of the orthodox veterans, as it offered a way forward while still giving the appearance of being socialist and enshrining party dominance in the next phase of China's development. Nevertheless, the neoconservatives were challenged by others who wanted faster growth, a greater role for the nonstate sector of the economy, and less party interference, albeit within the framework of authoritarian rule.

Shortly after the failed coup in the Soviet Union, Chen Yuan sponsored a piece by the Ideology and Theory Department of the *China Youth Daily* that summed up his group's position—namely, that both radical and delayed reform had to be avoided if China was to avoid the fate of the ex–Soviet Union.[7] The authors contended that China had to turn its back on the methods that had been used by the CCP in its struggle to gain power. It was high time to transform the party into a ruling rather than a revolutionary organization. Unlike Deng Liqun and Gao Di, the authors argued for a downgrading of class struggle, the use of populist measures, and mass campaigns to implement policy. Intellectuals, seen as vital to the process of modernization, were not to be treated as class enemies. The paper called for the party to return to carefully guided economic reform while retaining an authoritarian political structure to prevent possible social dislocation leading to chaos and upheaval.

---

[7] "Realistic Responses and Strategic Choices for China after the Soviet Upheaval," September 9, 1991. Long after Deng's views on renewed reform had been made public, Chen Yuan was still using this department to circulate his neoconservative views.

The paper's authors claimed that neoconservatism would be different from that of the "traditional diehard conservative forces," because it would incorporate what was useful in both the traditional and the present order, as well as gradually introduce some elements of Western institutions. Neoconservatives reject the program of wholesale privatization, the issuing of shares, and the opening of a stock market. They consider these measures unsuitable for the state sector and would restrict them to smaller enterprises with severe losses. Finally, with the disappearance of the state founded by the Bolshevik revolution, the authors proposed that the "Chineseness" of their own revolution be stressed and that China's particular situation and history be used to persuade people that "only socialism can save China."[8]

The Economic Imperative and the 14th Party Congress

Although it appears that Deng Xiaoping was initially pessimistic about the PRC's future following the collapse of the Soviet Union, he was soon convinced that the only hope for the party's survival was to push economic reform in order to raise living standards and to let people see that the party was at the forefront of the reform program.

The program of economic austerity imposed in late 1988 and tightened after June 4, 1989, very quickly revealed its limits.[9] It did not deal with the fundamental structural problems of the economy and, in fact, it exacerbated many of them by denying their existence. The economic squeeze dampened demand but did not improve productivity or remodel the irrational structure as had been promised. Already by early 1990 there were clear signs that the austerity measures were pushing the economy toward a major recession. In October 1989, for the first time in a decade, industrial output fell on a month-to-month basis by 2.1 percent. In the period January–March 1990, industrial output recorded no growth, while that of light industry fell 0.2 percent. The previously thriving collective sector was hit hard, and by September 1989 the growth in monthly industrial output had dropped from 16.6 percent to 0.6 percent. A number of large factories sat idle because of the slowdown in output. As a result, in the first two months of 1990 alone 1.5 million urban residents lost their jobs.

Shaken by the economic downturn and fearing social dislocation, officials quietly introduced measures to ease the austerity program de-

---

[8] Many students in Beijing preferred the joke "Only China can save socialism."

[9] See Barry Naughton, "The Chinese Economy: On the Road to Recovery," in *China Briefing, 1991,* ed. William A. Joseph (Boulder: Westview and The Asia Society, 1992), pp. 77–96.

spite resistance by fiscal conservatives at the center. Many policies associated with the disgraced former general secretary Zhao Ziyang again became key elements of policy. The role played by the collective and private sectors was recognized, and articles praising their contributions to economic growth began to appear. The coastal-development strategy closely associated with Zhao was reaffirmed, and the reputation of the Special Economic Zones was rehabilitated. After Tiananmen, the zones had been attacked by orthodox leaders on both economic and political grounds. They claimed that resources which might have been used to develop the economy more generally had been diverted to the zones. Further, they believed the zones had not brought in advanced technology as promised but constituted little more than low-grade, cheap-labor manufacturing areas. Politically they were seen as the main ports of entry for spiritual pollution and political corruption from the capitalist West. But, following a visit in early February 1990 to the Shenzhen Special Economic Zone, Premier Li Peng proclaimed that the establishment of SEZs and the further opening of coastal areas were still major components of the reform plan.[10] Government policy also began to deal with the problem of pricing and subsidies. In April 1991 the sharpest price increases in some 25 years were introduced for staple foods, with high-quality rice rising by 75 percent and wheat prices by 55 percent. In April 1992 the price of rice was increased again by 40 percent. These measures were necessary but still not sufficient to allow market forces to work properly in the Chinese economy.

By stealth, the program of economic retrenchment was gradually being rolled back. However, Deng Xiaoping obviously felt that policy-making by increment or by default was insufficient and that a clear statement of intent was necessary. Debates about the future direction were brought into sharper focus by the fact that the 14th Party Congress was scheduled to convene before the end of 1992. Party congresses and the fixing of five-year plans are always times of tense debate in China. Policy differences that previously could be contained often spill over into factional fighting and resultant purges. Once a document that will dictate policy for the coming five years has to be written, it becomes more difficult to paper over the cracks in the leadership, and political differences become increasingly public as the various policy proponents strive to set the agenda through newspaper articles and controlled leaks.

---

[10] "Li Describes SEZs as Part of Nation's Major Reform Plan," *China Daily*, February 10, 1990, p. 1.

The 14th Party Congress promises to be even more tense in this respect, since it will be the first party congress since Tiananmen. It will have to decide what, if anything, to do about the ousted reform leader Zhao Ziyang, who has remained in disgrace since June 1989. The Central Committee that was elected at the last congress in 1987 was thought of as Zhao's committee, and many of its number are believed still to support his policies. This also will very likely be the last party congress at which the generation of veteran revolutionaries will be able to exert real influence. They have been busy jockeying to ensure that their protégés are elected to key positions and to leave behind them a legacy that they find fitting. For Deng Xiaoping the 14th Party Congress is a critical opportunity to legitimize his call for revitalized economic reform.

Deng Xiaoping Takes a New Line

Deng Xiaoping seems to have been roused to action by the publication of an article in the *People's Daily* on September 1, 1991, that was interpreted as an attack on his program of economic reform.[11] On September 25, 1991, during a Central Work Conference, Deng called in Jiang Zemin and PRC President Yang Shangkun and warned them of the dangers of anti-reform leftism in China. Deng felt that the resurgence of the left since the events in the Soviet Union was damaging to China's future development. "Leftism" was Deng's code word for those opposed to his reforms either on ideological grounds, like Deng Liqun, or on economic grounds, like Chen Yun. The attack on leftism became the main theme of political life as 1992 progressed.

The first public indications of a resurgent reform effort came with Yang Shangkun's speech to mark the 80th anniversary of the 1911 revolution.[12] At the time, most of the foreign press concentrated on Yang's comments about Taiwan and reunification and overlooked the significance of his assertion that the core of all work was promotion of the economy. Yang's claim that work in all areas was to be subordinated to the needs of economic construction reconfirmed the policy line that Deng Xiaoping had laid down in December 1978. According to Yang, the party's attention was never to be shifted from this central task. This was a rebuff to those in the party who had been talking

[11] Chen Yepin, "Have Both Ability and Political Integrity, with Political Integrity as the Main Aspect—Comments on the Criteria for Selecting and Prompting Cadres," *Renmin ribao*, September 1, 1991. Chen was formerly a deputy director of the Organization Department of the CCP Central Committee and is a supporter of Chen Yun.

[12] A translation of Yang Shangkun's speech to a rally held on October 9, 1991, can be found in *Summary of World Broadcasts: The Far East* (*SWB:FE*), 1200, C1/1–4.

of the need for continued class struggle and who saw ideological correctness as the core of all work.

The most dramatic breakthrough came with Deng Xiaoping's inspection tour in South China in January and February 1992.[13] This trip provided the basis for a major report that was disseminated within the party as Central Document No. 2.[14] Given the forthright ideas expressed in the document, it is hardly surprising that Deng's opponents sought to stop its dissemination. Deng was clearly impressed with what he saw, especially in the Shenzhen Special Economic Zone, and called on Guangdong Province to catch up with Asia's "four little dragons" (Hong Kong, Singapore, Taiwan, and South Korea) within some 20 years. In a veiled criticism of Chen Yun, Deng remarked that he recognized now that one of his major errors at the beginning of the reform period was not to include Shanghai as one of the SEZs. Anyone reading the document would know that Shanghai was Chen Yun's bailiwick and that he had resisted pressures to turn it into another freewheeling economic zone, preferring to see it remain a socialist economic showcase in which orthodox notions of central planning held sway.

In the document, Deng stated that continued economic reform was vital for the party's legitimacy. He claimed that if China's economic reforms were reversed, the party would lose the people's support and "could be overthrown at any time," and he ventured the view that the party would certainly not have survived the trauma of Tiananmen if it had not already advanced down the path of economic reform. Interestingly, Deng absolved both Zhao Ziyang and Hu Yaobang, his first two choices as general secretary, of faults in the economic arena by stating that they had been removed from power because of their not properly opposing "bourgeois liberalization." Deng went beyond stating the general need for economic reform by implicitly criticizing those who sought to slow the pace of change. He claimed that economic reform should not "proceed slowly like a woman with bound feet" but should "blaze new trails boldly." This, Deng said, was what the experience of Shenzhen revealed.

Most important, Deng announced a major change in the CCP's political line. Ever since the events of 1989, the Chinese public had been told that the greatest threat to socialism in China came from bour-

---

[13] It seems that Deng sent an invitation to Chen Yun to accompany him on the trip, but his old adversary declined, preferring to vacation in Hangzhou. Between January 18 and February 12, 1992, Deng visited Wuchang, Shenzhen, Zhuhai, and Shanghai.

[14] The full text of the document can be found in the Hong Kong magazine *Zhengming* (Contention), April 1, 1992, pp. 23–27.

geois liberals, termed "rightists." As far as the party veterans were concerned, rightists were responsible for the unrest that had broken out in 1989. This unrest legitimized the attacks on Zhao Ziyang and his supporters as well as on outspoken pro-reform intellectuals throughout the system. Now Deng told his party members that it was the leftists, who opposed further reform, who now presented the greatest problem for China.[15] Deng turned his fire on those who argued that economic reform inevitably must lead to capitalism. According to Deng, a market economy did not necessarily imply capitalism any more than a planned economy implied socialism. He refused to accept arguments that the danger of "peaceful evolution" originated mainly in the economic sphere. Deng warned against sinking into another ideological impasse. For him, the basic line of rapid reform was clear, and it was to be upheld for 100 years.

In late February 1992 Deng's ideas began to be echoed in media articles the like of which had not been seen since before the suppression of the people's democracy movement in June 1989. The most dramatic one was published in the *People's Daily* on February 24.[16] This extraordinary piece argued for "boldly taking advantage" of capitalism and "appropriately expanding the domestic capitalist economy." The author suggested that far from aiding "peaceful evolution," the introduction of certain capitalist measures would provide a good supplement to China's "nascent" socialist system. What the writer had in mind were use of foreign trade and capital, production according to contract, rental markets, open bids for projects, enterprise mergers, and the issuing of stocks. Using Deng's argumentation, and indeed the logic put forward by Zhao Ziyang at the 13th Party Congress (1987), the writer argued that these were "class-neutral" methods to develop a commodity economy, be it capitalist or socialist.

Deng's Document No. 2 set the agenda for the Politburo meeting of March 9–10, 1992, which marked a decisive shift in the balance of power in favor of the reformists against their orthodox opponents.

---

[15] Reliable accounts claim that the disseminated version of the document toned down the general criticisms and removed negative evaluations of specific individuals among the party leadership. It is clear that among those for whom Deng was gunning were the acting minister of culture, He Jingzhi; the director of the *People's Daily*, Gao Di; Minister of Propaganda Wang Renzhi; Education Commission Party Secretary He Dongchang; Beijing Party Secretary Li Ximing; Politburo member Song Ping; and the hard-line ideologue Deng Liqun.

[16] Fang Sheng, "Opening Up to the Outside World and Making Use of Capitalism," *Renmin ribao*, February 24, 1992. See also the editorial from the same day, "Be More Daring in Carrying Out Reform."

Jiang Zemin made a self-criticism that he had neither sufficiently promoted reform in recent years nor sufficiently opposed leftism. This caused more-committed leftists in the Politburo, such as Li Ximing and Song Ping, to follow suit. The meeting accepted Deng's evaluation that "left deviationism" did in fact pose a greater threat than rightism, together with his view that development of the economy was the party's fundamental task.[17] It now remained for Deng to make certain that these gains were consolidated and that senior leaders did not merely pay lip service to his views while opposing or ignoring them in practice. This has proved difficult, and while it is clear that the agenda for the party congress is set, it is still unclear how far-reaching the changes will prove to be.

Two Groups Challenge Deng

Deng's policy initiative has been challenged by two main groups at the center. The first group consists of proto-Maoist ideologues such as the Central Advisory Commission member Deng Liqun; PRC Vice President Wang Zhen; and *People's Daily* chief Gao Di. These orthodox leaders are worried about the consequences of liberalization for the social fabric of China and have consistently insisted that the party reaffirm its leading role in the realm of ideology. They argue that socialism has moral and spiritual as well as material goals and that these goals can be defined only by the CCP. They feel that the party's role is to dictate the nation's ethical and moral values, and they have been at the forefront of campaigns against "spiritual pollution" and "bourgeois liberalization" in 1983, 1987, and 1989–90. Further, they see the policy of opening China to the outside world as a source of problems within the party. An official decision on party consolidation in October 1983 affirmed this point by stating that although the "open policy" had been entirely correct, there had also been an increase in the "corrosive influence of decadent bourgeois ideology and remnant feudal ideas."[18] Many of the orthodox leaders' supporters are in key positions in the ideological and propaganda apparatus and, as noted above, used the failure of the Soviet coup to argue for a tightening of ideological control in China.

The second group consists of those who are opposed on primarily economic grounds to Deng's renewed offensive and who represent

[17] See Xinhua, March 11, 1992 (in English).

[18] "The Decision of the Central Committee of the Communist Party of China on Party Consolidation," *Beijing Review*, no. 42 (October 17, 1983), p. 1. The decision was adopted at the Second Plenum of the 12th Central Committee.

the traditional central planning and economic apparatus. This group includes Chen Yun, former PRC president and head of the Chinese People's Political Consultative Conference; Li Xiannian (who died in June 1992); and Central Advisory Committee member Bo Yibo. Concerned about the destabilizing effect of pushing the marketization of the economy too far too fast, they are uneasy about overreliance on the market and worried that the economy may "overheat" as a result of the rapid growth of the collective sector, particularly the rural industries. Although Chen Yun is not opposed to an increased role for the market—indeed he has been one of its main proponents—he does view the too-rapid introduction of market forces as the cause of the recurrent economic problems during the 1980s. He has consistently argued for the importance and primacy of planning within the economic system. This defense of the state sector is reflected in his periodic criticisms of private enterprise and in his refusal to redefine property rights to allow a greater scope for private ownership in order to protect the state's privileged position in the economy. Chen and his colleagues also fear that current policies will deepen inequalities between China's poor hinterland and its more-advanced coastal regions. Finally, they are concerned about the mushrooming of corruption that has resulted from the liberalized policies and increased contacts with the West. This group retains support within the ministries and apparatus associated with the old central-planning system, particularly from those in the heavy-industrial sector.

These two groups have tried to frustrate Deng's plans. For example, it took several weeks to distribute Deng's report on his tour to South China through the party and state apparatus, with opponents such as Li Xiannian refusing to disseminate it through the network under his control.[19] Furthermore, the version that was distributed was sanitized to avoid naming names and making specific accusations about those leaders judged to be hampering reform. With access to the media in Beijing blocked, Deng Xiaoping, inspired by Mao Zedong's strategy in the early stages of the Cultural Revolution, got his supporters to publish supportive articles in the Shanghai press. To deflect the thrust of Deng's criticisms, his opponents circulated their own directives containing a selective interpretation of Deng's views. They called on their supporters to refrain from publicizing the shareholding and stock market system and from promoting the view that leftism was deeply rooted and could bring down socialism. On the contrary, they argued that the anti–"bourgeois liberalization" drive

[19] By contrast, the National People's Congress chairman and Deng supporter Wan Li made sure that the document was distributed widely throughout his network.

should be continued and called for pushing the viewpoints that "reform and opening up constitute the importation and promotion of capitalism" and that "the main danger of peaceful evolution comes from the economic sphere."[20]

Li Peng Tries to Walk a Tightrope

The annual meeting of China's legislature, the National People's Congress (NPC), which began its session on March 20, 1992, provided an immediate demonstration that leadership divisions over policy were serious. This was most evident in Li Peng's government work report to the meeting. Li, although cautious, basically followed the new economic line but, to his cost, strayed from Deng's most recent political warnings.[21]

In line with Deng, Li called for a bolder approach to economic reform and stated that China must assimilate the advanced technology of other countries, including that of the developed capitalist nations. He acknowledged that economic construction was the centerpiece of party work and parroted Deng by saying, "The purpose of revolution is to develop the productive forces." Of special importance was his confirmation that the Yangpu Open Development Zone on Hainan Island would be promoted and that new open cities in the border regions would be created to facilitate trade and investment. Yangpu is a project formerly associated with Zhao Ziyang and his supporters. Its objective is to attract foreign firms into joint ventures to produce high-technology products. Unlike in other zones, however, non-Chinese investors will be able to lease land for factories that they can own outright. Furthermore, Li gave the green light to the Pudong development in Shanghai, which had been wrestling with the central authorities for several years to be granted the same advantages as those of the Special Economic Zones.

While proposing these ambitious plans, Li was careful to stress that China's capacity for bringing them to fruition was severely constrained by the heavy deficit spending on inefficient state industries. This was interpreted as a reassuring signal to the orthodox economists that he would not countenance a return to the rapid development and resulting inflation that had brought on the economic turmoil of 1988. Although this may have been acceptable to Deng, Li

---

[20] Huo Sifang, " 'Leftist' Influence Unlikely to Give Up Turf Easily," *Jingbao*, April 5, 1992.

[21] For a translation of Li's report, see *SWB:FE* 1336, C1/1–12. For an account of the politics that went into its writing, see *Zhengming*, April 1, 1992.

broke ranks with the senior leader by rejecting Deng's call for 10 percent growth in GNP, offering instead the more cautious figure of 6 percent. Also, he did not give a high profile to Deng's rural policy of household-based production and the use of the market, but stressed instead collective service systems and ideological education campaigns.

Yet it was on political judgments that Li Peng diverged most radically from Deng. He dropped Deng's and the Politburo's assessment that leftism was the greatest danger at present and generally echoed the language more readily associated with the orthodox party leaders. Moreover, he did not promise that the policy line would remain the same for 100 years, but chose to say that China would become "a powerful, socialist country standing firm as a rock in the East."

Almost as soon as Li Peng had finished speaking, criticism of the report was voiced, and on April 3 the NPC adopted Li's work report with more than 150 amendments.[22] Governors from various provinces convened their own press conferences to criticize implicitly Li's projections for growth. The national media ran critical comments by delegates about the dangers of leftism, and appealed to leaders who did not clearly support reform to step aside for those who did. Most important, Li's political assessment was amended to note that, although "rightist deviation" had to be guarded against, the greatest danger came from leftism. On the economic front, the report was amended to praise stock markets and to give a generally more upbeat account of the private sector. Finally, Li's modest target for GNP growth was effectively discarded.

These amendments of Li's more orthodox assessment of the economy merely recognized the reality of what is now happening in China. First, while inefficient enterprises in the state sector stagnate and run up massive deficits, dynamic growth is taking place in the collective and private sectors. The output of state-sector firms grew 8.4 percent in 1991, compared with 19 percent for the collectives. Retail sales in the state sector increased by 14 percent, while those of the private sector increased by 18 percent, and those of joint commercial retailers, by 24 percent.[23] During the first four months of 1992, state-run industry lost US$2 billion, with just over 36 percent of the enterprises running a loss.[24] A view of the future can be gained from

---

[22] See *SWB:FE* 1347, p. i.

[23] *Far Eastern Economic Review*, March 12, 1992, p. 51.

[24] The majority of the losses were in the fields of oil, coal, nonferrous metals, tobacco, and the military-industrial sector. Reuter, May 26, 1992. At the end of June, the Chinese authorities announced that, for the first time, a bankrupt state-owned company would be auctioned off. Even foreigners would be able to bid. Not surprisingly, the enterprise was in Shenzhen. *China News Digest*, July 1, 1992.

Guangdong Province, where only 35 percent of industrial production comes from the state sector, and 38 percent from private or foreign-financed businesses, with the remainder coming from the collective sector.

Furthermore, growth rates moved rapidly beyond Li Peng's projections. Almost as Li was speaking, Guangdong Governor Zhu Senlin rejected his views, claiming that his economy would grow at double the officially planned target. In fact in 1991, while GNP grew nationally at 7 percent, Guangdong's GNP equivalent grew by 13.5 percent; in the same period its industrial output soared by 27.7 percent versus the national average of 14.2 percent.[25] By late April 1992, Chinese officials were already talking of growth reaching 9.1 percent for the nation as a whole, and when figures were announced for the first five months of 1992, GNP had already climbed to 11 percent. Once again, however, fears were expressed about the economy overheating and inflation edging up. In the first quarter of 1992, the cost of living in the 35 largest cities increased by 10.9 percent.[26] This is the maximum level that most economists feel is manageable for China's urban population.

Deng Attempts to Push Home His Advantage

With the tide shifting at least temporarily in their direction, Deng and his supporters tried to secure their advantage. Despite repeated rumors of major personnel changes, they initially made little headway in removing opponents from key positions. It was only in June 1992 that they began to make some progress, but major changes may still not occur until the 14th Party Congress or even later. On June 3 He Dongchang was dismissed as party secretary of the State Education Commission, although as a face-saving measure he was allowed to keep his position as deputy minister. Coming one day before the anniversary of Tiananmen, He's dismissal was a clear sign of appeasement to the restive students. He Dongchang was seen as an opponent of educational reform who had fully supported a tough line in dealing with the students and had sponsored other unpopular measures such as military training for students admitted to Beijing University. In mid-June unconfirmed rumors in the Hong Kong press claimed that two other noted orthodox members, Beijing party boss Li Ximing and

[25] For 1992 and 1993 an increase of 35 percent was being mooted by Guangdong officials. See Carl Goldstein, "Under Licence," *Far Eastern Economic Review*, April 23, 1992.

[26] This was in comparison with 8 percent for 1991 as a whole.

acting minister of culture He Jingzhi, had also been removed from their posts.[27]

At present, the health factor seems to be working to Deng's advantage. In June 1992 the former PRC president Li Xiannian (one of the foremost orthodox veterans and a major patron of Li Peng) died at the age of 82, thus removing a major obstacle from Deng's path. Other opponents such as Wang Zhen and Peng Zhen are reportedly in poor health; Chen Yun, although not at death's door, has not been as mobile as Deng in promoting his policy line.

The day-to-day control over the economy has also been effectively taken away from Li Peng and placed in the hands of Vice-Premier Zhu Rongji, who has been cited by some sources as a likely candidate to replace Li as premier. In June 1992 Zhu took over as head of the newly created Economic and Trade Office under the State Council, which superseded the Production Office. The new office is scheduled to be upgraded to commission level early in 1993.[28] The office will be the most powerful organ overseeing economic work, with control over state enterprises, joint ventures and stock companies, and foreign trade. Zhu is thus in a good position to forge ahead with Deng's plans to marketize further the Chinese economy.

The economic reform program was boosted by the circulation in late May–early June 1992 of Central Document No. 4, which extended the "open policy" from the coastal regions to the whole of China. The dissemination of this document followed Deng's visit to the Capital Iron and Steel Works in Beijing, where he complained that the party had not adequately implemented his calls for reform and faster growth. It seems that Deng pointedly criticized the Beijing party authorities for interfering with the enterprise's affairs. The document also granted all of China's provincial capitals as well as certain inland cities and border regions "preferential status" on a par with the zones and open cities along the coast. Initially 14 cities along the Yangtze River and on the border with Russia were assured of status equivalent to that of the Special Economic Zones.[29] The document outlined ways in which private and stock companies as well as joint ventures should be expanded. Following hard on the heels of this document came the proclamation in the *People's Daily* that private enterprise had "become an indispensable force in the economy."[30]

---

[27] *South China Morning Post*, June 16, 1992.

[28] *Ibid.*, June 12, 1992.

[29] *Ibid.*, June 3, 1992.

[30] Reported in *ibid.*, June 6, 1992.

This campaign from above has encouraged many pro-reform intellectuals who had been quiet since 1989 to speak up once more. Du Runsheng, a rural economist who was almost expelled from the party, has begun again to push publicly his ideas for increased marketization of the Chinese economy.[31] In April 1992 reform-minded party members, including Hu Jiwei, Li Rui, and Yang Xianyang, published a collection of articles constituting a sustained critique of leftism.[32] The book was quickly withdrawn under pressure from orthodox party leaders, but its contents were widely known. The most amazing development was a meeting in Beijing on June 15 convened by five unofficial organizations to criticize leftism and denounce unwarranted interference in cultural and ideological spheres. The attendance list reads like a "Who's Who" of pro-reform intellectuals still residing in Beijing. This tactic may yet backfire, as Deng Xiaoping has proved no friend to these people at critical times in the past.

Trouble with the Workers

Despite these trends in Deng's favor, the days of the orthodox party members may not be numbered if they can obstruct the reform process midway. This might allow time for groups worried about certain aspects of the reforms to rally around a return to a more centrally guided economic system. In particular, this applies to China's industrial working class, which was one of the major beneficiaries of Maoism in terms of a subsidized standard of living, a guaranteed job for life, and other relatively generous benefits.

Under Deng's reform package, urban workers are being offered a deal that involves giving up their secure, subsidy-supported, low-wage lifestyle for a risky contract-based system that might provide significantly higher incomes, but at the possible cost of rising prices for all and unemployment for some. Many urban workers have decided to reserve their judgment about economic reform. However, they seem generally concerned about the party's attempts to introduce housing reforms that would increase rents and to eliminate the so-called three irons that have come to define the terms of employment for state enterprise workers: the "iron rice bowl" (lifetime em-

---

[31] One senior party member known for his pro-reform views commented, "In the past when we were in Yan'an, we used the slogan 'use the countryside to surround the cities'; now I joke that we must 'use the company to surround the Party Center' " (*yong gongsi baowei zhongyang*).

[32] *Lishi de chaoliu* (Trend of History; Beijing: Chinese People's University Press, April 1992). Surprisingly, the book bears an inscription from hard-line leader Bo Yibo, but apparently he never saw the manuscript—only a selective summary of its contents.

ployment), the "iron salary" (guaranteed wages), and the "iron armchair" (guaranteed position for managers).

If pursued, the drive to make the state sector more efficient and responsive to the market would make redundant many of the 100 million people in the state sector. In June 1992 Vice-Premier Zhu Rongji estimated that this sector contained some 10 million surplus workers, although most would agree that this number is a major underestimation. To compound the problem, between 1991 and 1995 another 36 million people will enter the work force. Yet reforms are beginning to take effect: during the first five months of 1992, about 1.4 million workers were said to have lost their jobs through the reorganization of the state sector.[33] Fear of unemployment and worry about what the future may hold have led to many rumors of work slowdowns, strikes, walkouts, the murder of managers held responsible for the reforms, and suicides.[34] The increasing problem is reflected in the announcement in early June that, after 40 years, a labor arbitration system was to be reintroduced to deal with the growing number of disputes.

To counter this resistance, the party began a propaganda offensive in the press to convince the workers of the absolute necessity of reform. However, this seems to have cut little ice with the workers, who are still used to operating in the old-style state-socialist industrial culture. The party will have to gamble that it can hold the line until the collective and private sectors can absorb sufficient numbers of workers, until a proper social security system for the unemployed is set up, and until housing is no longer tied to the workplace for many urban inhabitants. To a large degree CCP leaders are likely to rely on instruments of authoritarian rule, which they hope will allow them to push through unpopular measures without facing the consequences of mass protest.

But this is at best a race against time, and orthodox party members may seize on worker unrest to slow down the reform process. In May 1992 it was rumored that local authorities in Tianjin Municipality had ordered such a slowdown following cases of unrest. In June the *Liaoning Daily* reported that officials were backing off from shaking up state enterprises. The paper stated that the government had stopped referring to "smashing the three irons" because workers' fears of a dramatic drop in their standard of living had promoted a "negative

---

[33] *Volkskrant*, Amsterdam, June 15, 1992.

[34] For details of such incidents, see *International Herald Tribune*, June 12, 1992; *Daily Telegraph*, June 3, 1992; *Far Eastern Economic Review*, May 7, 1992; and *Christian Science Monitor*, June 2, 1992.

attitude toward reform."[35] The CCP is in a catch-22 situation: the problem of worker discontent cannot be solved without a more thoroughgoing reform, which will in turn stir up more opposition. Its best hope is probably to get through this difficult phase quickly enough to avoid arousing opposition.

Personnel Change and the 14th Party Congress

As in other periods before a party congress, rumors of personnel change abound. Different factions are lobbying for support and leaking lists of their preferred choices internally and to the Hong Kong press in order to keep their opponents under pressure and to maintain momentum. Chen Yun and Li Xiannian got an early start by trying to control the election of new Central Committee members. Chen and Li had the Central Organization Department circulate a directive on Central Committee elections stating that only those with a good track record in opposing "bourgeois liberalization" should be considered. By mid-1992, however, Deng and his supporters appeared to be gaining the upper hand in the personnel stakes. In May, Chen declared grudging support for Deng's policies with the following two provisos: that key orthodox leaders keep their posts, and that Shenzhen not become the model for the whole country. While Chen Yun might achieve the first objective, the second is less certain, and other potential changes may weaken the orthodox camp.

The dismissals of a number of Deng's opponents, discussed above, and the death of Li Xiannian in June bode well for the reform camp in the jockeying prior to the 14th Party Congress. A further plus for Deng was Li Peng's poor performance at the meeting of the National People's Congress and his subsequent humiliation. His power has been blunted, and his days are very likely numbered, thus rendering less important the question of whether he remains premier. It might not be worth removing him and possibly upsetting his orthodox patrons when he is already implementing reform policies, albeit against his will. In contrast to Li, the fortunes of former Shanghai mayor and current Vice-Premier Zhu Rongji look bright, and most see him as the likely eventual premier.

---

[35] Reported by Reuters, June 10, 1992. This concern probably lay behind the Politburo Standing Committee member Li Ruihuan's call in May 1992 for leaders to pursue reform fully. Li noted that halfheartedness in implementation could prove disastrous for China, and revealed the existence of opposition to the reform program. *Renmin ribao*, June 29, 1992, p. 1.

Another vice-premier, Tian Jiyun, a protégé of Zhao Ziyang, has also recently enhanced his reputation. Tian has become very active in promoting the new policy line, even making use of humor as a weapon. In a speech at the Central Party School, after reiterating the gist of Deng's report on his southern tour, Tian suggested that perhaps the leftists in the party leadership might want to set up their own Special Economic Zone in which salaries and prices of goods would be low, and queuing and rationing would be commonplace. Further, there would be no foreign investment, all foreigners would be kept out, and no one would be able to go abroad.[36]

General Secretary Jiang Zemin has probably done enough to save his position by trimming his sails and coming out clearly on the side of reform. On March 10, 1992, he made his self-criticism to the Politburo meeting; in mid-May he also adopted the view that elements of capitalism could be used in China; and on June 9 he made his own pilgrimage to the Central Party School to express his complete support for Deng's policies. He defended Deng's view that fast economic development would save China's socialist system, and he soundly denounced leftism.[37]

Changes can be expected in the composition of the Standing Committee of the Politburo. Standing Committee hard-liners Yao Yilin and Song Ping will probably step down. The reformist Vice-Premier Zhu Rongji will likely be promoted to the Standing Committee and, in the name of balance, so will the orthodox Vice-Premier Zou Jiahua. As far as the next echelon of leadership in the Politburo is concerned, Li Ximing's career is over, and he may well be replaced by Chen Xitong, the mayor of Beijing.[38] Deng supporters Wan Li and Yang Shangkun will probably be retired to make way for a younger generation of reformers who will be able to sustain the policy for a longer period. Vacant Politburo places may be filled by Foreign Minister Qian Qichen, who has done a good job in promoting China's international interests in difficult times, and Yang Baibing, a half-brother of Yang Shangkun

---

[36] Tian's speech was delivered in late April 1992, and bootleg tapes of the speech were one of the hottest sales items in late May in Beijing. Interestingly, around this time Deng Liqun and Gao Di were dropped from the lecture circuit at the Central Party School, and its titular head, Qiao Shi, began investigations into the activities at the school of Li Ximing, Gao Di, and Minister of Propaganda Wang Renzhi and his deputy, Xu Weicheng.

[37] Reuters, June 15, 1992, and United Press International, June 16, 1992.

[38] Chen has shown himself more adept at moving with the times and has reportedly been pushing the reform line at meetings of the Beijing municipal authorities. Relations between Chen and Li were said to have become increasingly tense, and it seems that Chen opened one meeting by stating that it was convened specifically to discuss reform, only to see Li Ximing stand up and walk out.

and the general secretary of the Central Military Commission. Other possible Politburo candidates include the vice-chairman of the Central Military Commission, Liu Huaqing, as a reward for People's Liberation Army support for Deng. If the reformers really gain the upper hand, a rehabilitation for Zhao ally Hu Qili is not out of the question. Other possible candidates from the reform camp include Hu Jintao, the former party secretary of Tibet and a protégé of Hu Yaobang, and Wan Jiabao, the head of the General Office of the Central Committee, who is reportedly in charge of drafting the important political report for the congress that will spell out the party's official line.

Perhaps the most interesting personnel issue for the 14th Party Congress is whether something will be said about the case of Zhao Ziyang, the former CCP general secretary who was ousted for his soft stance on the pro-democracy demonstrations of 1989. Public criticism of Zhao at the party congress would certainly be interpreted as an attack on Deng's renewed reform drive. The orthodox groups have wanted all along to pin the blame for the demonstrations on Zhao and have sought unsuccessfully to have him expelled from the party and perhaps even subjected to a show trial for his alleged counterrevolutionary crimes. Zhao was first attacked by the orthodox faction for being weak in opposing "bourgeois liberalization" and then accused of pursuing West European–style democratic socialism in China rather than true communism. This was the same charge they had leveled against Gorbachev. A leading figure in this abortive campaign to discredit Zhao was the propagandist Deng Liqun; it was even rumored that Li Peng had set up a writing team to further general criticism of democratic socialism and of Zhao's tendencies in that direction.[39]

Unable to muster a sustained attack on Zhao Ziyang, reform opponents turned their attention to Bao Tong, Zhao's aide-de-camp. Bao, a member of the Central Secretariat, was arrested before June 4, 1989, and accused of leaking state secrets (concerning troop maneuvers) to foreigners. In spring 1992 Bao was expelled from the party in preparation for his trial, which took place in late July. He was sentenced to seven years' imprisonment—a relatively light sentence compared with those handed down to Wang Juntao and Chen Ziming one year earlier.[40] Bao has become the orthodox leaders' scapegoat for the events of 1989. They may even try to use his "guilt" to further discredit Zhao. However, this is unlikely to blunt the renewed reform drive. Indeed Deng may be secretly pleased with the trial, since he and his current supporters can use it to close the book on Tiananmen. The or-

[39] See "Notes on a Northern Journey," in *Zhengming*, February 1, 1992.

[40] Wang and Chen had been accused of being behind the demonstrations of 1989.

thodox leaders have been given a prominent victim, and further recriminations can be kept off the agenda of the 14th Party Congress.[41]

Beyond the 14th Party Congress

Over the short term the situation looks relatively positive for the reformers. The economy is on a fast track for growth, and the 14th Party Congress's political agenda seems to have been set in their favor. Success in economic reform, however, depends on the economy not overheating again or being derailed by energy shortages and on reforms not being stalled because of structural problems before genuinely new policy directions can be implemented. At present the momentum in favor of reform in the party center is still dependent on the continued good health of Deng Xiaoping. A few deaths in the wrong order could intervene to divert the reform program.

While Deng has acknowledged the need for rapid economic reform, he has drawn the line at political reform. However, a major overhaul of the political structure is inevitable if the economic reform program is to stay on track. Now, instead of invoking Marxism, China's next generation of leaders use arguments about economic development to justify their authoritarian rule. Citing the examples of Taiwan and South Korea, they claim that the modernization process requires a strong, centralized political structure, especially in the early phase of takeoff, in order to prevent social divisions from undermining the drive for economic modernization. Put simply, they equate democratization with chaos, and chaos with underdevelopment.

Yet some political reforms will be necessary to enable the regime to function efficiently. The party has not developed institutions capable of handling policy debate and sharp differences of opinion concerning the reform program. Thus, despite its outward robust appearance, the party remains vulnerable to internal convulsions and possible rapid collapse, as in the case of Eastern Europe.

In the past when the CCP was confronted by the major popular unrest that accompanied loosening up of the country's economy and society, the leadership displayed little understanding of the social processes and changes that its own program of modernization had set in motion. The next generation of leaders will be confronted by problems arising from new social and regional inequalities that China was not used to under the old Maoist model. In addition, the population time bomb is ticking despite important gains in controlling population

[41] It should be pointed out that Bao was closely involved with the issue of political reform, an area on which Deng's views are extremely ambivalent.

growth. China will still have some 15–20 million extra mouths to feed in 1993. Clearly, economic reform must continue to move fast just to keep the people fed.

Reforms will be necessary at all levels to ensure a smoother operation of the political system and a stable environment for economic development. One of the main emphases of the reform program has been the governing of China by a legal, predictable system with rules and regulations applicable to all. But individual power relationships built up over decades continue to be more important than the rule of law and the formal functions that people hold. At the center, the power still wielded by ostensibly retired veteran leaders continues to undermine the official stress on the institutionalization of Chinese politics and the idea that an orderly succession can be achieved. The party veterans still have an institutional power base with the Central Advisory Commission. By heading the commission, Chen Yun has been able to counter the pro-reform majority in the party's Central Committee. This explains Deng's desire to abolish the commission, and a major victory will be struck for the reformers if, as seems probable, it is scrapped at the 14th Party Congress. On the other hand, its retention would demonstrate the staying power of the orthodox forces.

Although continued economic reform is inevitable over the long term, its course over the short term still depends on the good health of Deng Xiaoping. Much hinges on who succeeds to the top leadership position, and Deng has been unable to deal with the issue of succession. He has repeated Mao's method of anointment by the paramount leader. Deng's attempt to boost the position of current General Secretary Jiang Zemin as his successor is merely the latest in a series of attempts to ensure that a successor is in place before the paramount leader dies. To date, however, all such efforts to manage succession by transfer of legitimacy from the paramount leader to his protégé have failed.[42] The suspicion remains that Jiang is doing no more than minding the shop until someone else comes along. The continual need to look over one's shoulder to judge what one's particular patron is thinking severely hampers the capacity of the younger generation of leaders to develop their own independent power bases that can survive their patron's death. The real power struggle for suc-

[42] During the Cultural Revolution, Mao Zedong had designated Lin Biao as his successor, only to have him purged, and before his death Mao chose Hua Guofeng to replace him as party chairman. However, Hua was too tied to the Maoist legacy to escape dismissal once the process of de-Maoization got into full swing in the late 1970s. Deng Xiaoping appointed first Hu Yaobang and then Zhao Ziyang to the position of general secretary, only to dismiss both later.

cession will begin only after this generation of veteran leaders has passed from the scene.

Political reforms will also have to occur if the center is to develop reasonable relations with the provinces, particularly those in the South. The central government has experienced major difficulties in extracting tax revenues and in controlling the investment strategies of the provinces. Threats, counterthreats, and the ignoring of central directives are not conducive either to devising a sensible macroeconomic policy or to ensuring that the provinces feel they can rely on consistent policy-making by the center.

If the center continues to flounder, regionalism will increase. A false parallel, however, should not be drawn with the regional disintegration of the Soviet Union. While there are genuine fears about secession in minority areas such as Tibet, Xinjiang, and Mongolia,[43] the rest of the provinces, including the increasingly economically independent South, see themselves quite clearly as a part of China. All they require is policy consistency and competence by their national leaders. Otherwise they will pursue their own policy agendas along with their nominal allegiance to Beijing. For example, in early 1992 Hainan opened an "internal" stock exchange, thus hoping to avoid the need for the center's approval. Beijing ordered it closed down, but once the center's emissary departed, it was simply reopened. In June Hainan Governor Liu Jianfeng floated the idea of making the province a duty-free zone using Hong Kong dollars as the official currency![44] Gradually China is moving toward a development strategy which accepts not only that different parts of the country will develop at different speeds, but also that different policy programs will be implemented in the search for wealth and power.

At the basic levels of society, the CCP has not come to terms with the new divisions and tensions that have arisen within China directly as a result of its economic policies. The party still tries to channel political activity into the existing outdated structures. But in both urban and rural China, much political activity takes place outside these formal structures and is to some extent anti-systemic. The regime is courting potential breakdown if the overwhelming majority of society has to rely on work slowdowns, withdrawal of labor, noncooperation, the beating up of tax officials, riots, and demonstrations in order to get its views across.

---

[43] For a recent account of the growing unrest in Tibet, see *International Herald Tribune*, June 22, 1992; for Xinjiang, *South China Morning Post*, June 1, 1992; and for Mongolia, *Far Eastern Economic Review*, April 9, 1992, pp. 18–19.

[44] *International Herald Tribune*, June 29, 1992.

It is clear that the PRC's overcentralized political system is no longer congruent with an increasingly decentralized economic system, or at least a system in which much economic activity occurs outside the centrally planned system. The economic reforms are giving rise to new forces within Chinese society. If the CCP continues to pursue economic reform, it will have to adopt strategies to accommodate the demands of these new forces. In addition, the party will be dependent on new strata such as professional managers, traders, and entrepreneurs, as well as on the technicians and scientists who were already important for the functioning of the centrally planned economy, to implement the more market-oriented policies. The development of effective institutions to accommodate the interests of these new strata will be a difficult task, given their diffuse nature. Unless the new generation of leaders can undertake a major institutional overhaul, they run the risk of crushing the very vitality and input needed to further their policies of economic modernization.

2 The Chinese Economy: Moving Forward

Gary H. Jefferson

The growth rate of China's GNP increased in 1991, following a three-year austerity program during which rates of inflation and real growth both fell. In 1992, GNP growth has further accelerated to match the double-digit rates characteristic of much of 1978–88, the first decade of China's reform program. With the end of austerity, the reform-minded elements of China's leadership are again taking an aggressive stand in an effort to broaden the economic reform program. Resurgent growth and a more open emphasis on reform are causing other countries that are moving toward a market-regulated economy to view China's economic reform program as a successful experiment worthy of study.

After the traumatic crisis of Tiananmen, the bottom-up nature of China's economic reform program became even more pronounced. While China's central leadership moved to consolidate political control, it effectively ceded the initiative on economic reform to provincial and local governments, particularly in the southern provinces of Guangdong, Fujian, and Hainan. Recent reform has been most notable in the areas of foreign trade and investment and, increasingly, in the development of financial institutions and markets. During the past year, industry and, despite serious flooding, agriculture have turned in respectable performances. Still, a number of critical issues remain to be resolved. Among these are the possibility of resurgent inflation due to underlying institutional weaknesses that threaten price stability, an explosive growth of the working-age population, expanding environmental degradation and associated health hazards, and the problem of political succession.

Renewal of Reform

The coincidence of an officially sanctioned austerity program in late 1988 (followed by the crackdown in Tiananmen Square during the spring of 1989) and the ascendancy of China's conservative leadership faction makes it difficult to distinguish between the economic and the political motives for reform. The absence of an independent central banking system and well-established financial markets, the principal instruments for carrying out macroeconomic policy in Western industrial countries, caused the Chinese government to rely extensively on heavy-handed administrative methods to implement the anti-inflation program initiated in the fall of 1988. Forced exchanges of wages for government bonds, the extension of price controls, and the forcible closing of many nonstate township village enterprises (TVEs), while consistent with short-run efforts to curtail inflation, could also be interpreted as a resolve to throw China's reform program into reverse.

Although the government did not formally end its three-year austerity program until March 1992, the Chinese leadership began to reflate the economy nearly two years earlier, in response to the nation's rising unemployment and the specter of political rebellion in the communist states of the Soviet bloc. Coincidentally, beginning in the winter of 1992, a "new wave" of reform was signaled by Deng Xiaoping's Chinese New Year trip to Shenzhen, China's booming city across the border from Hong Kong. A front-page commentary in the *People's Daily* praising the merits of capitalist methods, and Chinese Communist Party (CCP) General Secretary Ziang Zemin's public embrace of lessons to be learned by China from capitalism, have reinforced the impression that China's leadership is resuming forward momentum with its reform program.[1] The ruling 15-man Politburo, after a meeting in March, publicly committed China to keep unchanged "for 100 years" the policies of reform and opening to the outside world.

However, China's leadership is far from being of a single mind with respect to the pace of reform and economic growth. An 18.2 percent rise in industrial output during the first quarter of 1992 from a year earlier has rekindled worries about inflation. Reports persist of tensions between Deng and his supporters, who want to sustain economic growth at double-digit levels within an accelerated reform environment, and the more conservative State Council, which wants to restrict growth rates to the 6–7 percent range and establish a tighter grip over the economy.

Still, enthusiasm for reform has risen unmistakably. Specific reforms undertaken by the State Council for 1992 and those reported to be planned for subsequent years include: [2]

---

[1] "The Opening Salvo," *Far Eastern Economic Review*, March 12, 1992.

[2] The following list is drawn from *China Trade Review*, May 1992; *New York Times*, June 28, 1992; and *Economist*, June 20–26, 1992.

Price reform. After a suspension of significant price reforms, new initiatives are being taken to restructure China's price system, including substantial adjustments to urban food prices. During the first half of 1992, the price of noodles doubled relative to its level two years before, and, in Shanghai, electricity and water rates jumped by 50 percent. Coal prices around the country are scheduled to rise sharply from their current absurdly low levels.

Enterprise management reform. A second area of reform focuses on state enterprises, involving changes in their internal management and wage system. One element of this reform package gives money-losing state factories the power to set their own wages. The immediate aim is to create pay scales that reward individual effort and skill (instead of length of service and political performance) and thus boost productivity.

There are also expanded efforts to establish welfare provisions independent of state enterprises, including unemployment insurance, pensions, medical care, and housing. These further limit the functions of state enterprises to economic matters and create an independent safety net for workers, which would make it easier for enterprises to declare bankruptcy since employees would no longer have to rely on them for many welfare benefits.

More state-owned companies are being forced to merge, lay off workers, cut production if their goods are unmarketable, and make do with reduced subsidies if they are losing money. Although these measures are controversial, the government reported in June that it had already laid off 1.4 million workers. This is equivalent to about 1 percent of the urban labor force. Pro-reform Vice-Premier Zhu Rongji, the former mayor of Shanghai charged with bringing discipline to the state sector, estimates that there may be 10 million redundant workers in the system, which in all likelihood underestimates the magnitude of the problem.[3]

Enterprise finance. Experiments with stock issues are to be carried out on a much broader basis. According to one plan, more than one-half of state-owned companies will issue stock over the next five years or so. About 20 percent of the shares are expected to go to individuals and the rest to companies, universities, and government departments. This year five Beijing enterprises are scheduled to issue shares of stock to the public.[4]

---

[3] "China: Iron Rice Bowl Shows Cracks," *South China Morning Post*, June 16, 1992 (reported in *China News Digest* [hereafter *CND*, a computer-based electronic mail service], June 21, 1992).

[4] "Firms to Issue First Beijing Public Stocks," *China Daily* (Business Weekly Supplement), April 26–May 2, 1992 (reported in Foreign Broadcasting Information Service, *Daily Report, China* [hereafter FBIS-CHI], April 22, 1992).

Agricultural reform. China's agricultural sector continues to be increasingly subject to market regulation. The government now controls the buying and selling prices of only 25 percent of China's agricultural products; the rest are market controlled. During the past year, to boost wheat, maize, and rice production, the government has increased the prices of these crops.

These price incentives to promote increased production are necessary because China's population is growing at an annual pace of some 15 million, while the acreage of cultivated farmland is diminishing at an annual rate of about 333,000 hectares.

At the same time, the State Council has issued a circular decreeing, from April 1, 1992, raises in the state selling prices of grain to levels equal to state purchasing prices. The circular says that the raising of grain prices is an important step in accelerating the reform of the country's grain purchasing and selling system so as to move toward the elimination of state subsidies for marketable grain.[5]

Housing reform. Apartment rents have doubled, or by 1993 will double, in most Chinese cities, and they will quadruple by 1994. Many cities are also introducing plans to pressure occupants to buy their own homes, finally lifting key controls on rent after years of talk but little action. To rid itself of a large and poorly maintained housing stock, the state wants to sell off apartments at a subsidized cost. To keep a speculative secondary market from developing, the worker's place of employment is expected to retain partial ownership and, thereby, the right to control resale and profits. Rents, which in the past have represented about 1 percent of the average city-dweller's income, are likely to rise to about 20 percent.

Although in some locations, notably Yantai in Shandong Province, which has been on the cutting-edge of housing reform, the local government has provided income subsidies to offset increased rents, it is unlikely that many cities will replace the housing subsidy with another. In Guangzhou approximately 52 percent of the city's houses had been sold by early 1992 to individual buyers.

Foreign investment. Foreign investment will be allowed in new areas of the Chinese economy, particularly in the service sector. The first joint venture will be allowed soon in the insurance industry, a Japanese company is being allowed to open a joint-venture department store in Shanghai, and foreign banks will be allowed to open branches in several cities. For the first time since 1949, Chinese au-

[5] "State Grain Sales Price to Match Buying Price," Xinhua, March 18, 1992 (reported in FBIS-CHI, March 19, 1992).

thorities have agreed to allow a Taiwan bank—the Taipei Business Bank—to establish a branch in mainland China, in Shanghai. Despite a ban by their government, Taiwan banks are hoping that regulations will soon be relaxed so that they can offer services to Taiwanese doing business in China.[6]

Special policies to encourage foreign investment will also be extended to the interior of China, instead of simply to the coastal areas, where investment has already been concentrated. Among the 21 localities being authorized to offer tax breaks and other preferential terms to foreign investors are cities along the Yangtze River and provincial capitals in sensitive border regions next to Vietnam, ex-Soviet Central Asia, the Russian Far East, and Korea. This initiative demonstrates the leadership's understanding of the urgent need to spread the success of the coastal regions to poorer inland areas.[7]

Evaluation of the Industrial Reforms

Recently a number of articles in the Western press have emphasized the poor profit performance of China's state industrial sector. In 1991, 29.7 percent of all state-owned industrial enterprises turned in losses for the year. In that year industries directly controlled by the central government sustained a $5.7 billion loss, in addition to setting a record of $22 billion in delinquent taxes.[8] These reports strongly suggest that various reforms implemented in the urban industrial sector during the 1980s have been largely ineffectual.

However, different perspectives are now emerging on the achievements of China's state-owned industrial enterprises during the 1980s. Probably the most exhaustive study of productivity change in Chinese industry during this period concludes that in state industry, total factor productivity rose at an average annual rate of 2.4 percent from 1980 to 1988. During the same period the rate for the collective sector, not including TVEs below the village level, was estimated at 4.6 percent.[9]

One key source of efficiency growth would appear to be gains in allocative efficiency, that is, reallocations of capital, labor, and intermediate inputs (i.e., materials and energy) across sectors and enterprises

[6] "China Permits First Taiwan Bank to Open Branch in Mainland," Associated Press–Dow Jones, June 29, 1992 (reported in *CND*, June 30, 1992).

[7] "CCP 'Document No. 4' Promotes Further Reform and Opening Up," British Broadcasting Corporation, June 19, 1992 (reported in *CND*, June 24, 1992).

[8] "China Pursues Policy of the Bottom Line," *Asian Wall Street Journal*, March 2, 1992.

[9] G. H. Jefferson, T. G. Rawski, and Y. X. Zheng, *Economic Development and Cultural Change*, Vol. 40, no. 2 (January 1992), pp. 239–66.

to their most efficient uses. Evidence in support of this proposition includes a dramatic convergence of profit rates across 37 branches of state industry.[10] Another study, based on 226 large and medium-sized enterprises, indicates that even among those enterprises at the core of the state industrial system, the (marginal) productivities of capital, labor, and intermediate inputs have tended to become more equal.[11] Thus it would appear that a more efficient allocation of resources within the state system, motivated by greater market discipline and managerial incentives, is one explanation of gains in the measured productivity of state industry.

Is there any way of reconciling these apparently contradictory perspectives of declining profitability and rising efficiency? A substantial portion of the losses of state industry has little to do with its underlying efficiency. Rather, the increase in losses during recent years in part reflects the austerity program and slowdown in production. As a result of the recovery during 1991, losses that had grown by 19 percent during the first half of 1991 grew by just 3.6 percent during the second half. Moreover, 40 percent of these losses originated from the coal and petroleum extraction industries, in which prices are still controlled well below their market levels.

Furthermore, even as the productivity of state industry has risen with the expansion of competition with the nonstate sector, losses in state industry have persisted or even grown. Productivity *is* rising in the state sector, but it is rising even faster in the nonstate sector, allowing the latter to eat into the excessively high profits of the traditional state sector. Twenty-six percent of reported losses in the state sector are concentrated in Jiangsu and Zhejiang provinces, where the share of nonstate industry is largest and industrial competition is intense. Thus, even as state enterprises continue to show positive rates of productivity growth, the faster advance of productivity in the competing nonstate sector will result in a *relative* decline in the state-owned sector that is likely to generate growing losses in that sector and a continuing fall in its share of industrial output. At some point during 1992 the share of state industry in total industrial output is likely to fall below half of total industrial output as compared with a commanding share of about 90 percent in the late 1970s.

[10] Barry Naughton, "Implications of the State Monopoly over Industry and Its Relaxation," *Modern China*, Vol. 18, no. 1 (January 1992), pp. 14–41.

[11] G. H. Jefferson and W. Y. Xu, "Assessing Gains in Efficient Production among China's Industrial Enterprises" (Manuscript, November 3, 1991).

Foreign Trade and Investment

After running trade deficits between 1985 and 1989, China achieved a surplus in 1990. In 1991 China's two-way trade notched up a 17.5 percent increase to $136 billion, with a net surplus of $12.5 billion.[12] By the end of 1991, China reported having accumulated about $40 billion in foreign-exchange reserves, a figure that continues to grow in the face of persistent trade surpluses.

During the first decade of China's reforms, owing to its proximity to Hong Kong, Guangdong Province captured about two-thirds of foreign direct investment in China. Since the late 1980s, however, as Taiwan's investment role has grown, Fujian Province, the original home of many Taiwanese, has increasingly become the focus of foreign investment. Fully a third of the $3.5 billion total investment in Xiamen during 1986–91 is from Taiwan. However, during 1991 Taiwanese investment also spread to other major cities like Shenzhen (the number of Taiwanese joint ventures rose by 21 percent to 739), Guangzhou (rising 25 percent to 320), and Shanghai (doubling to more than 200). Recent reforms in the area of foreign investment—those described above authorizing joint ventures in the service sector and establishing Special Economic Zones in the interior—should result in a more geographically and sectorally diversified pattern of investment.

During 1991–92 the government began to take major initiatives toward dismantling barriers to trade that have also impeded its efforts to join the General Agreement on Tariffs and Trade (GATT), the world's ruling body for trade. One such major initiative now in the planning stage is the elimination of the current multirate exchange-rate system in favor of a single, convertible currency. Li Langqing, head of the Ministry of Foreign Economic Relations and Trade (MOFERT), said in January 1992 that China "will gradually rationalize the exchange rate . . . [and] apply a unitary floating exchange-rate system." In May, Chen Yuan, deputy governor of the People's Bank of China, reaffirmed this intent.

Trade negotiations between the United States and China during 1992 have focused on Washington's effort to make Chinese trade practices more consistent with general international trade practice. At stake is Washington's threat, made under Section 301 of the U.S. Trade Act, to impose up to $4 billion in punitive tariffs on Chinese goods if a range of barriers are not removed by October 1992.

Among other demands, U.S. negotiators want the Chinese side to take steps toward "transparency" in its murky trade system by agree-

---

12 "Warm Glow," *Far Eastern Economic Review*, March 12, 1992.

ing to publish or eliminate *neibu* (secret) rules used to limit trade, and to issue for the first time a comprehensive list of all import bans, controls, and quotas.[13] Attempting to move toward satisfying the GATT requirements, the Chinese government is reported to be undertaking the following specific measures:[14]

Gradually lowering the general tariff level to meet GATT requirements for developing countries and adjusting the rates of import duties on various commodities. During the first half of 1992, China lowered import duties on 225 products and expressed willingness to negotiate further tariff reductions in the course of recovering its status as a GATT signatory state.

Narrowing the scope of commodities subject to import-license management. At present 53 commodities are subject to import-license management, and the number will be dropped to only 37 in the near future, resulting in a total reduction of two-thirds in two years.

Formulating a "Foreign Trade Law" and an "Anti-Dumping Law" in order to make China's trade law and practices more transparent. Specifically, China has abolished import and export licenses on 205 goods for which licenses are issued by MOFERT commissioners stationed in various provinces and cities. The import and export of 29 remaining goods continue to be restricted by licenses that are directly managed by MOFERT. Henceforth all rules and regulations concerning import and export management will be made public by MOFERT.

Beginning to abolish export subsidies and allowing foreign-trade enterprises to take sole responsibility for profits and losses.

Supporting a proposal to join two international property-rights conventions: the Berne Convention for the Protection of Literary and Artistic Works and the Universal Copyright Convention. In addition, the Standing Committee of the National People's Congress is also expected to approve amendments to China's patent law to bring it more in line with international standards.[15]

These concessions, consistent with China's strategy to recover its place in the GATT, are being occasioned in large part by negotiations

[13] Reported in *CND*, from United Press International, May 22, 1992.

[14] The following information was drawn from "Import Reform Measures to Aid GATT Accession," *Da gong pao*, April 13, 1992, p. 2, and "Nation to Abolish Import, Export Licenses," *China chi jih pao*, April 10, 1992 (both translated in FBIS, April 16, 1992).

[15] Associated Press–Dow Jones, June 23, 1992 (reported in *CND*, June 25, 1992).

with the United States. "Our objective is to open the Chinese market and to bring the practices under investigation into line with international practice," stated U.S. Trade Representative Carla Hills.[16] Beyond these practices, since the Chinese government's crackdown in Tiananmen Square, China's most-favored-nation (MFN) status has provoked an annual debate in the U.S. Congress. For four successive years President George Bush has succeeded in his efforts to deflect Congress's attempts to void or condition China's MFN status. The persistence of a large and growing U.S. trade deficit with China, second only to that with Japan; continued human rights violations, including persistent reports of exports produced by prison labor (*laogai*); and Chinese arms sales are, however, making it increasingly likely that Congress will succeed in placing conditions on future renewals of China's special trade status.

Financial Markets

A key issue facing the Chinese economy is the public's rapid accumulation of financial savings and the need to diversify the nation's financial system to store this wealth and channel it into productive investment. According to government statistics, individuals now have accumulated some $260 billion in savings deposits, stocks, bonds, and cash. This is equal to 18 months' wages for every person of working age. The savings-deposit component alone totals *renminbi* (Rmb) 911 billion ($166.8 billion), a 30 percent rise from the end of 1990 and an astounding 140 percent rise from the end of 1988. Thus, as the government's budget deficit is growing ever larger, China's national savings rate (government plus private savings) remains at high levels.

Observers note that this savings glut represents either a bomb or a blessing for China's economy, depending on the government's reform of the nation's financial institutions. If the money is channeled into economic development through stocks and bonds and long-term savings deposits, it will hasten China's modernization. But if left in short-term savings, it could fuel rampant inflation and panic buying should the economy take a turn for the worse.

A high-level body, the Securities Association of China, has been established to coordinate the developing securities industry in China. Since 1986, bond trading has reemerged in major coastal cities such as Shanghai, Tianjin, Shenyang, Harbin, and Guangzhou. During the past two years, China's leadership has been allowing the steady ex-

[16] "U.S. Trade Authority Seeks Comment on Need for China Tariffs," Associated Press–Dow Jones, June 29, 1992 (reported in *CND*, July 1, 1992).

pansion of China's stock and bond markets. In 1991 a total of about Rmb 25 billion in bonds was traded in China, 40 percent of this by individuals. This compares with total bond trading of Rmb 11 billion in 1990 and Rmb 2.1 billion in 1989.[17]

There are only two securities exchanges in China that have been formally authorized to trade company shares. Both the Shanghai and Shenzhen securities exchanges were established by similar legislation approved in late 1990 by the People's Bank of China. This may provide some indication of a basic pattern of legislation to be expected in the event of other exchanges opening throughout the country. It is expected that the central government will draft comprehensive national legislation in the future and exchanges will be established in other major cities. In the meantime, unwilling to wait for Beijing's authorization, Hainan Island has established its own renegade stock exchange.

During 1992, share trading in China has become less restricted and more open. The Shanghai stock exchange has abolished limits on daily price fluctuations; the price of one stock immediately climbed 470 percent. As part of a renewed endorsement of Deng's policy of opening to the outside world, and 43 years after the expulsion of foreign investors following the Chinese revolution, the Shanghai and Shenzhen stock exchanges have begun issuing "B" shares to overseas investors. These shares are denominated in *renminbi,* but are sold for foreign exchange.

On the heels of the establishment of China's first stock markets, initiatives are also being taken to establish futures markets. The Shanghai metal exchange, expected to be China's first real futures market, opened in late May 1992. At the same time, Shanghai's Foreign Exchange Transaction Centre is working toward regular trading of currency-forward contracts (a kind of futures market for foreign exchange), although officials acknowledge that few people inside or outside the exchange are yet familiar with the concept. Finally, city officials in Shanghai want to set up a grain and edible-oil exchange that would trade futures contracts on these crucial commodities.[18]

So far China has opened only Shanghai to foreign-branch banking, having given six banks permission to establish branches there in 1991, including the aforementioned Taiwan bank. More recently the Chinese government has given its approval for foreign banks to set up branches in Guangzhou, Dalian, and Tianjin. Previously branches had been restricted to operate mainly in the Special Economic Zones and

---

[17] "China Pursues Policy of the Bottom Line," *Asian Wall Street Journal,* April 2, 1992.

[18] "Shanghai Is Economic Reform Battlefield," Reuter, June 24, 1992 (reported in *CND,* June 28, 1992).

in Shanghai. At present 47 foreign financial institutions have opened branches in China, including Citibank, Bank of America, Crédit Lyonnais, Banque Indosuez, and Sanwabank.

The Chinese leadership expects that the expansion of the role of foreign banks in China can help ease funds shortages, enable them to serve as go-betweens by introducing foreign clients to investment opportunities in China, help promote the country's fledgling securities markets and real-estate industry, and transfer advanced and effective banking management methods to domestic banks.[19]

Lessons from China's Reform Experience

Recently, analyzing the experience of a full decade of reform during the 1980s, economists have been attempting to draw lessons from China's economic reforms. Three of the studies—"Lessons from China's Economic Reform," by Chen, Jefferson, and Singh (1992); "How to Reform a Planned Economy: Lessons From China," by McMillan and Naughton (1992); and "What Is Special about China's Economic Reforms?" by Xiao Geng (1991)—have a surprisingly similar emphasis.[20] The first, by Chen et al., identifies six key lessons, used here to organize the principal observations of all three papers.

The importance of a leading sector. Few of the achievements or failures of China's reform program can be viewed in isolation; dynamic change in one sector has invariably spilled over into change in other sectors.

Specifically, the rapid transformation of China's communal agriculture to family-based farming resulted in dramatic increases in farm output and labor productivity. Rapid increases in labor productivity and savings created surplus supplies of rural labor and capital that were channeled into nonfarm activities, particularly the development of rural industry. Even as China's state industrial output was growing at an average rate of 8 percent per year during the 1980s, the share of rural industrial output in total industrial production expanded from 13 percent in 1980 to its current share of more than 25 percent.

---

[19] "Expanded Foreign Bank Activities Viewed," Xinhua, May 6, 1992 (reported in FBIS-CHI, May 7, 1992).

[20] Chen Kang, Gary Jefferson, and Inderjit Singh, "Lessons from China's Economic Reform," *Journal of Comparative Economics*, June 1992; John McMillan and Barry Naughton, "How to Reform a Planned Economy: Lessons from China," *Oxford Review of Economic Policy*, Vol. 8, no. 1, pp. 130–43; Xiao Geng, "What Is Special about China's Economic Reforms," Research Paper Series no. 23, Socialist Economies Reform Unit, World Bank, November 1991.

This explosion of rural industry has caused it to become a leading sector, now lubricating other dimensions of reform and generating intersectoral benefits. Rural industry has expanded the scope of market activity, bringing competitive pressures to bear on state-owned enterprises. At the same time, rural industrial enterprises have become competitive exporters, accounting for more than one-quarter of Chinese exports. Finally, the development of the TVE sector has both mitigated the problem of rural surplus labor and the flight of workers to the cities and diffused the potential under the reforms for a growing division between urban and rural areas.

The efficacy of gradual and partial reform. China's urban industrial reforms are a model of piecemeal, on-again, off-again reform, involving profit retention and management contract systems rather than outright privatization, and a dual-track pricing system rather than complete marketization. The two-tier pricing system has made state enterprises more sensitive to market signals while also creating a competitive link between the more rigid state sector and the dynamic nonstate sector. In 1991, 80 percent of the products of rural enterprises were sold on the open market.

McMillan and Naughton arrive at a key conclusion about the lesson of China's economic success: "Privatization is not crucial; competition is." According to these authors, the success of China's industrial reforms resulted from the following developments:

> First, massive entry of non-state firms; second, a dramatic increase in competition, both among state firms and between state firms and non-state firms; and, third, improvements in the performance of state-owned firms resulting from state-imposed market-like incentives.[21]

China's experience shows that privatization need not be the centerpiece of a reform policy. As indicated by the rapid growth of the nonstate sector, "entrepreneurs set up new firms." In addition, as discussed above, "state-owned firms' performance can be improved." And finally, as enterprises restructure and the nonstate sector grows, "the state-owned sector acts as a safety net," retaining redundant labor while more-productive jobs within and outside the state sector are created. Thus China has created a reform process in which the state sector must perform on a par with the nonstate sector to retain its output share; if it does not, it withers away.

[21] McMillan and Naughton "How to Reform a Planned Economy," p. 131.

The importance of a kindred economic model. Both Chen et al. and Xiao emphasize the important contribution of Hong Kong, Macao, and Taiwan to China's reform program. One conspicuous feature concerning the internationalization of the Chinese economy, particularly the outwardly oriented provinces of the Southeast, is the dominant role of these kindred regions. As trading partner, financier, and intermediary and facilitator, Hong Kong, in particular, has had a pervasive effect on the developmental path of a country with 200 times the population of this small but dynamic entrepôt.

In southern China, economies are booming beyond all expectation. Hong Kong serves as the management and financial hub of a region where economic growth tops 13 percent a year. At this rate an economy doubles every six years. Twenty percent of Hong Kong's bank notes circulate in Guangdong Province, where some 16,000 Hong Kong–owned factories employ 3 million workers and export almost $11 billion worth of goods a year. Guangdong's estimated GDP is $78 billion, or $1,230 per capita, roughly the equivalent of Thailand's and almost double that of Malaysia.[22]

Hong Kong accounts for three-quarters of Guangdong's foreign trade, and Guangdong itself accounts for more than 40 percent of all of China's exports. Hong Kong is also responsible for the lion's share of direct foreign investment in the province: 80 percent of the $17 billion worth approved by the Chinese authorities.

Hong Kong and Guangdong stand in mutually reinforcing stages of development. Labor in Hong Kong costs at least five times as much as labor in Shenzhen (which has the highest wages in Guangdong). A 50-year lease on land in Hong Kong costs 30 to 50 times as much as in Shenzhen. Hong Kong is fast becoming a high-wage service economy, the marketing and management headquarters for manufacturing in southern China.[23] This deepening link between Hong Kong and Guangdong is creating a level of confidence in Hong Kong's future that would have been unimaginable in the wake of the Tiananmen crisis. "The combination of the Hong Kong–Guangdong connection is exciting the imaginations of a lot of people," commented John C. Wilson, cochairman of the American Chamber of Commerce's trade and investment committee.[24]

Finally, the presence of Hong Kong in many ways requires Beijing to pursue market-consistent policies. The widespread use of the Hong

[22] *Transition*, World Bank, February 1992.

[23] *Economist Yearbook*, 1992, p. 110.

[24] "Confidence Increases in Hong Kong," *International Herald Tribune*, June 10, 1992 (reported in *CND*, June 16, 1992).

Kong dollar in Guangdong and the crossing of an average of 100,000 persons a day between Hong Kong and Guangdong impose a certain discipline on the government's official valuation of the *renminbi*. In recent years the official exchange rate of the Rmb has become increasingly consistent with the underlying black-market rate. At the same time, the Chinese government has established government-run swap markets in major cities where Chinese and foreign businesses can exchange large amounts of currency at rates that reflect market conditions. In the absence of the swap markets and reasonable similarity between the official and market rates, black market transactions in Guangdong would overwhelm efforts to maintain the exchange rate of the Rmb at unrealistically high levels.

The critical distinction between managed reform and bottom-up (or spontaneous) reform. Economic reform usually has a proactive connotation, suggesting that the central government designs, initiates, and implements a reform program. In the case of China, notable among the initiatives of the central government have been the establishment of Special Economic Zones, provisions for the retention by enterprises of profits and the distribution of bonuses, and the enterprise contract responsibility system. Although the direct impact of these initiatives has been substantial, in the case of China reform from the bottom up has played a major role. Three points deserve emphasis.

First, it is critical to realize that many of these reforms are enabling reforms; that is, they authorize local initiatives but do not guarantee their success. In order for reform initiatives from the central government to be successful, households, enterprises, and localities must respond to them. Certain labor reforms have been widely adopted by state enterprises, including the authority to contract labor and rationalize the work force (optimal labor combination program). Once they receive the go-ahead, local agents in China show an impressive capacity to "run with the ball."

Second, many reforms have followed de facto change; the government consented to or sanctioned important reforms only after they had become widespread. These include China's highly successful agricultural reforms. The two most important components of the household production responsibility system—leasing land for household farming and setting quotas on a household basis—were in 1979 explicitly banned by China's leadership and not formally sanctioned until these key agricultural reforms had been almost universally implemented. The most recent example of the central government sanctioning bottom-up reform is Beijing's decision in 1991 to authorize formally trading on the stock markets of Shanghai and Shenzhen.

Third, many reforms remain unsanctioned, including private banking as well as more-surreptitious undertakings. It is widely understood that enterprises develop counterpolicies (*duice*) that are formulated to counter or thwart government policy (*zhengce*) or regulations that inhibit local initiative or profit. Hainan Island's renegade stock exchange began operating during the spring of 1992. Following a three-day closure said to be needed to resolve operational problems but coinciding with a visit by Chinese government authorities, the bourse reopened and remains without official authorization. More recently, local leaders in Xiamen, Chongqing, and Liaoning have all ignored the official approval process and started selling stocks or stock purchase certificates without permission.[25]

These bottom-up initiatives are critical for China's reform strategy, because they provide an important complement to the gradual, partial strategy of the center. Reform bottlenecks can often be resolved by spontaneous initiatives from below.

Obstruction of reform by flawed institutions and bad policy. Economic reform is impeded not just by the lack of a feasible strategy, the lack of political will, or the fear of economic dislocation. At certain junctures of China's reform process, flawed institutions (or policy instruments) and bad policy have also made key reforms difficult to initiate or to sustain.

During China's recent austerity program, the absence of a strong central bank and well-developed financial markets required the use of intrusive administrative measures to curtail inflation. Forced distribution of government bonds to urban workers in lieu of cash wages, resort to price controls, administrative allocation of scarce raw material supplies, and the forcible closing of rural enterprises—all clumsy administrative means employed during 1989–90—impaired microeconomic efficiency.

A central underlying cause of China's recurrent inflation is an inefficient fiscal system that has contributed to declining revenues and chronic government budget deficits, thereby necessitating borrowing and money creation, with inflationary consequences. The introduction of the system of giving local government responsibility over finances resulted in localities obtaining a surplus of revenue over expenditures and in chronic deficits at the center. Although reforms to strengthen the central government finances have been proposed, they have been shelved owing to strong opposition from the fiscally healthy local regions. No solution is therefore in sight.[26]

---

[25] Reuters, July 2, 1992 (reported in *CND*, July 4, 1992).

[26] As both Xiao and McMillan and Naughton point out, however, some gains have been made in this critical area of fiscal reform. The growth of revenues from the non-

Like flawed institutions, bad policies can inhibit reform. For example, the Chinese government persists in granting capital and energy subsidies to state-owned enterprises. The result is an insatiable thirst for investment goods to support capital- and energy-intensive production techniques, which reduce the demand for labor. As a consequence, granting profit-maximizing enterprises unfettered autonomy to lay off workers would, at prevailing distorted factor prices, result in intolerably high levels of urban unemployment. As Chen et al. emphasize, persistent distortions in relative factor prices are undermining efforts to move forward with aggressive labor market reform.

The importance of economic checks and balances and the difficulty of achieving these under a communist system. Even though China has made impressive strides in its reform program, it is unlikely that the Chinese government can establish a world-class economy without a unified system of law and the checks and balances needed to protect enterprises from the arbitrary bureaucratic interference and the unequal rules of doing business that prevail throughout China. Among the most critically needed reforms are banking and collateral law, commercial law, enterprise law, and property rights law. It is unlikely that enterprises can achieve the requisite autonomy without widespread ownership reform, that is, a move toward more private ownership of the major means of production.

Xiao demonstrates the relationship between ownership reform and productivity gains. Analyzing the relationship between the combined productivity of capital and labor (total factor productivity) and the share of nonstate industrial output in 30 provinces, he finds a strong association between productivity and the share of nonstate industry. It may be that, ultimately, a system of private-property rights will be the only way to shield enterprises from the arbitrary bureaucratic interference that inevitably takes its toll on economic efficiency.

McMillan and Naughton argue that policymakers concerned with transition strategy for East European countries and former Soviet republics have not sufficiently appreciated the relevance of the successful Chinese experience. While economic theory predicts that the introduction of markets and incentives will result in rising output and efficiency, among the many formerly centrally planned economies making the transition, only China's has performed in a manner consistent with this prediction. "While the exact sequence of events in

---

state sector, both relative and absolute, has helped to offset shrinking revenues from the state sector. While Xiao sees a broadening of the tax base, McMillan and Naughton applaud the development, albeit more slowly than they consider desirable, of a more diversified tax system.

China cannot and should not be replicated elsewhere," McMillan and Naughton point out, "the key features of China's reforms can be adopted in other countries."[27]

China's Economic Prospects

The review given above paints a rosy picture of the current state of the Chinese economy and the prospects for continued reform. Indeed, during the past year, inside and outside China, investors and analysts have become more "bullish" about the Chinese economy. Having survived the combined shock of economic austerity and political retrenchment, economic reform in China is now widely viewed as irreversible.

While the restoration of economic growth and the renewed emphasis on reform by the central government are impressive, observers should also heed difficult near- and long-term problems that the Chinese government must address.

Rekindled inflation. During the first quarter of 1992, China's industrial output increased 18.2 percent over last year. The April 1992 cost-of-living index in China's 35 major cities jumped 14 percent over the same month in 1991.

As suggested earlier here and by Barry Naughton in his review of the Chinese economy in *China Briefing, 1991,*[28] this recurrent tendency of policymakers to overinflate the economy relates in substantial part to the absence of a well-developed system of macroeconomic controls, including a weak fiscal system and, underneath that, the persistence of government subsidies to the state sector. According to Western accounting methods, China suffered from a deficit of Rmb 66.6 billion last year. This figure—nearly 4 percent of GNP—is a record high for the PRC. The 1992 budget revives the specter of inflation with its prospect of further stepped-up government spending and credit expansion.[29] The principal danger of another round of accelerating inflation is that it will undermine the credibility of the resurgent reformers while, in the absence of well-established instruments of macroeconomic management, also necessitating the use of clumsy administrative interventions with adverse effects on efficiency.

Rapid labor-force growth. Following the Cultural Revolution baby boom, record numbers of persons are now reaching working age. According to

[27] McMillan and Naughton, "How to Reform a Planned Economy," p. 131.

[28] Barry Naughton, "The Chinese Economy: On the Road to Recovery?" in *China Briefing, 1991,* ed. William A. Joseph (Boulder: Westview Press and The Asia Society, 1992).

[29] "Business As Usual," *Far Eastern Economic Review,* April 2, 1992.

the Ministry of Labor, nearly 23 million new workers (7.2 million in the cities and towns and 15.6 in the countryside) are expected to join the labor force each year for the next five years. In 1991, 4.3 million new jobs were created in China's cities and towns, a substantially smaller number than the forecast growth of the work force.[30]

In the meantime, efforts to promote labor reform by "smashing the three irons"—the "iron rice bowl" (lifetime employment), the "iron salary" (guaranteed wages), and the "iron armchair" (guaranteed position for managers)—are encountering resistance through strikes and other signs of labor unrest. The combination of accelerating growth in the labor force and continuing distorted factor prices makes it highly unlikely that in the foreseeable future China can succeed in establishing a competitive, mobile labor market. A critical step in resolving this contradiction is the elimination of subsidies for capital and energy consumption that motivate producers to employ inefficient labor-saving techniques.

Ecological pressures. Plentiful supplies of coal and a skewed pricing system that discourages investment in alternative energy sources have made China the most coal-dependent country in the world. Coal now fuels two-thirds of China's commercial industry, compared with about 19 percent in Europe and 53 percent in India. The country's remarkable economic growth during the 1980s was fueled almost entirely with coal. Now its cities are among the most polluted in the world.

There are two main environmental consequences of China's dependence on coal. The first is the high level of "total suspended particles" and sulphur dioxide in the air. This poses a serious health hazard to residents of Beijing, Chongqing, Shenyang, and other industrial cities. The second problem is global—the so-called greenhouse effect, the concern of leaders attending the Rio Earth Summit in June 1992.

In 1965, according to World Bank statistics, China produced only 5 percent of the carbon dioxide emitted into the atmosphere. By 1985 its share had more than doubled, now standing at around 12 percent and making China the third biggest producer of greenhouse carbon gases.[31] Although this figure is not high in per capita terms, the sheer size of China's population, the current growth rate of output and emissions, and the prospective size of China's GNP will make it vulnerable to international pressure to transform its production process, thus requiring, at least in the short run, tradeoffs with economic growth.

---

30 *Wall Street Journal,* March 2, 1992.

31 T. M. Tong, *Independent,* May 25, 1992 (*CND*).

The succession problem. China's leadership still lacks a stable way to transfer power. This is an old problem for China, which over the ages has typically been ruled through a highly personalized authoritarian system. The anticipated or actual demise of the reigning ruler triggers a power struggle. Each new struggle delays China's quest to become a modern economy.

Deep divisions persist within the Chinese polity regarding the pace of reform and the ultimate vision of the roles of the market and private ownership within the Chinese economy. During the spring and summer of 1992, the dismissal or death of key hard-liners gave Deng Xiaoping a freer hand to position reformers in the government. It remains the case, however, that the return to reformist policies rests largely on the acumen and stature of a single person, Deng, whose passing will almost certainly once again unsettle China's political scene and threaten the country's near-term economic progress.

In sum, 1992 is emerging as the year in which the Chinese government is moving the country back on the track of economic reform. Economic growth has again become robust. This is a historic year for China, since industrial output from the nonstate sector will for the first time eclipse that from the state sector; industrial output produced and sold under the state plan will shrink to about 20 percent of total industrial output. This is an important indication that China has indeed moved substantially toward a market-regulated economy.

Whereas economic reform is clearly accelerating, political reform remains stalemated. Rapidly rising living standards, particularly in coastal urban areas, are likely to rekindle demands for human rights and democratic processes as they did during the spring of 1989. Furthermore, dramatic democratic reforms in other formerly socialist countries have demonstrated to China's intelligentsia that popular pressure can lead to the elimination of the Communist Party's monopoly over political power. The interplay of China's inexorable drive toward economic modernization and the hesitant reform of its political system promises to be a key focus of world attention during the 1990s.

3
China and the New World Order

John W. Garver

For some 20 years, the leaders of the People's Republic of China (PRC) have believed that China, Japan, and Western Europe were emerging alongside the United States and the Soviet Union as independent and roughly coequal partners in a multipolar world order. According to this view of the world, old cold-war alignments were breaking down and new patterns of international relations forming. In Beijing's view, these developments were good for China: a multipolar global system would give the PRC more room for diplomatic maneuver and put China on a more equal footing with the world's front-rank powers. China still lauds trends toward a five-power multipolar system, but the collapse of the Soviet Union has left the United States as the world's only superpower, a fact that is clearly unsettling to the policymakers in Beijing.

China in a Unipolar World

China's leaders are unhappy with the emergence of U.S. global preeminence, primarily because they believe that it makes more likely U.S. pressure to overthrow the Chinese Communist Party (CCP) and move China toward a capitalist economic system. As Deng Xiaoping told his comrades in a Politburo meeting convened in April 1990 to discuss the recent anti-communist upheaval in Eastern Europe, "Everyone should be clear that under present international circumstances all enemy strength will be directed against China and [the enemy] will use every sort of pretext to create new difficulties and pressures for us."[1] After the collapse of the Soviet Union and the overwhelming allied victory in the 1991 war against Iraq, China became even more vulnerable. In the words of one senior Chinese analyst:

---

[1] "Deng Xiaoping Reads the Future for the CCP," *Zhengming* (Contention), Hong Kong, no. 151 (May 1, 1990), p. 7.

> The changes in the world today provide strong evidence for the United States to consider that its values have prevailed. Judging by the speeches of some American politicians, people have reasons to worry about that. Faced with fewer obstacles, the United States will be more inclined to consider itself the only strong leader in the world, able to force its will on others. [Recent international events] make onlookers wary and skeptical of possible future actions by the United States. Worry and doubts about a "Pax Americana" arise in the rest of the world.[2]

In the CCP worldview, U.S. foreign policy remains animated by a fundamental hatred of communism and embodies a relentless crusade to destroy socialism around the world. According to Beijing, in the early 1950s Washington's monopoly-capitalist rulers thought they could accomplish this by outright military force. After their defeat in Korea, however, they abandoned this illusion. John Foster Dulles then worked out a more subtle, long-term strategy in which China's younger generation would be subverted by ideological and cultural means. In three or four generations China's youth would be ready to reject communism and embrace "bourgeois liberalism." According to the CCP view of the world, the "counterrevolutionary rebellion" that China experienced in early 1989 was a product of just such a strategy of "peaceful evolution" and was the result of collusion between domestic and foreign counterrevolutionaries seeking to overthrow the CCP.

The Chinese leadership believes that unipolarity is dangerous primarily because it tempts U.S. leaders to pursue more vigorously their scheme of bringing about "peaceful evolution" in China. Revocation of China's most-favored-nation (MFN) status is the most immediate action threatened by the newly supreme United States.[3] From Beijing's perspective, such a move, should it occur, would be an effort to destabilize CCP rule of China; it would be tantamount to a U.S. effort to impose American-style bourgeois-liberal values and institutions on China. It would be an expression of a U.S. drive for global hegemony. Should U.S. leaders conclude that their country has power adequate to change China into a bourgeois-liberal country, their efforts will certainly fail in the end, according to Chinese analysts, but they

[2] Zi Zhongyun, "Will a 'Pax Americana' Prevail?" *Beijing Review*, North American Edition, May 4–10, 1992, pp. 34–37.

[3] The deterioration of Sino-U.S. relations following the Beijing massacre was covered in David Zweig, "The Downward Spiral: Sino-American Relations Since Tiananmen," *China Briefing, 1991*, ed. William A. Joseph (Boulder: Westview Press and The Asia Society, 1992), pp. 119–42.

could inflict severe injury on China's development effort in the process. Aside from the revocation of MFN, a newly arrogant United States might intervene more forcefully and with more anti-communist motivation in Tibet, Hong Kong, and Taiwan. It might block China's entry into the General Agreement on Tariffs and Trade (GATT), step up "subversive" radio broadcasts into China via a Radio Free Asia, begin funding for Chinese dissident groups, or take a number of other moves antithetical to Chinese policy objectives.

The purported U.S. strategy of "peaceful evolution" figured prominently in the anti-liberal ideological indoctrination campaigns of 1989 through 1991. By mid-1992, however, it seems that "peaceful evolution" is on the way out. The theme is disappearing from the media, and new polemics against it are not appearing in the bookstores. Deng Xiaoping has apparently concluded that emphasis on foreign efforts to subvert Chinese socialism runs contrary to the renewed push for opening and reform that he desires. This does not mean that Deng no longer fears the penetration of Western liberal ideas into China—there is no evidence of that. Rather, he has apparently concluded that too much emphasis on this danger will allow his conservative opponents within the CCP to thwart the further economic reform that he believes can alone save Chinese socialism. The new anti-U.S. strategy is more subtle.

Propaganda

One important instrument of China's national policy is propaganda. With the reimposition of tight party control over the media after June 1989, one can again speak of a general "line" for Chinese foreign propaganda. This line has consistently belittled the national power and prestige of the United States. Chinese media is full, for instance, of exposés of America's problems of homelessness, violence, unemployment, drug use, and economic decline. The Los Angeles riots of April 1992 produced a torrent of articles explaining the fundamentally racist nature of American society. There are multiple reasons for the consistently negative coverage of the United States. The most important probably has to do not with foreign relations, but with countering the fascination and appeal that American society has for a great many Chinese. But there is also a foreign policy rationale. The perception of power is an important component of power, and by tarring the image of the United States, the CCP hopes to lessen American prestige. Xinhua, China's national news service, is one of several truly international news services whose dispatches are syndicated around the world. Especially in the developing countries, Xinhua dispatches receive significant play.

Another major theme of Chinese propaganda is the fragility of U.S. global preeminence. A growing economic challenge from Germany and Japan, Russia's continued possession of a nuclear arsenal adequate to destroy the United States, and the processes of European unification and a loosening of the transatlantic link combined with the recession of the Soviet threat are among the factors cited. According to one Chinese analyst: "The cold war pattern has collapsed and international relations will probably return to maneuvering among various . . . nations. The *former* allies will not always be in agreement with the United States. . . . The possibility for realizing a 'Pax Americana' is weaker, not stronger, than in the cold war period."[4] In short, the U.S.-led Western alliance is at an end. Such statements are designed to cause people to doubt the ability of the United States to impose its will. It is interesting to note that this article on "Pax Americana" appeared in the North American edition of *Beijing Review*, China's main foreign propaganda organ. If Americans have doubts about the extent of their nation's power, they are less likely to try to impose their will and values on China.

Diplomacy

China's diplomacy during the Persian Gulf War of 1991 reflected a subtle but distinct opposition to U.S. global supremacy. Beijing quickly condemned Iraq's invasion of Kuwait in August 1990 and called for an immediate end to Iraqi military actions and a peaceful settlement of Iraqi-Kuwait disputes. In the U.N. Security Council China voted for 11 resolutions directed against Iraq, including Resolution 661, which provided for mandatory economic sanctions. Despite Iraqi lobbying and a visit to Beijing by Iraqi officials, China did not use its veto power to block Security Council actions against Iraq or join Cuba and Yemen in voting against some of the resolutions. When the vote came on Resolution 678, setting a deadline for Iraqi withdrawal from Kuwait and authorizing the use of force thereafter, China abstained.

China was critical, however, of the military buildup by the United States and other powers in the Persian Gulf region, advocating a political solution to the crisis by peaceful means. It spoke out against the Western naval blockade of Iraq and condemned the U.S.-led coalition's war against Iraq after January 15, 1991. It lauded the mediatory

[4] Zi Zhongyun, "Will a 'Pax Americana' Prevail?" p. 36–37. Emphasis added.

efforts of U.N. Secretary General Javier Pérez de Cuéllar, India's attempts to come up with a "nonaligned solution," efforts toward an "Arab solution," and the cease-fire proposal broached by Soviet Foreign Minister Aleksandr Bessmertnykh. Beijing also tried its own hand at mediation, dispatching special envoy Yang Fuchang to Syria, Turkey, and Iran in February with a six-point peace plan providing for the withdrawal of Iraqi forces from Kuwait along with the removal of all foreign troops from the gulf region and a resolution of the Arab-Israeli conflict.

Beijing's Gulf War diplomacy sought conflicting objectives. On the one hand, Beijing wanted to use the opportunity of the crisis to court international goodwill in hopes of overcoming the Western sanctions imposed after the Beijing massacre. Beijing's reasonably cooperative role during the crisis confirmed President George Bush's assertion that China was an important power with which the United States needed to maintain a good working relationship, which had been Bush's chief argument against congressional proposals for revocation of MFN status. Beijing seized on Bush's desire for Chinese support at the United Nations to arrange an official visit by Foreign Minister Qian Qichen to the United States in December 1990, the first by a high-ranking Chinese official to the United States since June 1989. Beijing also wanted to court the Middle Eastern governments arrayed against Iraq, especially Egypt, Saudi Arabia, and Iran. This too mandated Chinese support for the anti-Iraq coalition.

But Beijing also feared that the military subordination of Iraq would be a step in the direction of U.S. global supremacy. From Beijing's perspective, the Gulf War was fundamentally a conflict between global and regional hegemonisms. The real U.S. objective in waging war against Iraq was to bring the Middle East and its oil wealth more fully and completely under U.S. hegemony. The destruction of Iraq's military power and/or the establishment of a pro-U.S. regime in Baghdad would be, Beijing concluded, a major step toward U.S. hegemony in the region. On the other hand, the continued existence of a powerful, anti-Zionist, doggedly independent Iraq would limit U.S. regional influence. Thus Beijing opposed the U.S.-led war against Iraq.

The U.S.-initiated Arab-Israeli peace talks that began in the aftermath of the Gulf War led to the establishment of PRC-Israeli relations on January 24, 1992. China and Israel had long conducted substantive but covert relations, especially in the area of weapons development. Those relations slowly grew in prominence, culminating in the establishment of crypto-embassies in mid-1991. But Beijing balked at instituting full diplomatic relations, fearing that this would damage its status among Arab countries. Growing U.S. influence in the Middle East in the aftermath of the Gulf War, along with the disintegration of the Soviet Union, prompted Beijing to conclude that it should not be locked out of the Middle East peace process. Increased Japanese activism in the Middle East pushed Beijing in the same direction. Israel insisted, however, that full recognition be the price of inclusion in the peace process. In the normalization agreement, Israel recognized Beijing's position that "Taiwan is an inalienable part of the territory of the People's Republic of China."[5]

China and the Collapse of the Soviet Union

China's response to the collapse of the Soviet Union in 1990–91 was also deeply influenced by a desire to counter the trend toward U.S. global supremacy. Ideological concerns were probably not the most important motivation here. Rather, the CCP apparently concluded that a USSR led by neo-Stalinists was likely to remain independent of the Western alliance system and semiconfrontational toward the United States, whereas a USSR or its successor state led by the likes of Boris Yeltsin would move into the Western camp and align itself with the United States.

As the confrontation between liberal reformers and neo-Stalinist conservatives deepened in the USSR in 1990–91, the CCP did what it could prudently do to assist the hard-liners in the Communist Party of the Soviet Union (CPSU). Caution was in order, however, because the CCP had already been chastened by the failure of efforts to support embattled neo-Stalinists in Eastern Europe in the fall of 1989. East Germany was the most important in this regard because of the pivotal role Mikhail Gorbachev had played in pushing East German leader Eric Honnecker toward reform, and because of Honnecker's turn to China in an effort to check Soviet pressure.

As a consequence of these developments, Beijing sided solidly with the East German government during the summer and fall of 1989. CCP Politburo Standing Committee member Qiao Shi told a visiting East German delegation in September 1989 that China "would support [East Germany] in the . . . defense of state sovereignty and the struggle against all efforts to undermine socialism in [East Ger-

[5] The normalization communiqué is in Chai Shikuan and Feng Xiuju, "Nations Establish Diplomatic Ties," Foreign Broadcast Information Service, *Daily Report, China* (hereafter FBIS-CHI), January 24, 1992, pp. 5–6. For background, see Jonathan Karp and Lincoln Kaye, "Shalom to China," *Far Eastern Economic Review*, January 16, 1992, pp. 12–13.

many]."[6] The next month another Politburo Standing Committee member, Yao Yilin, visited East Berlin to endorse Honecker's embattled East Berlin regime. In a joint statement, Yao and Honecker said that the lesson of both the "counterrevolutionary riot in Beijing and the current defamation campaign" against East Germany was that "socialist values should be staunchly upheld." Yao also probably gave assurances of support should Honnecker order a repression of mounting dissent.

Beijing later opposed the move toward German unification as Honnecker's communist successors struggled to stem the tide in that direction at the end of 1989.[7] Beijing quickly realized the potentially great costs of such diplomatic missteps and swiftly shifted course. Beijing's experience during the East European revolutions of 1989 encouraged greater caution when the stakes became even higher in the Soviet Union during 1990–91.

CCP leaders were outraged by Gorbachev's "betrayal of the proletariat" in Eastern Europe in 1989 and launched an internal campaign condemning his apostasy. They also debated open criticism of Gorbachev, but caution prevailed. Beijing feared that Taiwan would exploit any breach that opened between China and the new East European governments. Beijing also wished to protect the substance of its economic relations with Eastern Europe. Open polemics against Gorbachev would not have served Beijing's efforts to regain international respectability after the Beijing massacre. Nor would this approach have been in line with the de-ideologicalization of Sino-Soviet relations that had been agreed to during the Gorbachev–Deng Xiaoping summit of May 1989 and that served China's development needs. Yet the CCP decided to support the CPSU's hard-liners in subtle ways camouflaged by repeated, prominent declarations of noninterference in the internal affairs of the Soviet Union.

Chinese support for the CPSU took three major forms: exchange of delegations with the CPSU; a decision for a summit meeting between Jiang Zemin and Gorbachev in June 1991; and economic diplomacy in the form of a $720 million commodity credit extended to the embattled Soviet communist government in early 1991.

Between the time of the May 1989 Deng-Gorbachev summit and the failed Soviet coup of August 1991, there was a steady stream of top-level party and governmental delegations traveling between Beijing

[6] " 'Fully Grateful' Visit to China by DDR Delegation," *China aktuell*, Hamburg, September 1989, p. 665.

[7] "China Speaks Out—Indirectly—against German Reunification," *China aktuell*, Hamburg, January 1990, p. 8.

and Moscow. Fifteen high-level Soviet leaders visited China during this period. Virtually all of the Soviet visitors were hard-liners in the political struggle then intensifying in the USSR. Several, including Deputy President of the Supreme Soviet Anatoli Lukyanov and CPSU Russian Republic chief Ivan Polozkov, were key conservative leaders. Two, Defense Minister Dimitri Yazov and Minister of Internal Affairs Boris Pugo, were subsequently members of the eight-person State Emergency Committee set up by the August 1991 coup leaders.

It was apparently the Soviet hard-liners who pushed these exchanges. According to the account by a former Soviet diplomat specializing in relations with China, in response to mounting Chinese criticism of Gorbachev, Soviet hard-liners around Gorbachev seized on the "China card" to try to persuade their boss "to discontinue *perestroika* and put the Soviet house in order."[8] Yuriy Prokofyev, head of the CPSU's Moscow committee, for instance, opined in early 1991 that "China has found the right orientation for its reform which started in the rural areas to solve the problem of food first and which links the market economy with socialism."[9]

The political intent of this delegation diplomacy was also indicated by the scheduling of a visit to China by Ivan Polozkov, Boris Yeltsin's most direct rival for control of Russia, shortly after Yeltsin's landslide victory in the Russian presidential election in early June 1991 and following the announcement of Yeltsin's upcoming visit to the United States for talks with President George Bush. Polozkov's visit to China was timed to coincide with Yeltsin's visit to Washington.[10] Increasingly on the defensive, the CPSU's neo-Stalinists were trying to use the CCP and the Chinese model to counter their liberal opponents. China served the Soviet conservatives as an example of successful "reform" within the framework of continuing communist hegemony and of "principled defense" of Marxism-Leninism.

The CCP responded enthusiastically to the Soviet hard-liners' push for a rapid expansion of exchanges. CCP leaders understood the game being played, and played it well. By their comments and actions during visits to the USSR, Chinese leaders made clear their support for continued communist rule and socialist economics in that country. During his visit to Moscow in March 1991, for example, CCP Beijing chief Li Ximing praised the Soviet people for having a glorious tradition of the October Revolution, and the CPSU for leading the Soviet people to surmount numerous difficulties in the course of socialist

[8] "Policy by Fiat," *Far Eastern Economic Review*, June 11, 1992, pp. 16–18.

[9] Xinhua, March 27, 1991, in FBIS-CHI, March 27, 1991, p. 2.

[10] *South China Morning Post*, June 20, 1991, in FBIS-CHI, June 20, 1991, p. 10.

revolution and construction. "We sincerely hope," Li Ximing said, "that the comrades of the Soviet Communist Party will surely resolve the current problems . . . and move the situation into a track of steady and healthy development."[11]

The high point of CPSU-CCP diplomacy was CCP General Secretary Jiang Zemin's visit to Moscow in May 1991. Jiang's visit reflected an important shift in the CCP's evaluation of Gorbachev. As noted earlier, following the East European revolution of 1989 the CCP had been extremely hostile to Gorbachev, viewing him as a class traitor. Following Boris Yeltsin's abandonment of the CPSU at that party's 28th Congress in July 1990, however, the CCP's analysis shifted. The congress had revealed the relative isolation of hard-liners and the wide support for Gorbachev within the CPSU. Moreover, the newly independent radical forces led by Yeltsin began to grow rapidly. Thus by late 1990 the CCP concluded that the real alternative to Gorbachev was likely to be Yeltsin and that the prime task was to block the anti-communist Yeltsin radicals. There were three dominant groups in the Soviet Union, the CCP now concluded: the radicals led by Yeltsin, moderate reformers led by Gorbachev, and conservatives led by Polozkov. The CCP sympathized with the conservatives but realized that their power was declining. Under these circumstances, it was best to unite with Gorbachev. This led to the rescheduling of Jiang's visit to Moscow, which had initially been planned for early 1990 but had been canceled by Beijing in December 1989 as a show of displeasure with Gorbachev's "betrayal" in Eastern Europe. The meeting of the general secretary of the CCP with his CPSU counterpart, still Mikhail Gorbachev, was a symbolic endorsement of the latter. In his talks with Soviet leaders, Jiang again conveyed the CCP's hope that the Soviet Union would adhere to the socialist road and the leadership of the Communist Party.

A $720 million commodity credit extended in February 1991 was another important aspect of CCP support for the CPSU. This was twice the size of a short-term loan extended to Moscow for the purchase of Chinese consumer goods during Li Peng's April 1990 visit to Moscow. CPSU deputy general secretary Vladimir Ivashko, who was informed of China's willingness to extend the loan during a visit to Beijing, stressed the political significance of the credit, saying that the offer came at the initiative of Jiang Zemin rather than as a result of a request from the Soviet side. Beijing's demonstration of "moral support for the renewal process" in the USSR was of "great importance,"

[11] Xinhua, March 27, 1991, in FBIS-CHI, March 27, 1991, p. 2.

Ivashko said.[12] Ivashko, of course, had his own reasons for stressing the political significance of the loan; he was part of the CPSU's neo-Stalinist group that was playing the "China card" against the reformers. Nonetheless, Beijing's loan did provide Ivashko and his comrades with political ammunition.

China's loan must be seen in an international context. Early in 1991 Soviet-Western relations deteriorated badly under the impact of Moscow's crackdown in the Baltic states, Soviet maneuvers regarding negotiations on the reduction of conventional forces in Europe, and strategic weapons talks. In January the Group of Seven (G-7) suspended $1.5 billion of food aid and technical assistance to the Soviet Union and canceled a scheduled meeting to discuss further assistance. The United States reacted coldly to a Soviet request for $1.5 billion in agricultural credits and then postponed the scheduled Moscow meeting of Bush and Gorbachev. In February the chief spokesman for the Soviet Foreign Ministry warned against outside intervention in the internal affairs of the Soviet Union in the Baltics, and Gorbachev told foreign visitors that the United States and the Soviet Union were headed for a "new cold war." In this context, Beijing's extension of three-quarters of a billion dollars in credits was a strong demonstration of support for Moscow in its renewed confrontation with the West.

When CPSU hard-liners moved against Yeltsin and Gorbachev in August 1991 with their attempted coup d'état, the CCP was warmly enthusiastic. Various foreign sources reported statements lauding the coup made privately by top CCP leaders, including Deng Xiaoping. Chinese media gave extensive coverage to the declarations and activities of the coup leaders and to the socioeconomic problems that had led to the move. It did not give similar coverage to those resisting the coup. No official statement of endorsement was made—although one had reportedly been prepared and was stopped from release only by the rapid unraveling of the coup.

The promptness and breadth of the Chinese media's response to the Soviet coup strongly suggest that CCP leaders had foreknowledge that CPSU hard-liners were planning some sort of move. It is probable that Soviet Defense Minister and coup participant Dimitri Yazov conveyed in general terms the intentions of the plotters to People's Liberation Army Chief of Staff Chi Haotian during the latter's visit to Moscow immediately before the coup attempt. During a final, hastily arranged meeting, Yazov reportedly asked Chi how the CCP viewed the Soviet situation. Chi replied that China was very worried about

---

[12] Foreign Broadcast Information Service, *Trends*, March 6, 1991, pp. 16–17. This FBIS publication is different from its *Daily Report*.

the deterioration of the Soviet economy and the possibility of a split in the nation. Yazov then said that some comrades in "our army" were ready to "take action." Chi reportedly replied: "We adhere to the principle of not interfering in the internal affairs of the Soviet Union, but we express our understanding."[13]

When the Soviet coup collapsed, the CCP issued internal circulars explaining to party members the reasons for the failure. The reasons given were tactical: failure to move swiftly against Yeltsin and the Russian parliament, failure to secure control immediately over all media and over lines of communication with the outside world, and so on. Lack of popular support was not, of course, among the reasons cited for the coup's failure. Press coverage while the coup was under way had indicated that the Soviet masses had been alienated by the consequences of Gorbachev's reforms and favored the restoration of "stability."

The failure of the Soviet coup touched off renewed debate within the CCP. Conservatives argued that events in the USSR demonstrated the need to maintain tight control and to intensify ideological indoctrination. Any reforms that might trigger instability, such as further moves toward the market or opening to the outside world, should be avoided, they maintained. Deng Xiaoping contended, however, that the differing fates of socialism and communist rule in China and the USSR demonstrated that only reform and opening could save socialism. This debate was not resolved until March–April 1992, when Deng's position prevailed.

As the USSR disintegrated after the coup, China responded quickly and pragmatically. By that point there was little to be gained by acting otherwise. Moreover, Beijing feared that if it did not move swiftly, Taiwan would exploit the situation and China's relations with the West would further deteriorate. On September 7, 1991, Beijing recognized the independence of Estonia, Latvia, and Lithuania. This was the day after the State Council of the Soviet Union formally recognized the independence of the Baltic states, and ten days, five days, and one day after the European Community (EC), the United States, and Japan respectively recognized those states.[14] Before the end of the month, agreements had been reached regarding the establishment of diplomatic relations. These agreements endorsed Beijing's

---

[13] Yeh Lu-ching, "CPC Holds Up Communism on Its Own, Launches Protracted War against Capitalism," *Dangdai* (Contemporary), Hong Kong, no. 6 (September 15, 1991), in FBIS-CHI, September 26, 1991, p. 23.

[14] Lithuania had declared independence on March 11, 1990, and Estonia and Latvia on August 21, 1991.

position on Taiwan, which holds that Taiwan is an inalienable part of the territory of China, whose sole legitimate government is the PRC.

As the USSR entered its terminal crisis in December 1991, Beijing again moved swiftly and pragmatically. On the 12th, four days after the leaders of Belarus, Russia, and Ukraine formed the Commonwealth of Independent States (CIS), a Chinese Foreign Ministry spokesman said that China was prepared to develop good-neighborly relations with both the Soviet Union and the Soviet republics. On December 24, three days after the five Central Asian republics signed the CIS agreement, an official Chinese spokesman talked for the first time of the "former Soviet Union," saying that China was ready to forge relations with all members of the CIS. On December 27, the day after Gorbachev resigned as president of the USSR and the Supreme Soviet dissolved itself and the USSR, Foreign Minister Qian Qichen sent telegrams to the foreign ministers of Russia, Ukraine, Belarus, Kazakhstan, Uzbekistan, Tajikistan, Kyrgyzstan, Turkmenistan, Georgia, Armenia, Azerbaijan, and Moldova declaring China's recognition of the independence of those countries and its willingness to begin negotiations regarding the establishment of diplomatic relations.

A delegation headed by Ministry of Foreign Economic Relations and Trade (MOFERT) head Li Lanqing and Vice–Foreign Minister Tian Zengpei visited the eight former Soviet republics of Belarus, Russia, Ukraine, Uzbekistan, Kazakhstan, Tajikistan, Turkmenistan, and Kyrgyzstan from December 26, 1991, through January 7, 1992. In Moscow, Li Lanqing conveyed China's recognition of Russia as the successor to the membership of the USSR in the U.N. Security Council. By the end of January agreements were reached with each of these countries and Moldova regarding the establishment of ambassadorial-level relations. Diplomatic relations with Azerbaijan and Armenia were established on April 2 and 6. Relations with Georgia were not established until June 9. Instability in these three states was the reason given for the delay in establishing ties. Beijing pushed for endorsement of its position on Taiwan in the various bilateral communiqués and, with the significant exception of Ukraine, succeeded in obtaining it. Ukraine insisted on more ambiguous wording, merely recognizing the PRC's desire to safeguard territorial integrity and promising to establish ties only with the PRC.[15] Meanwhile, Beijing sent additional military forces to China's western borders to prevent infiltration and subversion.

The collapse of the CPSU regime and the USSR appeared to CCP rulers as a calamity of epic proportions. To the CCP's remaining true believers in Marxism-Leninism, the "proletariat's loss of state power"

[15] The Sino-Ukraine communiqué is in FBIS-CHI, January 6, 1992, p. 12.

in a major state and the demise of the world's first socialist state were major setbacks for the revolutionary struggle of the world's working classes. World progress had taken a tremendous step backward, they believed. Moreover, the victory of imperialist subversion in the USSR could well lead to an intensification of imperialist efforts to overthrow proletarian state power and socialism in China.

Of even greater concern to CCP leaders, the demise of the CPSU and the USSR gravely delegitimized communist rule in China. The USSR had, of course, been China's "big brother" in the 1950s, when popular slogans had proclaimed, "Learn from the USSR" and "The USSR of today is the China of tomorrow." These slogans were remembered, often maliciously, by Chinese in 1991–92. The course of China's revolution in the 20th century had been profoundly influenced by the Bolshevik revolution; Marxism-Leninism came to China in part through the USSR. Now the final failure of the Bolshevik revolution encouraged many Chinese to conclude that their country had taken a wrong turn in 1949 when the CCP came to power.

At the global level, the dramatic improvement in U.S.-Russian relations that came about in 1992, together with Russia's growing orientation toward the West, has meant a major augmentation of U.S. global influence. Not only is Beijing much less able to play off Moscow and Washington against each other, but it faces the increased possibility of Russian-U.S. collaboration in ways antithetical to Chinese policy interests. Soviet-U.S. "collusion" against China was the CCP's strategic nightmare throughout the post-1945 period. In the post–cold war world, such "collusion" is even more likely on issues ranging from territorial disputes in the South China Sea, to Korean unification, to Taiwan.

Yet the CCP also gained in some respects from the demise of the USSR. The national disintegration and severe economic decline that followed the failed August coup convinced many Chinese that continued rule by the CCP was the only realistic alternative to a similar national calamity befalling China. Even many who had been critical of the government's brutal crushing of dissent in June 1989 now concluded that that move might have forestalled chaos such as now beset the former Soviet Union. CCP propaganda, of course, encouraged people to reach these conclusions.

China's Emerging Central Asia Policy

The emergence of a half-dozen independent nations in Central Asia in the aftermath of the Soviet collapse also represented a fundamental geopolitical gain for China's national security. While future relations between Russia and the new Central Asian states are uncertain, if these countries evolve in the direction of military and political independence from Moscow the result could be very positive for China's long-term strategic situation.

Along its far western borders, China was previously confronted with the possibility of opposing powerful Soviet armies operating relatively close to major Soviet industrial and population centers and supported by a fairly robust transportation system. Chinese forces defending Xinjiang, by contrast, were operating at the end of long, thin logistic lines vulnerable to incursions from Mongolia. This situation has been fundamentally altered by the independence of the Central Asian republics. Where previously the world's greatest conventional military power threatened, a series of weak buffer states independent of Moscow now seems to be developing along Xinjiang's borders. As of June 1992, CIS military forces under Moscow's control had not yet withdrawn from Kazakhstan, Kyrgyzstan, and Tajikistan, which border on China, but if, as seems likely, this does occur, China's national security will be greatly enhanced.

China moved quickly to consolidate ties with its new Central Asian neighbors. Kazakhstan's prime minister made a five-day official visit to China in February. Eight agreements were signed during that visit, including one allowing Chinese entrepreneurs to set up operations in Kazakhstan and another regarding promotion of the rail line between Urumqi in Xinjiang and Alma Ata in Kazakhstan. This line was opened in September 1990, and both sides hope it will emerge as a second trans-Eurasian rail link rivaling the trans-Siberian line as a conduit for international commerce. China also agreed to provide commodity loans to Kazakhstan. In March 1992 when the ruling Kazakh Socialist Party held a congress in Alma Ata, the CCP liaison department sent a delegation. The same delegation visited Uzbekistan and Turkmenistan. Also in March the Uzbek president paid a three-day state visit to China. During that visit too, a series of agreements were signed.

Kyrgyzstan President Askar Akayev paid a five-day official visit to China in May 1992. The usual economic and cultural agreements were signed, but the visit also took on significant political coloration. The joint communiqué signed at the conclusion of Akayev's visit pledged both countries to maintain "peace and stability" in Asia, but added that the development of Sino-Kyrgyzstan relations was not directed against or harmful to the interest of any third country. In separate comments in Beijing, Akayev said his country was concerned with the security of Central Asia and that in this regard China was an important factor. Therefore the establishment and development of relations of friendship and trust between China and Kyrgyzstan would be important for the stability and security of the entire region. Elsewhere in Beijing, Akayev said that China was a major guarantor of stability on the continent of Asia.

Mongolia also figures prominently in the mosaic of China's new Inner Asia policy. While always nominally independent of the USSR, Mongolia was a Soviet satellite from the time of its creation in 1921 until about 1989. The withdrawal of Soviet forces stationed in Mongolia since 1963 was one of the conditions Beijing set for the normalization of Sino-Soviet relations in the 1980s. Gorbachev eventually accepted this demand. The first limited withdrawal came in the spring of 1987, and the first large-scale withdrawal began the day Gorbachev arrived in Beijing for talks with Deng Xiaoping in May 1989. The last Soviet forces are scheduled to leave Mongolia by September 1992.

The withdrawal of Soviet forces from Mongolia, along with the collapse of Mongolia's Stalinist political system in 1989, led to a rapid improvement in Sino-Mongolian relations. A foreign ministers' meeting in March 1989 resulted in the restoration of economic, political, and cultural exchanges. Border trade, suspended since the 1960s, was resumed four months later. Mongolia's president visited China in May 1990; PRC President Yang Shangkun paid the first-ever visit by a Chinese head of state to Mongolia in August 1991. During the latter visit several agreements were signed, including one allowing Mongolia to use port facilities near Tianjin. The rail route to the Pacific Ocean via Beijing is considerably shorter than that via Khabarovsk in Russia. This increases Mongolia's advantage in exporting to Japan (which provides half of Mongolia's hard-currency trade) and the rest of the Pacific littoral. China has refused to pass this full-cost savings on to Mongolia, however, charging Mongolian firms transport fees only slightly lower than those incurred by the much longer Khabarovsk route. Some analysts have suggested that security problems in its own territory of Inner Mongolia lead Beijing to prefer that the Republic of Mongolia ("Outer Mongolia") not become too prosperous. There are strong ethnic ties between the two Mongolias, and if Inner Mongolia remains substantially more prosperous than Outer Mongolia, Mongols in the former are less likely to desire independence and union with the latter.[16]

During a visit by Mongolian Prime Minister Dashiyn Byambasuren to China in May 1992, China officially stated its respect for Mongolia's sovereignty. In the context of an exchange of views on the regional

[16] Lincoln Kaye, "Faltering Steppes," *Far Eastern Economic Review*, April 9, 1992, pp. 16–18.

situation after the disintegration of the USSR, Chinese Premier Li Peng assured Byambasuren that China respects the independence and sovereignty of Mongolia and the inviolability of its borders. China had claimed sovereignty over Outer Mongolia until 1945, when that claim was relinquished only reluctantly by Chiang Kai-shek's government under extreme Soviet pressure. Mao Zedong had also asked first Stalin and then Khrushchev in 1950 and 1954 respectively to permit the "return" of Outer Mongolia to China. For such reasons Mongol leaders had long looked upon the Soviet Union as their protector against a revanchist China. In this context and coming shortly after the USSR's demise, Li Peng's statement was an important declaration of principle.

The Special Sino-Japanese Relation

China's relations with Japan are as deeply ambivalent as its relations with the United States and Russia. This ambivalence has become even more pronounced with the end of the cold war. On the one hand, Beijing has invited Tokyo to enter into a sort of *entente cordiale* in which the two powers will cooperate politically and economically to foster peace, stability, and economic development in Asia. On the other hand, Beijing is deeply apprehensive about the growth of Japanese power. It also fears that Japan's emergence as Asia's dominant power and as a major global actor will thwart China's own aspiration to become a leading world power and condemn it to second-rank status for the foreseeable future.

Since 1987 China's foreign policy community has been engaged in a reassessment of Japan's role in the evolving structure of power in Asia. A number of developments, especially Tokyo's announcement in January 1987 that its defense expenditures would surpass 1 percent of GNP, convinced Chinese analysts that Japan intended to pursue a more assertive political and military role in Asia. These developments came at a time when both the United States and the Soviet Union were reducing their military commitments in Asia. Other trends pointed to an unraveling of the Japan-U.S. alliance. Trade frictions and nationalist passions were mounting in both countries, while the rapid improvement of Soviet-U.S. relations and a general decline in the Soviet threat eliminated the overarching security imperative that had previously helped keep Japan-U.S. economic conflicts manageable during the cold war.

Chinese analysts differed in their assessments of the stability of the Japan-U.S. alliance, but even those who believed that it would persist for some time were convinced that latent contradictions would increase over time and that Japan would act more independently. The question thus emerged, What should China's relation to the developing Japanese power be?[17] The proposal of a Sino-Japanese entente was Beijing's official answer to this question. This conclusion seems to be the result of an analysis of the profound changes that have remade the international order. It represents Beijing's best-case scenario for development of the post–cold war Asian power system.

A Chinese initiative to Japan was impossible as long as Japan kept in place its post-Tiananmen sanctions. Economic sanctions were lifted by the end of 1990, however, and Prime Minister Toshiki Kaifu's official visit to China in August 1991 marked the restoration of high-level bilateral contacts. In Beijing's view, Kaifu's visit marked the renormalization of Sino-Japanese relations.

The first top-level Chinese visitor to Japan after this "normalization" was Jiang Zemin in April 1992. In the keynote speech during his visit, Jiang made public China's proposal of a broad Sino-Japanese political partnership. The breakdown of the old international order had created great instability in many regions of the globe, Jiang noted, with territorial, religious, and national conflicts long suppressed by the cold war bipolar structure now emerging. East Asia, however, was an exception to this trend, with peace and stability reigning. This was good for China, for Japan, and for the entire region. Beijing and Tokyo should step up their cooperation to consolidate and strengthen these positive trends and prevent the disorder currently plaguing other regions of the globe from spreading to Asia. Jiang enumerated the resolution of the Cambodian and Afghanistan conflicts and the reduction of tension in the Korean peninsula as examples of successful diplomatic cooperation that China and Japan might undertake. There was also a danger, Jiang said, that "hegemonism, big and small, of all kinds" might emerge in Asia in the aftermath of cold-war bipolarity. China and Japan should also cooperate to prevent this.[18]

An article in *Beijing Review* during Jiang's visit elaborated further on the logic of a Sino-Japanese partnership. Stability in the Asia-Pacific region depended on three factors, according to the article: China's own stability, "Japan's adherence to peaceful development" (i.e., nonmilitarism), and the expansion of Sino-Japanese relations. "In the emerging world order, the United States and Russia will reduce their military presence in this region, while the political and economic clout

[17] Jonathan D. Pollack, "The Sino-Japanese Relationship and East Asian Security: Patterns and Implications," *China Quarterly*, no. 124 (December 1990), pp. 714–29.

[18] *Renmin ribao* (People's Daily), April 8, 1992, p. 1.

of China and Japan . . . will increase. This prospect calls for closer China-Japan coordination of effort in developing their relations." The article stressed that China and Japan should step up their cooperation in the Asian-Pacific Economic Cooperation (APEC) Council and otherwise promote multilateral regional cooperation "in response to the worldwide trend toward forming regional economic blocs." Japan faced mounting trade frictions with Europe and the United States that were forcing it to "adjust its mode of economic development." The article concluded:

> In the end Japan might become a market for manufactured goods from the Asian-Pacific region and a supplier of capital and technology to other nations in the region. This provides China an opportunity. . . . Once China increases its exports, it can expand imports from Japan. This will open new channels for Japan to expand its foreign trade at a time when its trade with the United States is in trouble.[19]

But lurking behind Beijing's bid for an *entente cordiale* with Japan is deep mutual suspicion. China suspects that Japan hopes to transform its regional economic predominance into political and military predominance. Such a development could threaten China's security. It might also lead to the formation of a Japanese-led economic bloc that would exclude China and hobble its economic growth. China points to Japan's large (in absolute monetary terms) defense budget and high level of technological sophistication and maintains that Japan is already the third largest military power in the world. In this context, recent moves by Japan to alter its laws to permit the deployment of Japanese military forces overseas, even if only in support of U.N. peacekeeping missions, are extremely troublesome to Beijing.

Tokyo's perceptions mirror those of Beijing. Japan is troubled by the PRC's current military buildup (12 percent in real terms in 1991), its increasingly active and powerful long-range high-seas navy, and its nuclear development program, which apparently continues unabated in spite of the dramatic reductions in U.S. and Russian nuclear arsenals. China's test detonation of a mammoth 1-megaton hydrogen bomb in May 1992 was a manifestation of this last threat. Tokyo is also troubled by China's large weapons sales to such countries as Burma and Pakistan, its claim to most of the sea floor of the Yellow and East China seas, its sweeping territorial claims in the South China Sea, and its claim to the Senkaku Islands. The last issue erupted again

---

[19] Liu Jiangyong, "Sino-Japanese Cooperation in a Changed Situation," *Beijing Review*, April 6–12, 1992, pp. 16–17.

in February 1992 when China promulgated a law specifically enumerating "Diaoyu tai" (China's name for the Senkakus) as among its maritime territories. A forcible Chinese incorporation of Taiwan would also adversely affect substantial Japanese interests.

One important objective of Beijing's entente proposal is to draw Japan to China's side in confrontations with the United States. Following the April 1990 Politburo talk by Deng Xiaoping, China's Foreign Ministry formulated a diplomatic strategy on the basis of Deng's guidelines. Toward the West, China would follow a strategy of division. Relations should be developed with Japan in order to offset pressure from the United States and Western Europe.[20]

This strategy fits with Japan's own self-perception. Japan sees itself as a mediator between China and the West, uniquely positioned by geography and history to facilitate Sino-Western understanding. During the post-Tiananmen period, Tokyo led its Western allies in restoring ties with China. During the July 1989 Group of Seven summit, for instance, Tokyo lobbied strenuously against the isolation of China through heavy economic sanctions. At the next G-7 summit a year later, Tokyo announced its decision to resume government lending to China and urged the other G-7 countries to do likewise. Japan's lobbying was instrumental in persuading the other G-7 countries to modify their criticism and sanctions of China. Japan then led the West in resuming intergovernmental economic relations with China. In November 1990 Japan agreed to lend China 36.5 billion yen as the first stage of Japan's third loan package to China totaling 810 billion yen for the 1990–95 period. That loan had been suspended after the Beijing massacre. The next month new long-term trade agreements were signed covering the 1991–95 period and involving the exchange of $8 billion in Japanese equipment and technology per year for large amounts of Chinese coal and crude oil. Kaifu's August 1991 visit to China was also the first visit by the leader of a major Western power after June 1989.

It is in China's interest to encourage Japan to place itself between China and Western pressure and sanctions, and to lobby with its Western friends on China's behalf—especially as this apparently costs Beijing nothing. Thus PRC Vice-President Wang Zhen expressed gratitude for Kaifu's stance at the July 1990 G-7 summit, and during a visit to Tokyo in June 1991 Foreign Minister Qian Qichen asked Japan to lobby again on China's behalf during the upcoming G-7 summit. Japan has also agreed to lobby with the advanced industrial democracies for Chinese admission to GATT prior to Taiwan's entry.

---

[20] *Zhengming*, no. 151 (May 1, 1990), p. 7.

A somewhat different but not entirely contradictory explanation of Beijing's entente offer to Tokyo is that it is a ploy to awaken Washington to its need to use China as a counterbalance to Japan in Asia. Chinese analysts often assert that the United States should develop relations with China as a way of offsetting Japan's growing power. Beijing's ostensible bid of a political partnership with Japan may be a way of alerting Washington to the danger of a Chinese-Japanese condominium that would minimize U.S. influence in the region. Richard Nixon, among others, has raised the possibility of such a development.[21] The proposal of entente with Japan may be designed to exacerbate such fears, prompting the United States to repair its ties with Beijing. Beijing's preferred long-term structure of power in Asia, in other words, might be Japanese and U.S. rivalry for China's favors rather than a Sino-Japanese partnership excluding the United States.

Still another objective underlying Beijing's entente with Tokyo has to do with persuading Japan not to move forward with the creation of some sort of Pacific economic bloc that excludes or adversely affects China. There has recently been considerable debate within China's elite and media about global economic regionalization and its impact on China. On the one hand, Chinese leaders are apprehensive that for various reasons China might become the stepsister of such a Pacific bloc; on the other hand, they see China's inclusion in the right sort of bloc as a vehicle for fueling further foreign trade and investment. The crux lies in the orientation and purpose of the bloc. A Japan oriented toward partnership with China will heed Beijing's concerns as it proceeds to build a new economic community in the Pacific. This will ensure China's inclusion in that community on terms favorable to China. Thus in March 1991 MOFERT head Li Lanqing proposed to his Japanese counterpart a joint feasibility study of the creation of an East Asian economic sphere centered on China and Japan.

A final objective underlying Beijing's broaching of a Sino-Japanese entente has to do with China's fear of Japan's drifting toward a greater military and political role in Asia. If U.S.-Japan relations sour because of trade frictions, Japan might feel compelled to enhance its military strength further. If, however, Tokyo feels that China is a friendly power and can be counted on to cooperate with Japan to deal with future problems of peace and stability, then the chances of Japan moving in this direction will be lessened.

Cooperation in furthering the reduction of tension on the Korean peninsula has been a major dimension of Sino-Japanese cooperation

[21] Richard Nixon, "Paying the Price," *Time*, April 2, 1990, p. 47.

during the past several years. Here the crux has been parallel diplomacy vis-à-vis North Korea. While all the powers of the region—the USSR and the United States as well as China and Japan—favored and facilitated the rapprochement between North and South Korea, it was China and Japan that had the most at stake and the greatest leverage in Pyongyang. With Sino-Soviet rapprochement, Kim Il-sung's traditional strategy of playing Moscow against Beijing was fatally undermined. When the USSR collapsed, North Korea moved closer to the sole remaining communist power, China. Beijing, for its part, has sought to consolidate ties with North Korea. While turning down Pyongyang's requests for large-scale aid to help North Korea out of its serious economic decline, Beijing has given Pyongyang a range of political support. Simultaneously, it has pushed Pyongyang toward moves to reduce tensions with South Korea. Only Japan was in a position to supply substantial economic aid to North Korea, and Tokyo used this as leverage to push Pyongyang toward improved relations with the South.

The question of North Korea's clandestine nuclear weapons program was the most important issue in this regard. As international concern with North Korea's nuclear program mounted in 1990 and 1991, China was drawn into diplomatic activity. Beijing explicitly opposed the possession of nuclear weapons by either North or South Korea, but rejected U.S. suggestions of sanctions designed to force Pyongyang to forego the development of nuclear weapons and open its nuclear facilities to inspection by the International Atomic Energy Agency (IAEA). Chinese spokesmen also opposed the notion of a military strike against North Korea's nuclear production facilities when this was broached in various contexts. Beijing argued that it did not want to force North Korea into a corner and preferred "dialogue" to coercion.

Dialogue over the nuclear issue apparently occurred during a ten-day visit by Kim Il-sung to China in October 1991. South Korean papers had reported the previous month that, following the collapse of the USSR, Pyongyang had informed Beijing that it intended to develop nuclear weapons to bolster its security. Be this as it may, during talks with Kim in October, Chinese leaders urged North Korea to sign a safeguards inspection agreement with the IAEA, assuring the world that it was not developing nuclear weapons. Jiang Zemin reportedly went so far as to tell Kim that if the United States took military action against North Korea's nuclear facilities, China had no intention of interfering. This had important implications for China's role in the U.N. Security Council should South Korea, Japan, and the United States bring before that body the question of North Korea's nuclear weapons along with a request for various international sanctions. Kim could not expect China to block Security Council endorsement of action against North Korea. Chinese leaders also denied Kim's request for large increases in economic assistance. While this was probably related, as Li Peng explained, to China's own pressing economic needs, it nonetheless left Pyongyang with few options but to accede to foreign demands on the nuclear issue if it wanted economic assistance. Meanwhile, Tokyo insisted that resolution of the nuclear issue was a prerequisite for the normalization of North Korea–Japan relations.

As a result of Chinese, Japanese, and other international pressure, Kim Il-sung incrementally brought his nuclear program under international supervision. In December 1991 North and South Korea signed an agreement mutually renouncing the possession of nuclear weapons. The next month Pyongyang signed a safeguards accord with the IAEA. In May it hosted the first IAEA inspection team. Major problems remain, of course, but substantial progress has been made. During a January 1992 visit to Beijing, Japanese Foreign Minister Michio Watanabe conveyed his government's appreciation for recent developments on the Korean peninsula. He also said that Japan was keenly interested in seeing North Korea submit to unconditional inspection of its nuclear facilities at an early date.

China had its own reasons for not wanting the nuclearization of the North-South Korean confrontation. One major reason is the probable impact of such a development on Japan. If North Korea goes nuclear, there will be great pressure on South Korea to follow. The existence of nuclear states on both halves of the Korean peninsula would, in turn, push Japan toward pursuing greater military strength, possibly including nuclear armaments. This would mark a major step toward Japan's reemergence as the dominant military power in East Asia. Korean and Japanese possession of nuclear arms would greatly constrain China's freedom of military action in the Northeast Asian region, while increasing the cost to China of any possible war. It would also eliminate the prestige Beijing currently enjoys as one of only five recognized nuclear powers.

China and the European Pole

Beijing welcomed progress toward West European unification during 1991–92. Following the conclusion of the December 1991 Maastricht agreements on European Community political and economic union, a Chinese Foreign Ministry spokesman conveyed China's congratulations. The agreements marked new progress toward European integration, the spokesman said, a development that would "contribute to the peace and stability of Europe and the world . . . and also to mutually beneficial cooperation between the European Community and the developing countries."[22]

Chinese commentary generally places the trend toward European unity in the context of declining U.S. global influence, often depicting Western Europe as achieving greater unity and integration in the face of U.S. opposition. While Europe struggles to control its own destiny, Washington is trying to impose a "new Atlanticism" on it in hopes of maintaining U.S. domination over Europe. The Europeanist trend definitely has the upper hand, according to most Chinese commentary, a situation that receives implicit praise from the PRC. According to a long article in *Shijie zhishi* (World Knowledge; a semiofficial publication of the Ministry of Foreign Affairs), for instance, the decline of the Soviet threat to Europe has destroyed the strategic foundation of the NATO alliance and the basis for the U.S. political and military presence in Europe:

> [This] has offered Western Europe a new opportunity to cast off United States control and minimize U.S. presence and influence in Europe. . . . The most important fact is that the European-U.S. confrontation has been extended from economic conflict to a contention for dominance over European affairs. The United States wants to establish a new order in Europe under its dominance, while Western Europe wants to build a "European Europe" under its own control. This is the very crux of the Euro-U.S. contradictions under the new situation.[23]

In October 1990, a year after the imposition of economic and political sanctions following the deterioration of Chinese–West European relations in the wake of Tiananmen, the EC, following Japan's lead, decided to resume economic assistance and ministerial-level visits to China. Visits by British and Italian Prime Ministers John Major and Giulio Andreotti took place in September 1991, and in January–February 1992 Li Peng made official visits to Italy, Switzerland, Portugal, and Spain. According to Qian Qichen, speaking to the German Foreign Policy Association in March 1992:

> The main reason why relations between China and West European countries would not stay cool for long is that the two sides share many

---

[22] FBIS-CHI, December 12, 1991, p. 2.

[23] Yi Yin, "Impact of Tremendous Changes in Soviet Union on Europe," in FBIS-CHI, November 5, 1991, pp. 1–4.

> parallel interests . . . and . . . hold identical or similar views on some major international issues. . . . Both Western Europe and China are of the view that, with the end of the bi-polar structure, the world is moving towards multi-polarity. As a big country . . . China is playing a role that cannot be ignored. . . . West European countries are becoming a major force in a multi-polar world by strengthening . . . their political and economic integration with the European Community as the core.[24]

Support for European unity is a long-standing Chinese policy. In the 1960s, as in the 1990s, the rationale was to weaken U.S. influence in Europe. During the 1970s the objective was to constrain the USSR in the East by maximizing the threat it faced in the West. It is doubtful whether Chinese analysts have thought through the implications for China of a united Europe. Should a truly united Europe emerge, China's hopes of achieving first-class power status would be set back considerably. China has a much better chance of being in the same league with Germany, France, or Britain than with a united Europe. Beijing's logic seems to be that the stronger the possible opponents of the United States, the more Washington will need Chinese friendship.

Along with much of the rest of the world, Chinese analysts recognize united Germany as the center of gravity in the new Europe. Consequently, Beijing has stressed developing Sino-German relations. After being caught on the losing side on the question of German unification in 1989, China shifted position quietly—and reverted to China's more traditional supportive position on German unification—in February 1990, when a Foreign Ministry spokesman announced that China "understands the desire of the German people for the reunification of [their] nation."[25]

The slow disintegration of Yugoslavia in 1991–92 presented China with the difficult choice of acquiescing to German-led international efforts to force the government of a sovereign country (a communist one to boot) to accept the secession of various nationalities or to oppose those efforts, thereby possibly antagonizing Germany. The demise of yet another socialist regime was not itself a major concern to Beijing, even though Belgrade, then chair of the Non-Aligned Movement, had facilitated China's application for observer status in that organization, which was approved in May 1992. But international intervention to coerce Belgrade to accept the secession of Yugoslavia's various republics presented a major problem for Beijing. Since Tiananmen, Beijing has laid great stress on the principle of nonintervention

---

[24] "An Independent Foreign Policy of Peace," *Beijing Review*, March 30–April 5, 1992, pp. 13–15.

[25] Xinhua, in FBIS-CHI, February 8, 1990, p. 3.

in the affairs of a sovereign state. Indeed, this has become the paramount principle of Chinese foreign policy. Moreover, to the extent that the Western-led international community succeeded in compelling repressive communist states to concede the right to self-determination to various nationalities within their boundaries, the temptation would be greater to apply a similar policy to China regarding Tibet or Taiwan. Yet to oppose German-European efforts with respect to Yugoslavia ran the risk of antagonizing Germany.

Bonn took the lead in pushing the European Community toward recognition of Slovenia and Croatia in December 1991, when it concluded that Serbia was the main violator of the Geneva cease-fire agreement and that recognizing the breakaway republics would force Belgrade to a settlement by showing it that the world no longer considered those entities as rebel states. In spite of its repeated proclamations about support for noninterference in the affairs of sovereign states, Chinese spokespersons or media said nothing critical of German or EC policy toward Yugoslavia. Beijing's displeasure with German-led Western intervention in Yugoslavia's dismantlement was reflected, however, in its belated recognition of the breakaway Yugoslav republics. In contrast to its swift recognition of the ex-Soviet republics, only on April 17, 1992, ten months after Slovenia and Croatia declared independence, did China recognize them, securing explicit endorsement of Beijing's position on Taiwan in the process. In May 1992 when the U.N. Security Council voted sanctions against Serbia and Montenegro for their military actions in Bosnia-Herzegovina, China announced that it would not join in the sanctions.

Beijing's strategic nightmare is that the Western alliance led by the United States, including Japan and reinforced by Russia, will hold together, and that China, because of its neo-Stalinist political system, will be ostracized. In such a scenario China would be the odd country out, with eerie similarities to its international situation more than 100 years ago. In the words of a pamphlet produced by the theoretical department of *Zhongguo qingnian bao* (China Youth Daily) and analyzing the impact of the demise of the USSR on China:

> A foreseeable near-term result of the changes in the USSR is the accelerated formation of a "7 plus 1" pattern made up of the seven industrialized Western nations plus the USSR, a world trend toward "collective Western hegemony" emerging, [and] the external climate for China's modernization becoming extremely unfavorable. . . . [In such a situation China should] maneuver among various political groupings in the Western world, using the contradictions that exist between the United States

> and Europe and between the United States and Japan to cause more divisions and undermining, so that they cannot coalesce to work against China.[26]

Chinese analysts prefer to speak of what the international system is becoming, rather than what it is. The old bipolar system has broken down, they say, and a new multipolar system has not yet fully formed but is rapidly emerging. The fact that the United States is currently the only superpower and enjoys a unique global position is a temporary phenomenon, an aberration that will soon disappear. There is a strong normative component to these seemingly empirical propositions: the PRC clearly believes that things would be a lot better for China and the world if U.S. global power and influence receded.

China's fundamentally anti-U.S. orientation is currently manifest primarily at the rhetorical level and in the United Nations. A more forceful application of this impulse is constrained by the need not to endanger the extensive economic and cultural interactions with the United States that facilitate China's development. Consequently, Beijing's opposition to U.S. global preeminence now operates subtly, indirectly, and covertly. However, if the constraint imposed by substantial positive Sino-American economic ties were removed—for example, by the revocation of China's MFN status as punishment for human rights violations—it could be expected that Beijing would pursue a much more vigorously anti-American foreign policy.

---

[26] "Realistic Responses and Strategic Choices for China after the Soviet Upheaval," September 9, 1991.

4
Courts, Justice, and Human Rights

Margaret Y. K. Woo

The Preamble to the U.N. Universal Declaration of Human Rights proclaims, "It is essential, if man is not to be compelled to have recourse, as a last resort, to rebellion against tyranny and oppression, that human rights should be protected by the rule of law."[1] This guarantee of basic rights requires protection—in particular, protection through legal institutions. Legal institutions can provide both procedural regularity to challenge the violations of rights and checks on arbitrary decision making.

This discussion explores the legal and judicial institutions reestablished in China in the aftermath of the Cultural Revolution and on the heels of the economic reforms of 1978. To what extent has China become a "rule-of-law" state that protects the rights of its citizens? What kinds of legal institutions and legal procedures have been established in China, and what are the limits of their protection of the basic rights of citizens?

These questions will be examined from a systemic perspective, not through an analysis of particular legal provisions or procedures. The recent development of the legal system in China will be surveyed, and then several phenomena that characterize that system—bureaucratization, authoritarianism, and a preference for informality—will be examined. These underlying strands point to a legal system that, from a Western perspective, affords only limited protection to the rights of individuals.

However, the inquiry cannot end there. It is necessary to understand the ways in which the Chinese have sought to reform their le-

[1] Universal Declaration of Human Rights, signed December 10, 1948, G.A. Res. 217A(III), U.N. Doc. A/810, p. 71 (1948). China has adopted the following human rights conventions: International Convention on the Elimination of Racial Discrimination; Convention on the Elimination of Discrimination against Women; Convention against Torture and Cruel, Inhuman, and Degrading Treatment or Punishment; Convention against Genocide.

gal system to provide, at a minimum, greater procedural regularity. These reform efforts are placed within the context of China's philosophical emphasis on the rights of the collective, which must be balanced against the interests of individuals. When these additional points are considered, what emerges is a legal system that remains an instrument of the state but is also a place in which individuals in ordinary cases can find recourse.

Changes in the Legal System Since 1979

During the Cultural Revolution, "Smash the police, the procuracy, and the judiciary" had been the slogan of the day, creating a situation of chaotic lawlessness in which abuses of citizens' rights were many. With the end of the Cultural Revolution and the rise of Deng Xiaoping in the late 1970s, there was a shift to a pragmatic focus on economic development. Among the first reforms implemented was the reestablishment of legal institutions previously abolished. This focus on legal reform stemmed from a recognition that a coherent legal system was critical for economic development and also from a rejection of the concept of "rule of men, not of law" that had characterized the Cultural Revolution.

Specifically, the Chinese government resurrected the judiciary, the office of the procuracy (public prosecutor), and the practicing bar. By 1984 more than 140,000 judges had been reinstated or trained to serve in the four-level Chinese court system (consisting of the Supreme People's Court, the 29 higher people's courts, the 300 intermediate people's courts, and the nearly 3,000 lower [basic] people's courts). The country trained a total of 16,000 lawyers and established about 2,500 legal advisory offices. By 1989 these numbers had increased to a total of 195,000 court workers and 26,584 registered lawyers at 3,653 legal advisory offices.[2] Counting unregistered and part-time lawyers may produce an even higher figure. Additionally, China reopened its 9 law research institutes and 69 law journals and newspapers.

From 1979 to 1989 the National People's Congress (NPC) and its Standing Committee also promulgated 80 laws, 20 amendments, and 40 regulatory decisions. During that same period the State Council enacted more than 900 administrative regulations and decrees, and the various provinces, autonomous regions, and municipalities directly under the central government adopted more than 1,000 local laws and regulations. While the majority of the laws were directed at economic

---

[2] *Zhongguo falu nianjian 1990* (China Law Yearbook 1990; Beijing: Falu Chubanshe, 1990), p. 1009.

reform, some of the legislation asserted the existence and protection of "basic rights of the person."

Perhaps even more important than these declarations were a number of institutional protections that were adopted. New criminal and civil procedure codes were promulgated to regulate the prosecution of criminals and the proceedings in civil cases. Other laws, such as the Arrest and Detention Law and the Organic Law of People's Courts, were also implemented. There was also a constitutional promise of judicial independence, ensuring courts freedom from interference in their work. There was, for a short time, a Committee for Internal and Judicial Affairs that was formed to tackle the problem of Chinese Communist Party (CCP) interference in the judiciary.[3]

In short, during the decade 1978–88 China undertook efforts to establish a state "ruled by law, not by men." There was a promise of formal public hearings before impartial, professional adjudicators and, in criminal cases, a right to a defense with notice of the charges, with an opportunity for both parties to present their positions. To be sure, the reformed Chinese legal system was not an adversarial system dependent on two legal advocates presenting conflicting stories, as in the American model. Rather, it was derived from the European model of civil-law countries, in which results turn on the competence and truth-finding skills of the procurator and the judge involved in the case.

Despite all these reforms, serious problems remained in the Chinese legal system, particularly in the area of criminal law. Criticism continued of China's failure to ensure a presumption of innocence, of limitations placed on the role of defense lawyers, and of persistent arbitrary arrests and detentions. Moreover, the use of so-called administrative sanctions and detentions enabled the government to circumvent the protections of the formal legal process.[4] China's Public Security Bureau (PSB) still had authority to "administratively" impose monetary fines and short detentions ranging from a few months to three years, called reeducation through labor (*liaodong jiaoyang*), for offenses such as prostitution and juvenile delinquency.[5] China also con-

[3] Separation of party from state was part of the reform agenda suggested by then-prime minister Zhao Ziyang's 13th Party Congress address delivered in October 1987. Zhao Ziyang, "Advance along the Road of Socialism with Chinese Characteristics: Report Delivered to the 13th National Congress of the CCP," *Beijing Review*, Vol. 30 (November 9, 1987), pp. 1–27; see also Deng Xiaoping, *Deng Xiaoping Xuanli* (Selected Works of Deng Xiaoping; Beijing: Beijing Renmin Chubanshe, 1983), p. 34.

[4] See Margaret Y. K. Woo, "The Right to a Criminal Appeal in the P.R.C.," *Yale Journal of International Law*, Vol. 14, no. 1 (1989), pp. 118–154.

[5] "Reeducation through labor" is often indistinguishable from the punitive sanction of "reform through labor" that is imposed on criminals convicted of more severe

tinued to employ detentions called shelter and investigation (*shourong shencha*), which allow the PSB to detain people for investigation without a formal charge for an unlimited period. While both administrative and quasi-administrative sanctions could theoretically be appealed to the courts, they were imposed without the protections of a prior judicial proceeding, leaving a clear potential for abuse by the public security authorities.

The avenues for circumventing the formal protections of the legal system were drawn into focus most strikingly in the spring of 1989. In June of that year, the Chinese government used military force to stop student demonstrations for democracy in Tiananmen Square and arrested many of the protesters. In the crackdown, law enforcement authorities apparently followed the rule of swift round-up, swift interrogation (*kuaibu kuaixun*), under which people were held and detained for examination without formal arrest. Thereafter, the central government failed to follow the 1979 criminal procedure code in its prosecution of those involved in the demonstrations, utilizing arbitrary arrests, warrantless arrests and searches, secret trials, and the imposition of administrative rather than criminal sanctions.[6] China's selective use of the judicial apparatus to quell the democracy movement drew international attention and brought criticism from the international human rights community.

In the months following Tiananmen, there were few signs of renewed legal and political reform. Laws passed in the immediate aftermath of Tiananmen emphasized continued economic development but also greater restriction on individual liberties and a more intense focus on the use of law as a instrument for ensuring stability and preventing future social unrest.[7] The central government tightened its control

---

crimes. The power of the Public Security Bureau to impose administrative penalties was reaffirmed in 1980 when the 1957 Security Administrative Punishment Act was republished. The Chinese have tried to bring administrative sanctions within the ambit of judicial supervision in recent years. The Administrative Litigation Act and, specifically, the 1986 Security Administration Punishment Act provide that an accused may seek judicial review of a public security sanction.

[6] See Asia Watch Report, *Punishment Season: Human Rights in China after Martial Law* (New York: Asia Watch Committee, 1990); Department of State Report, *Country Reports on Human Rights Practices for 1989* (Washington, D.C.: U.S. Government Printing Office, 1990), pp. 803–907; Department of State Report, *Country Reports on Human Rights Practices for 1991* (Washington, D.C.: U.S. Government Printing Office, 1992), pp. 810–17.

[7] The legislation passed at this time included, for example, a demonstration regulation, which restricted how public demonstrations could be conducted and by whom, and a "social organization" law, which required all social organizations to register with the state and provide detailed information. Margaret Y. K. Woo, "Legal Reforms in the Aftermath of Tiananmen Square," *Review of Socialist Law*, Vol. 17, no. 1 (Winter 1991),

over the legal institutions and increased its rhetoric on the importance of laws and legal institutions as an effective weapon against social unrest and chaos, rather than for the protection of basic rights.[8]

Facing pressure from the international human rights community, China attempted to address its human rights record and published a 1990 white paper on human rights,[9] in which it defended its judicial institutions and its work in guaranteeing the rights of the people. To some, the white paper represented a whitewash; to others, it was a grudging acknowledgment by the Chinese government of the concept of international human rights and of the opinion of the international community. But ultimately the white paper reflects a cultural and political divide between the West and China.

Multifaceted economic reform seems to be on the country's agenda again, as Deng Xiaoping and his supporters appear to have the upper hand in Beijing.[10] There are also signs of renewed interest in legal reform in China. Critical articles discussing criminal procedure, and the legal system generally, have resurfaced in legal periodicals. The Chinese government even acknowleged 472 cases of illegal confessions obtained by torture and 3,509 cases of unlawful detention filed for investigation and prosecution in 1990.[11] China has also initiated academic exchanges and discussions on the Chinese concept of human rights—the latest turn in the winding road of legal reform in China.

Characteristics of the Chinese Legal System

The post-Tiananmen developments should not be viewed in isolation, but rather as an extension of unresolved issues in the legal reforms begun in 1978. To understand the problems inherent in the Chinese legal system, it is important to grasp several of its fundamental characteristics and to understand its philosophical underpinnings.

---

pp. 95–119; see also *The Aftermath of the 1989 Tiananmen Crisis in Mainland China,* ed. Bih-jaw Lin (Boulder: Westview Press, 1992).

[8] In speaking to the Legal Affairs Committee of the NPC, Jiang Zemin again praised the loyalty of the legal workers during the "recent political storm, counterrevolutionary turmoil" and emphasized the importance of strengtening legal work. "Maintaining Stability Requires the Party," *Fazhi ribao* (Legal System Daily), March 6, 1990, p. 1.

[9] "Human Rights in China," *Beijing Review*, Vol. 34, no. 44 (November 4–10, 1991), pp. 8–46.

[10] Nicholas Kristof, "Support for Move to Freer Markets Is Growing in China," *New York Times*, June 28, 1992, pp. 1, 10.

[11] Department of State Report, *Country Reports on Human Rights Practices for 1991* (Washington, D.C.: U.S. Government Printing Office, 1992), p. 812; "Procuratorate Urge Tough Penalties for Torturers," Foreign Broadcasting Information Service, *Daily Report, China* (hereafter FBIS-CHI), April 17, 1992, p. 39.

These reflect a combination of Soviet socialist legal practice and theory, China's own Maoist revolutionary values, and the long history of Chinese social structures and traditions.

Judicial Independence and Bureaucratization

It is often said that an independent judiciary is one guarantee of an impartial legal system. Indeed, the constitution adopted by the Chinese in 1982 guarantees that "the people's courts" shall exercise their powers independently and not be subject to interference by "any administrative organ, public organization, or individual." However, the dominance of the Chinese Communist Party has caused many to question the extent of judicial independence in China. The guarantee of judicial independence does not mean independence from the CCP. Moreover, the work of judges in China is subject to an elaborate grid of internal and external supervision, even apart from the party. This supervisory structure reflects the traditional Chinese penchant for formal bureaucracy, but also demonstrates a growing concern about balancing procedural regularity with discretion in judicial decision making.

First, numerous actors are involved in judicial decision making other than the judge who hears the case. Chinese courts operate under the principle of the court as an organic whole (*youti zhengti*). The judge in China is not an individual empowered to decide cases independently, but rather is merely one component of the judicial system. It is the court in China that is ensured independence, not the individual judge.

As in the Soviet legal system, the judge in China sits as part of a collegiate panel. As noted earlier, China has a four-tiered court system, consisting of basic, intermediate, and higher-level people's courts, topped by a Supreme People's Court. In the basic court, the judge hears cases together with two "people's assessors," or jurors; in the intermediate court, three judges hear each case. By and large, the judges follow the lead of the presiding judge of the collegiate panel. Moreover, all important judicial decisions must be examined and approved by the court president, the administrative head of the court.

Additionally, difficult or important decisions must first be reviewed by the court's judicial committee. The judicial committee, composed of the court's president, vice-presidents, chief judge, associate chief judges, and the chief procurator as a nonvoting member, is responsible for "sum[ming] up judicial experience and discuss[ing] difficult and important cases and other issues relating to judicial work."[12] According to Chinese scholars, the judicial committee is a court's highest research and adjudication unit.[13] Because it is the judicial committee, and not the collegiate panel or the individual judge, that actually discusses and decides difficult and important cases, some judges have entirely deferred decision making to the judicial committee, relegating to themselves merely administrative tasks.

Beyond the layers of internal court supervision, the Chinese also assert the importance of supervision of judicial work by the "masses," by the procuracy, and, most recently, by the people's congresses, the system of elected (under CCP supervision) bodies from the local to the national levels that are the closest China comes to representative government. Peng Chong of the National People's Congress defined supervision by the people's congresses as follows: "In major cases, the people's congress may request a report from the people's procuracy and the courts, and also conducts its own investigation. If [the people's congress] finds error, it may ask the procuracy or the courts to correct the case according to law."[14] China's 1982 constitution provided for such supervision by the people's congresses.[15] The provision, however, has been brought into active use only in the last few years and remains controversial.

It is unclear how members of the people's congresses, who usually are not legally trained, are to "supervise" the work of the courts. Nevertheless, in August 1989 the Shanxi Provincial People's Congress formed a subcommittee to review cases adjudicated by the intermediate people's courts. The intermediate people's court corrected 26 of the 38 cases that the subcommittee found to be incorrect.[16] Moreover, the recent (1992) Law Governing Deputies for the NPC and People's Congresses includes a detailed article on inspection activities and supervision by the people's congresses of governmental organs, including the courts.[17] Of course, supervision by the people's congresses of judicial work challenges the Western principle of separation of pow-

---

[12] People's court law, ch. I, art. 11.

[13] Ka Changjiu, "Court Reform," *Faxue* (Jurisprudence), no. 1 (1990), p. 150.

[14] "A Discussion of the Various Kinds of Supervision by the People's Congresses and the Standing Committees," *Fazhi ribao*, November 1, 1990, p. 3.

[15] 1982 constitution, ch. I, art. 3.

[16] "To Complete the Workings of Law," *Fazhi ribao*, October 15, 1990, p. 2; see also "Shandong Province Correctly and Voluntarily Accepts People's Congress Supervision," *Fazhi ribao*, February 24, 1992; "Shanghai Court Sets Example," *Fazhi ribao*, January 31, 1992, p. 2.

[17] After three years of revision, the law was passed at the fifth session of the Seventh NPC. The Law Governing Deputies to the National People's Congress, reprinted in FBIS-CHI, April 14, 1992, pp. 1–5.

ers, in which the three branches of government (judicial, executive, and legislative) each has its own sphere of authority, and reflects the Chinese attitude toward the mutually coordinating functions of all legal institutions. More problematically, supervision by people's congresses may be another means through which the CCP can exercise control. Indeed, like all other activities, inspection of the courts by the people's congresses must theoretically be carried out under the "guidance" of the Communist Party.[18]

Party Dominance and Politicization of Law

The Chinese Communist Party dominates all aspects of Chinese life and public policy. This dominance is a legacy of the 1949 revolution, which promoted the belief that the CCP is the key to China's modern progress and resulted in the party's effective control of the government since that date. As a result of this philosophy, the CCP controls the state apparatus from the national down to the most local level, creating a hierarchical party bureaucracy parallel to the system of local, provincial, and national governmental organs. For example, the National People's Congress, although theoretically elected by the people and enshrined in the constitution as "the highest organ of state power," still serves primarily as a conduit for party policies.[19]

The dominance of the CCP over China's legal system can be seen in a number of ways. Judges and lawyers are expected to serve the interests of the Communist Party. Judges remain under the control of the party's Political and Legal Commission. In early 1992 Qiao Shi, the commission's head and a member of the party's Standing Committee, reaffirmed that judges should conduct their work "within the legal framework and under the party's leadership" Qiao held up as models those judges who are "loyal to the party, to the masses, and to the socialist cause."[20] Similarly, lawyers are viewed as legal workers of the socialist state and are expected to protect its interests, which may sometimes be in conflict with the interests of the individual litigants, whom the lawyers are also expected to serve. Often the obligations of the lawyers and judges are expressed in terms of adherences to the "four cardinal principles" that underlie the Chinese con-

---

[18] *Fazhi ribao,* February 11, 1992, p. 1.

[19] Kevin J. O'Brien, "Legislative Development and Chinese Political Change," *Studies in Comparative Communism,* Vol. 22, no. 1 (Spring 1989), pp. 57–73; Francis Foster-Simon, "Codification in Post-Mao China," *American Journal of Comparative Law,* Vol. 30 (1982), pp. 413–14.

[20] "Maintain Stability, Serve Economic Development," *Fazhi ribao,* January 11, 1992, p. 1.

stitution: adherence "to the socialist road, to the people's democratic dictatorship, to leadership by the Communist Party of China, and to Marxism-Leninism and Mao Zedong Thought."

Most important, the CCP retains its power to appoint and dismiss judicial workers. Party committees have exercised the power to dismiss leaders from judicial departments, as from other departments of the government, including the legislature.[21] In the post-Tiananmen crackdown, liberal members of the legal system were removed, and the party instituted greater political education for judicial and other legal workers. Stringent ideological guidelines for procurators and judges alike were announced, and procuratorial offices were urged to set up political departments to address ideological issues in their work.

Despite efforts at reform, there are also continued instances of the party directly interfering in or taking over the work of judges on individual cases. In the early days of the People's Republic of China (PRC), party committees reviewed all decisions, from arrest to sentencing, under a practice called "review by party secretary" (*shuji pi'an*). This is a practice that legal reformers in China have long fought. At its worst, such interference can mean that a crime goes unpunished simply because influential party members prevent the punishment. At other times, however, the intervention of the party has been touted as beneficial to individual petitioners. Thus, for example, in 1989 a legal periodical proudly noted a case involving a petitioner who had filed numerous petitions to reverse a 26-year-old conviction rendered during the excesses of the Cultural Revolution, but could not succeed until a party official intervened.[22]

Party dominance is also manifested in the application of substantive provisions of law, party policy and ideology often taking precedence over statutory codifications. Moreover, a change in party policy can result in an immediate change in interpretation and implementation of law. This is particularly true in the area of criminal law, where the declaration of "anti-crime" campaigns has led to significant reinterpretations of existing criminal laws.

Anti-crime campaigns have been declared periodically, typically in periods of government retrenchment, in order to reinforce the state's power and "to defend against criminals and reactionary forces, and to

[21] Li Maoguan, "Why Laws Go Unenforced," *Beijing Review*, Vol. 32, no. 37 (September 18–24, 1989), p. 18; "Each Level of People's Congresses Must Vigorously Supervise According to Law," *Fazhi ribao*, February 26, 1992, p. 1 (on the problem of local officials invalidating elections).

[22] *Minzhu yu fazhi* (Democracy and Legality), no. 9 (1989), pp. 4–7.

maintain the stability of the state."[23] When China has launched national campaigns to combat crime, some of the procedural protections guaranteed by the criminal code have received short shrift. Thus, during the 1983 anti-crime campaign, emergency measures were adopted for the purpose of "swiftly and severely punishing criminals who jeopardize public security."[24] In particular, the courts sidestepped required time periods for notice to defendants; the ten-day period for filing appeals was shortened to three days; and certain death sentences, which ordinarily must be approved by the Supreme People's Court, were considered final after approval by a provincial higher people's court. Indeed, during the 1983 anti-crime campaign, even these abbreviated procedural protections were sometimes ignored.

Similarly, after the 1989 democracy movement, the Chinese government again called for vigorous prosecution of crime. The government moved to emphasize the need "to deal severely with crime" and instituted an "anti-crime campaign against the six vices," those of gambling, prostitution, pornography, trafficking in women and children, the sale and abuse of drugs, and the use of feudal superstition to defraud.[25] As a result of this emphasis on the prosecution of crimes, the people's courts passed judgment on 482,658 accused people, marking an increase of 30.88 percent from the previous year. Again, for many of the democracy movement participants, some of the procedural protections guaranteed by the Chinese legal codes were ignored.

Informality and Implementation of Law

A major characteristic of the legal culture in China is a preference for extrajudicial methods and the flexible application of law. Individuals and even institutional actors in China often avoid the use of formal procedure.[26] If the focus is on substantive justice—the outcomes of particular cases—informality may sometimes be desirable. Yet excessive informality can also undermine the predictability of procedural

---

[23] Liu Fazhu, China's top prosecutor, recently revealed that Deng Xiaoping is the driving force behind anti-crime campaigns. "Crackdown Said Deng's 'Brainchild'," FBIS-CHI, January 13, 1992, p. 27.

[24] Decision of the Standing Committee of the National People's Congress Regarding the Procedure for Prompt Adjudication of Cases Involving Criminals Who Seriously Endanger Public Security (September 2, 1983), trans. in *Laws of the P.R.C., 1983–1986* (Beijing: Foreign Languages Press, 1987), p. 35.

[25] "On the Work of Eliminating the 'Six Vices'," *Fazhi ribao*, November 14, 1989, p. 1.

[26] In 1988 the procurator's office conducted an investigation of 11,300 reported cases of prosecutorial and police misconduct. The investigation revealed that 4,454 cases involved false accusation, extraction of confession under torture, illegal arrest, and search and seizure without due process. *Renmin ribao* (People's Daily), January 18, 1989, p. 4.

regularity and lead to arbitrariness and abuse of discretion in the legal system. Additionally, while China has made efforts to develop a practice and a culture of law in its populace and has most recently instituted its second five-year plan for mass legal education, most people still have a tendency to look at laws and legal procedures skeptically. This problem is nicely summarized by the Chinese saying "We have law, but no obedience; we implement law, but not strictly; we have violations of law, but no investigation" (*youfa buyi, zhifa buyan, weifa bujiu*).[27]

At a fundamental level, the reluctance to follow formal laws has roots in traditional Chinese culture itself, which prefers social pressure to the use of force by the state. Confucian morality places tremendous emphasis on maintaining social harmony through the preservation and regulation of personal relationships. Although formal law existed in traditional China, its focus was on instances where social norms had failed.

This traditional preference for informality was later reinforced by Marxism-Leninism-Mao Zedong Thought, which emphasized a "mass-line" approach to administration of justice. Hence, in the early years of the PRC, disputes were often resolved through mediation within families, villages, and neighborhood committees. This system continues in active use today. People's mediation committees are still employed extensively and are generally preferred to legal procedure as a less adversarial means of resolving disputes. In 1989 about 69 percent of the civil cases filed with the courts were ultimately resolved through mediation.[28] Many people in China would still prefer to solve problems through personal relationships rather than go through a formal legal process. Similarly, in adjudicating cases, Chinese judges are more inclined to preserve relations than to uphold the strict prescriptions of law.[29]

Complementing this preference for informality is widespread ignorance of the requirements of formal law. This lack of awareness of law is attributable in part to the fact that many of the laws on the books are general and abstract, leaving much room for variations in understanding and interpretation. Interpretation has been largely depen-

---

[27] This is a play on the official version, "Youfa biyi, zhifa biyan, weifa bijiu," which means, "We must obey laws, we must implement laws strictly, and we must investigate violations."

[28] *Zhongguo falu nianjian 1990*, p. 994.

[29] According to a study by Arthur Rosett and Lucie Cheng, economic court judges cited the old adage "Heqing, heli, hefa" (according to relationship, rightness, and the law) as their guideposts in decision making. Lucie Cheng and Arthur Rosett, "Contract with a Chinese Face: Socially Embedded Factors in the Transformation from Hierarchy to Market, 1979–89," *Journal of Chinese Law*, Vol. 5, no. 2 (1991), pp. 224–25.

dent on the development of internal regulations and only recently on the growing interpretive role of the Supreme People's Court.

Lack of awareness of law has, unfortunately, not always been limited to ordinary citizens. Many judges in China lack formal legal training. At one time, judges in China were appointed from the ranks of the military, and they had little or no training in law or adjudication. It is only recently that judges have been required to pass a competency test. Still, in 1989 only 10 percent of the judges and procurators at all levels in the whole country had an education above college level, and in 1991 only 65 percent of the court personnel were college educated.[30] Yet, undeniably, the country continues to promote legal training, and a body of young legal professionals with a greater consciousness of law is growing in China.

Still another factor in the limited implementation of law is corruption. Corruption and the growth of economic crime are perhaps among the biggest problems facing the Chinese government today; conservatives attribute them to reforms and "deficient" ideological training. Corruption is, of course, the flip side of the preference for informality and personal relations. Litigants who are encouraged to resolve disputes through the use of personal relations and favors may come to believe that such personal relations and favors should best be directed to judicial officers themselves. Indeed, there has been some recognition of this problem, and an effort has been made to redress it in the amended 1991 civil procedure law, which prohibits judges from "accepting dinner invitations or gifts from litigants or their legal representatives" and subjects judges who take bribes or play favorites to criminal prosecution.

Finally, limited implementation of law is also attributable, in part, to local abuses of power and local protectionism. As Vivienne Shue has pointed out, Chinese society is not so dominated by the central state as most people think. Rather, localism and cadre departmentalism have a distinctive influence in the implementation of central policy and laws.[31] Localism is even more prevalent with the damage to the central government's legitimacy in the aftermath of the Tiananmen massacre. Peng Chong recently spoke on this problem of localities and departments being ignorant of law, failing to enforce law, giving orders in place of law, and exercising authority to overrule the

---

30 Li Maoguan, "Why Laws Go Unenforced," *Beijing Review*, Vol. 32, no. 37 (September 18–24, 1989), p. 18. The goal is to have 70 percent of court personnel, 80 percent of all judges, and 90 percent of heads of courts be college educated by 1996. *Fazhi ribao*, August 27, 1990, p. 1.

31 See Vivienne Shue, *The Reach of the State: Sketches of the Chinese Body Politic* (Stanford: Stanford University Press, 1988).

law.[32] This tendency has combined with a reluctance by local governments to follow the legal dictates of the central government.

Similarly, local protectionism (*difang baohu zhuyi*) is a predominant problem in economic courts, the branch of the judicial system responsible for handling economic disputes involving the state. Local protectionism can be seen when a court refuses to accept or delays a case brought by a party from outside the area, competes with other courts for jurisdiction over cases, or favors local parties in adjudication and mediation.[33] This problem is accentuated when the budget for the local court is in the hands of the local government and many judges of the court are drawn from the local area.

Law and Rights in the Chinese Context

Even beyond bureaucracy, party dominance, and the preference for informality in legal affairs, any understanding of rights in the Chinese system requires an examination of the differing conceptions of rights and law in Chinese tradition and culture and of the philosophical underpinnings of the Chinese legal system. The failure to address or to reconcile the reality of cultural and philosophical differences between China and the West has sometimes led to self-righteous and unproductive discourse about human rights that has been interpreted by the Chinese as cultural imperialism. On the other hand, understanding how the Chinese conceive of rights, law, and the legal system can further the task of applying universal concepts of human rights to China's social, cultural, and institutional realities.[34]

China's conception of law and rights is distinctly different from traditional Western concepts, particularly from the concept of natural law and rights. According to the natural law view, certain rights are, by nature, inherent in the human being and cannot be transgressed by the state or others. Human rights, under this conception, are held by individuals as against competing claims by the state and society.

---

[32] "Views on Law Enforcement, Constitution," FBIS-CHI, March 27, 1992, p. 26.

[33] "Oppose Local Protectionism in Adjudication of Economic Cases," *Minzhu yu fazhi*, no. 6 (1990), p. 2, and no. 1 (1991), pp. 14–15.

[34] See, for example, William Alford, "Building a Goddess of Democracy from Loose Sand: Observations on Human Rights in China," in *Cross-Cultural Perspectives on Human Rights*, ed. A. An-Naiem (Philadelphia: University of Pennsylvania Press, 1992), pp. 65–80; Wei-chin Lee, "Heaven Can Wait? Rethinking the Chinese Notion of Human Rights," *Asian Thought and Society*, Vol. 16, no. 46 (January-April 1991), p. 28.

By contrast, Chinese legal philosophy defines "law as the state's will and rights as the state's creation."[35] Rights may be expanded and contracted at will by the state on the basis of the needs of the collective. Under this view of law and rights, the Chinese people are free because state laws represent the will of the proletariat, which is in turn (theoretically) represented by the Chinese Communist Party, while laws in capitalist societies reflect only the will of the ruling class, the capitalist owners of the means of production.

According to Andrew Nathan, this view stems not only from the Marxist concept of law as an instrument of the ruling class, but from the traditional Confucian ethic of selflessness.[36] The Confucian tradition emphasizes social harmony and order, often at the expense of individual liberties. In China, persons are viewed primarily as members of a family or a community, rather than as autonomous isolated individuals. Social order and harmony are achieved when each person understands and abides by his or her rights as well as obligations in relation to others. "In the Confucian view, a man is born into society and cannot prosper alone: the individual depends on the harmony and strength of the group."[37]

This tradition is bolstered by Chinese Marxism, which subordinates individual interests to the higher interests of party, class, and nation.[38] Hence, Mao wrote, "the individual is an element of the collective. When collective interests are increased, personal interests will subsequently be improved."[39] Members of a socialist society should behave selflessly and make sacrifices for the greater good. Chinese Marxism attributes an additional element of class nature to law. As one Chinese scholar has explained, "While Americans understand rights as innate, the Chinese hold that rights are the products of class struggle and are granted by the state. Second, Americans think that rights should be apolitical or non-ideological in a civil society while Chinese hold that all rights bear the political nature of socio-economic class. Third, Americans believe rights should be applied universally.

[35] See A. Nathan, "Sources of Chinese Rights Thinking in Chinese Constitutions," in R. Edwards, L. Henkin, and A. Nathan, *Human Rights in Contemporary China* (New York: Columbia University Press, 1986), p. 130.

[36] See *ibid.*, pp. 137–47.

[37] *Ibid.*, p. 138. Self-interested individualism was not defended even during the revolutionary period when rejection of Confucian values was widespread.

[38] *Ibid.*, p. 141.

[39] *Ibid.*, citing "Miscellany of Mao Tse-tung Thought (1949–1968)," *Joint Publication Research Service*, June 12, 1969, part 2, p. 250.

The Chinese believe rights are subject to the political interests of the ruling class."[40]

The Chinese conception of rights and laws also emphasizes the imposition of duties on the individual citizen.[41] In this view, law is designed not simply to protect individual interests, but rather to enable individuals to meet their duties to the state. Particularly after Tiananmen, the government has made a point of emphasizing the dualities of "democracy and law, freedom and discipline, rights and duties."[42]

In the Chinese legal system, then, law defines rights, and individual rights are tied to collective rights, with collective rights taking precedence over individual ones.[43] Further, under Chinese Marxism the collective right is encompassed by the right of the proletariat and its "vanguard," the Communist Party. This formulation provides little comfort to concerns about bureaucratization, party dominance, and informality of the law in China. For example, if law defines rights, then the state or party can readily change or withdraw an individual's right. The state can limit the enjoyment of rights to citizens in "good standing" and deny it to those who have been identified as political "enemies." Rights thus are treated as rewards that can be withdrawn as a form of punishment.[44] In this view "deprivation of political rights" is justified as a form of punishment for certain crimes, particularly "political" crimes. Similarly, a philosophy in which collective rights always take precedence over individual rights can be said to justify party intervention in even ordinary legal cases and the use of social and personal relations in place of legal processes.

Chinese scholars have recently attempted to square China's emphasis on collective rights with notions of international human rights. Some have attempted to develop a distinctly Chinese concept of human rights, separate from law and deriving from social relations among people.[45] In this view, rights are grounded in economic, political, and cultural relations and exist only when social conditions have

[40] Wang Xi, "Constitutional Culture: A Comparison Between P.R.C. and U.S.," *Human Rights Tribune*, Vol. 2, no. 3 (June 1991), p. 21.

[41] Qiu Ye, "On the Unity of Rights and Duties in Law," *Faxue yanjiu* (Studies in Law), no. 3 (1990), p. 16.

[42] "Article Compares Bourgeois, Proletarian Rights," FBIS-CHI February 23, 1990, supp. 4, p. 9.

[43] Recent publications reaffirm this conception of rights in China. See *Zhongguo fazhi bao* (China Legal News), November 8, 1989, front-page article entitled "Law Is Freedom's Boundaries," meaning freedom is the freedom to act within the bounds of the law.

[44] Wang Xi, "Constitutional Culture," p. 22.

[45] Li Buyun, "Discuss the Three Formulations of Rights," *Faxue yanjiu*, no. 4 (1991), pp. 15–16.

been safeguarded. By contrast, another scholar has argued that there is a place for law in China that is "relatively independent" of politics and economics, and that the activities of the party and government departments must be circumscribed by law.[46] Indeed, some scholars would find a higher authority for law in the traditional "mandate of heaven."

Others have explored the ways in which the priority given to collective rights and interests in China can lead to recognition of rights that are also broadly acknowledged internationally. China's constitution, like most socialist constitutions, contains a litany of guarantees of positive social and economic rights, which rest on the primacy of the collective rights to security, subsistence, and development. The Chinese government claims that, in order to guarantee these economic and social rights, it must uphold as paramount the nation's collective right to survival and continuing economic development. Viewed in this light, there can be a role for the collective in legal affairs and there can be room for informality in the resolution of disputes. There can be certain spheres, such as the economic one, in which the interests of the collective in stability and development justify protection for the individual. For example, because of the need to provide economic development, the government may have to ensure procedural regularity for individuals and others engaged in commerce.

To be sure, this is not where China is now. China today has been characterized as a "rule-*by*-law" state, not a "rule-*of*-law" state. The Deng regime has used law as an instrument to "safeguard national and social stability, and to ensure the advances of economic construction,"[47] irrespective of the protection of individual rights. The possibility of convergence of these two objectives is only beginning to be explored by Chinese scholars and certainly remains to be worked out in the legal system itself.

How the Legal System Works in Ordinary Cases

If one looks at all the underlying influences on the Chinese legal system that we have examined, the picture that emerges is rather bleak from the perspective of individual rights. Judges in the system operate in a complex and constraining bureaucratic web. The Communist Party exercises tight control over lawyers and judges and, at

[46] Hao Tiechuan, "The Relative Independence of Law and Its Concrete Meaning," *Faxue*, no. 4 (1991), pp. 1–4.

[47] "Supreme Court Head Cited on Judicial Function," FBIS-CHI, January 8, 1992, p. 25.

times, over the actual interpretation of law; there is also strong preference for informal means of dispute resolution, which can lead to ignorance of the law.

Chinese reformers have, however, made efforts at change in each of these areas. As already noted, these efforts have been more vigorous at some times than at others and have met with varying degrees of resistance from hard-liners within the central government. Prior to 1989 there were attempts to bring to fruition the promise of judicial independence set forth in the 1982 constitution through the elimination of the party's political-legal committees in the courts. During his tenure, Zhao Ziyang put in a motion calling for the separation of party from government. Similarly, there was a continuing struggle to prevent party interference in particular cases (as opposed to broad categories of cases), though it had limited success. So have the efforts to educate the public, through various campaigns, about the need to follow law, and the attempts to encourage use of formal legal process.

Most recently, the Chinese government has articulated its primary goals as "social stability" and "economic development." In the criminal justice system, this has translated into imprisonment of those who threaten the authority of the state. In the civil and economic area, however, the effect has been different. Indeed, efforts have been made to stabilize the legal system in order to encourage private citizens to pursue economic and civil cases, with some success. In 1989 the Chinese courts received 1,815,385 civil cases and 690,765 economic cases. Among the changes implemented in the civil justice system was a 1991 amendment to its civil procedure code. Changes to the code included new provisions directed at ensuring consistency and enforceability of civil judgments, clarifying procedures for multiparty litigation, and delineating the appropriate jurisdiction of the court. The changes were designed in part to increase confidence in civil litigation by ensuring protection for the interests of the participants.

Even in the area of criminal law, there are indications that the legal system can render justice for ordinary citizens who do not threaten the authority of the state. The system can, for example, serve as a check on local bureaucratic abuses. Indeed, in this context the individual citizen and the central government may share the same goal of checking such abuses.

To assist in achieving this goal, the Chinese government enacted an Administrative Procedural Law in 1990. While it is still too early to judge how effectively this new procedure has been implemented, its promulgation does formalize a process by which an individual can bring a complaint against local cadres. This kind of litigation may be supported by the central government if it helps to rein in the excessive autonomy of local officials. As Harold Berman pointed out in his analysis of the former Soviet Union, the repressive Soviet legal system was an autocratic central authority that had been successful in crushing human rights, but nevertheless was also "an effective system of control over abuses of human rights by intermediate administrative officials."[48] China may be moving in a similar direction.

Discussion of particular cases may help to demonstrate some of the competing interests within the Chinese legal system and give a glimpse of how the system functions for ordinary Chinese people. Of course, no single case or even two cases can completely illustrate the intricacies of how the system functions, but the following two examples at least raise some of the issues now being discussed by the Chinese themselves. Moreover, unlike most officially reported cases, which give only a bare recitation of facts and procedure, these examples reveal the mindset of the parties and actors involved toward law and the legal system.

The first is a 1989 case involving a woman accused of the crime of "rumor mongering."[49] The defendant, Qian, was a team leader in the No. 134 Central Machine Shop in Hunan Province. In 1988 Qian reported on a coworker, Fung, whom she believed was drawing sick pay beyond the 100-day limit. Qian allegedly wrote three letters concerning Fung, who in turn pressed charges of "rumor mongering" against Qian in the basic people's court. The city and provincial procuracy (the prosecutors) investigated the three letters, determined that they had been written by Qian, came to handcuff and arrest her at her factory, and demanded to search her home.

In September Qian was put in protective detention and was hospitalized for illness. In December the procuracy brought Qian to the basic people's court for a nonpublic hearing. The evidence presented by the procurator was limited to the three letters allegedly written by Qian. Witnesses, however, testified that Qian would not have been the kind of person to use such words. Following the criminal procedure code, Qian requested an additional inquest to obtain a supplementary expert evaluation of the handwriting in the letters and testimony by additional new witnesses. The court, however, denied the request and instead sentenced Qian to imprisonment for one year.

Qian appealed to the intermediate court, which requested that the public security authorities conduct a new investigation. After looking at the letters and taking additional evidence from Qian's daughter,

[48] Harold Berman, "Human Rights in the Soviet Union," *Howard Law Journal*, Vol. 11 (Spring 1965), pp. 339–40.

[49] "Was the Procedure in This Case Legal?" *Minzhu yu fazhi*, no. 7 (1990), pp. 6–7.

the intermediate court remanded the case to the basic court for retrial on the ground that "the facts were unclear." The basic court sent the case back to the procurator for additional investigation, which was reviewed by the national people's procuracy. The local procuracy finally dismissed the case and released Qian on September 23, 1989. Yet, in the dismissal document, the procuracy continued to maintain that there was evidence of criminality, but stated that the case was being withdrawn for insufficient evidence. As a result of this lack of clarity, Qian has suffered in her pay and work; she has petitioned the procuracy for clarification, but without success.

This case demonstrates some of the problems still experienced by litigants in the Chinese legal system. At the local level Qian faced procedural violations by officials who failed to follow the mandate of the law. The case was criticized by the journal in which it appeared for Qian's improper arrest, the court's failure to grant a new inquest, and the procurator's decision to prosecute a minor rumor-mongering case that certainly did not endanger public safety. Additionally, it does not appear that Qian had legal representation, as guaranteed by the constitution. All of this demonstrates that the implementation of procedural regularity in the legal system is still incomplete.

However, it is an encouraging sign that the issue of procedural violations is being discussed openly. Moreover, in this case at least, the legal system ultimately functioned to acquit Qian. Qian made use of the layers of internal review and the procedural guarantees, for example by requesting additional testimony. Through the system of formal appeal, she was given additional investigation and review, resulting in the higher court reversing the decision of the basic people's court. Importantly, Qian was able to have a new set of decision makers hear her case, apart from the local officials who had acted questionably in the first place. It may be that there were extrajudicial forces leading to her acquittal. Yet another plausible conclusion is that with competent judicial officers who work to uncover the truth, the skeleton of procedure in place in China can be called upon to render justice in individual cases. To be sure, regularity in procedure, including the provision of a credible appeals process, can also serve the state's purposes by helping to centralize state policies and check local abuses.

The second example is a 1991 civil case involving an official who brought suit for libel against a retired schoolteacher.[50] Libel has achieved some prominence in recent years, because in conjunction with the Administrative Procedure Act it has been used as a vehicle

---

[50] "Should This Litigation Have Been Brought?" *Minzhu yu fazhi*, no. 2 (1992), pp. 6–9.

for offensive action by intellectuals, such as Wang Meng, against central government criticism and control.[51] This case, by contrast, shows how an official attempted to use libel law and the legal process against an ordinary citizen instead of (or perhaps along with) the usual party and political channels.

In 1990 a retired teacher, Chen, wrote a letter to the local party committee to complain that the city's vice-mayor, Wang, had used his position to obtain better housing for his family and a job and relocation from the countryside to the city for his sister, and that Wang was lazy, incompetent, and self-serving. Chen also asserted that Wang had mismanaged the city's educational system. In response, Wang filed suit against Chen for libel, asking for damages of Rmb 2,000.

After receiving the case, the basic court solicited the advice of the intermediate courts and conducted several months of investigation before deciding to hold an open hearing. The court considered the impact of the case upon society and tried to be objective. In offering an opportunity to both parties to present their positions, the court held an unprecedented ten-hour hearing on June 23, 1991. After the hearing, the court extended the time to render a decision pursuant to article 135 of the civil procedure code. What is most interesting about the case is the thoughts of the relevant parties and actors about it and about the legal process.

The defendant, Chen, expressed concern that his complaint would lead to such a lawsuit. He contended that the constitution ensured his right to report misconduct, and that the party had encouraged the "masses to report real conditions." He perceived bias in the legal system favoring Wang, the official, as in the Chinese saying "Officials protect each other" (*guanguan xianghu*). The plaintiff, Wang, meanwhile, also saw bias in the legal system. He felt disadvantaged because the "masses" saw this as a case of an official suing a citizen and wished to see the citizen prevail over the official. He argued therefore that this was a case of a citizen suing a citizen, since he was suing in the capacity of citizen. Apparently Wang also received pressure from party members who believed that he, as a party member, should have considered not simply his own individual circumstance, but also the reputation of the party.

The members of the court commented that they too had received pressure and some interference. According to one judge, some of the "masses" suspected that the court was prejudiced in favor of the vice-mayor. Party officials, meanwhile, believed that it was not desirable for a vice-mayor to sue a citizen, and that it was damaging to the

51 "Wang Meng: The Litigating Official," *China Spring*, no. 12 (1991), p. 52.

party and the government's authority. Hence the court hoped that this case could be resolved through mediation.

This case illustrates the tension of converging forces within the legal system. For one, what is the right of a citizen to criticize governmental officials? While the right to criticize is guaranteed by the constitution, is the right limitless? What are the boundaries to the criticism? The case also seems to raise the substantive legal issue of the conflicting rights of speech versus privacy.

Another significant issue dealt with in this case is the status of a party official vis-à-vis the ordinary citizen in a private civil suit. This issue is important in light of the dominant role of the party in China and the socialist principle that sees a unity of interest between citizens and the government and that otherwise would negate a citizen's right to sue officials. Yet the message promoted by this case seems to be that not only can a citizen sue an official, but an official must use legal channels rather than his or her official position to pursue the vindication of any personal rights. An official is no more than an ordinary citizen in the courts when suing to vindicate his or her private interests. Nevertheless, the line between party and ordinary citizen is still not clearly drawn, as some people continue to see the dispute as a "contradiction between the party and the masses" that should have been politically resolved through party channels and responsible party officials.

Ultimately this case may also demonstrate the still profound hesitation of the Chinese public to use the courts, and the view that courts are the last resort. Even when courts are invoked, social harmony and personal relations must be considered, and informal resolution is preferred. Hence it is not surprising that in handling this case, the court solicited advice from higher courts, listened to the opinion of the public, and postponed rendering a decision, hoping for a mediated result. Rather than the rigid application of law, then, the Chinese judges considered the social milieu surrounding the case and opted for informal resolution. As such, the rights of the individual remained dependent on the particular social circumstance.

China's legal system is becoming more established. This is evident in the growing body of legal professionals as well as in the rising expectations of the people for the efficacy of the legal system and the protection of rights.[52] Yet the legal system will necessarily continue to

[52] Ann Kent, "Waiting for Rights: China's Human Rights and China's Constitutions, 1949–1985," *Human Rights Quarterly*, 1991, p. 171.

reflect certain tensions: judicial independence versus party control, law as an instrument of the state versus law as protector of individual liberties, and rigorous formality versus preference for informal resolutions.

At present, law and legal institutions are still primarily an instrument of the Chinese Communist Party state. Despite the intentions of some reformers, the legal system is more a function of party policies to ensure the power of the state and less a catalyst for effectuating fundamental change. Political cases, defined as any opposition to party policy, remain beyond the protection of due process. In such cases the legal system and procedural regularity will bend for the needs of the state as defined by the CCP.

Yet in everyday cases, there may be a convergence of goals between the state and the Chinese people. To the extent that procedural regularity can guarantee consistency of central policy, China has done much and will continue to do more to pursue legal procedural regularity, which will in turn benefit individuals in ordinary cases. Indeed, individuals in China are increasingly turning to the courts for resolution of their disputes, revealing a growing, albeit still nascent, "legal culture."

As we have seen, a number of forces are moving China in the direction of internationally recognized legal rights. However, far-reaching legal reform that would truly loosen the party's grip on society will have to wait for deeper political reform. To many, the best hope is that the past decade of partial political reform and the renewed force of economic reform will lay a sufficient foundation so that any future retrenchment may retard, but will not eliminate, the slow tide of progress that has characterized the Chinese legal system.

5
Public Health in China

Gail Henderson

Public health trends are never unidimensional. It is entirely possible for health to improve in some respects but deteriorate in others. Overall health indicators can show positive trends at the same time as differences among groups increase. The incidence of some infectious diseases can decline while that of others increases. Protein-deficient diets can improve, then become overly rich in animal fat. In China, although general health indicators have shown continued, substantial improvement over the last four decades, less-aggregated data reveal many of these more complex patterns.

Recent trends in public health in China have been affected by three powerful forces. First, economic development has improved living conditions, and thus health, and promoted the modernization of medicine. However, development has also exacerbated inequalities in access to costly medical care. Second, in contrast to the view of health care as a public good that prevailed in the Maoist era, fiscal reform has shifted the focus toward health care as an economic commodity, introducing incentives that have encouraged hospital-based, technology-dependent medicine. Third, changing demographic patterns, including lower birth rates and a rise in the number of persons surviving to old age, have fostered new demands for pre- and postnatal care and for medical care for the elderly.

Assessment of health trends in China is complicated by two additional factors. First, because the quality and availability of health data have not been constant over time, we have much more information, both positive and negative, about recent health patterns than about those in the past. This makes interpretation of long-term trends or the impact of recent economic developments problematic. Second, health is not neutral territory. Just as the diagnosis of a particular disease can be highly stigmatizing to an individual, data on the health of a nation are often accompanied by some kind of moral evaluation. In most societies, health is—simply put—politics.

The Transformation of Public Health

During the 20th century, the most poignant and powerful metaphors in our collective understanding of China have been images of health and disease. In the first part of this century, China was literally the "Sick Man of Asia," with health needs so great that Christian missions and foreign philanthropic agencies in China devoted themselves to medical service and education.[1] The economist R. H. Tawney described the scene in 1932:

> An eminent Chinese official stated that in Shensi [Province] at the beginning of 1931, three million persons had died of hunger in the last few years, and the misery had been such that four hundred thousand women and children had changed hands by sale. . . . There are districts in which the position of the rural population is that of a man standing permanently up to the neck in water, so that even a ripple is sufficient to drown him.[2]

The overall health of the Chinese population was typical of many less-developed nations. The leading causes of disease and death were acute infectious conditions, and those at greatest risk were young children and women of child-bearing age. Life expectancy was 35. One of every four or five children died before reaching age one, and 80 percent of these deaths resulted from tetanus, a preventable condition. Fecal-borne diseases such as dysentery, typhoid, cholera, and schistosomiasis were endemic. Tuberculosis accounted for 10–15 percent of all deaths, and sexually transmitted diseases were the fourth most common admitting diagnosis in urban hospitals.

Literature, missionary letters, and journalists' first-person narratives from that time period were littered with accounts of unimaginable poverty and disease. The English surgeon Joshua Horn quoted a fellow countryman who ran a hotel in pre-Liberation Shanghai for more than 20 years, on his return in 1965:

> "I searched for scurvy-headed children. Lice-ridden children. Children with inflamed red eyes. Children with bleeding gums. Children with distended stomachs and spindly arms and legs. I searched the side-

[1] See, for example, Mary Brown Bullock, *An American Transplant: The Rockefeller Foundation and Peking Union Medical College* (Berkeley: University of California Press, 1980), and Yueh-wah Cheung, *Missionary Medicine in China: A Study of Two Canadian Protestant Missions in China before 1937* (Lanham, MD: University Press of America, 1988).

[2] Cited in Shiela M. Hillier and J. A. Jewell, *Health Care and Traditional Medicine in China, 1800–1982* (London: Routledge and Kegan Paul, 1983), pp. 76–77.

> walks day and night for children who had been purposely deformed by beggars. . . . I looked for children covered with horrible sores upon which flies feasted. I looked for children having a bowel movement, which, after much strain, would only eject tapeworms. I looked for child slaves in alleyway factories. Children who worked twelve hours a day, literally chained to small press punches. . . ." In 1965 he searched without finding, but in the 1930s, there was no need to search far for such sights were everywhere to be seen.[3]

In 1948 the United Nations Relief Organization stated, "China presents perhaps the greatest and most intractable public health problem of any nation in the world." Two decades later the dominant image of Mao's China was one of healthy, red-cheeked babies, born to a nation that seemingly provided health care for all. In 1971 two Americans visiting China, Victor and Ruth Sidel, observed that in stark contrast to Shanghai in the 1930s, "China's cities [are] clean and calm, with people showing little or no sign of boredom, cynicism, or irritability."[4] Victor Sidel, an activist physician practicing in the Bronx, spent years writing about China's extraordinary achievements in health, often lecturing with two slide projectors running simultaneously—the photographs of China on one side overshadowing in all respects those of the Bronx on the other.

In the years during and immediately after the Cultural Revolution (1966–76), "official briefings" given to foreign visitors substituted for factual information about all spheres of life, including statistics on birth rates, death rates, and the leading causes of morbidity and mortality. In fact, systematic data were simply nonexistent. The first survey that would provide information about leading causes of death was the 1976 Cancer Epidemiology Survey, and those results were released only years later.[5] Nevertheless, during the 1970s it became clear to many Western observers that major advances had been made in the battle against infectious and parasitic diseases that had plagued prerevolutionary China.

---

[3] Joshua Horn, *Away with All Pests: An English Surgeon in the People's Republic of China* (New York: Monthly Review Press, 1969), p. 19.

[4] Victor W. Sidel and Ruth Sidel, *Serve the People: Observations on Medicine in the People's Republic of China* (Boston: Beacon Press, 1974), p. 5.

[5] According to Judith Banister, "China: Recent Mortality Levels and Trends" (Paper presented at the annual meeting of the Population Association of America, Denver, May 1992), "This was a nationwide attempt to record the cause of death, age, and sex of the decedent, and other details for all the 18 million deaths recorded in China during the three-year period 1973–1975. This must be the largest mortality survey in human history" (p. 7).

According to a World Bank study mission to China in the early 1980s, by the 1970s, except in the very poorest areas, the leading causes of morbidity and mortality had shifted from infectious diseases to chronic conditions (such as cancer and heart disease), the so-called epidemiologic transition.[6] Those at greatest risk were no longer infants and young women but middle-aged and elderly people. Because most infants were surviving into childhood, life expectancy increased, and by the 1970s the national average was reported to be above 60 years. In the span of several decades, China had indeed transformed itself from one of the least-enviable of all nations into a model for the delivery of primary-care services. How was this accomplished?

For industrialized countries in the developed world, this shift in health and disease patterns—which generally occurred prior to the 20th century—had more to do with rising standards of living and better nutrition than with medical progress.[7] In contrast, in the 20th century "epidemiologic transitions" in developing nations have been initiated by medical progress, organized health care, and disease-control programs that have usually been funded by international agencies rather than being a result of general improvements in living standards.[8]

In the case of China, although there was substantial redistribution of resources, average per capita income remained quite low, and there was no massive input of foreign programs or technology. Rather, on the national level there was a series of economic, educational, and organizational policies which created a system that defined health as part of the broader economic and social objectives of the regime. In 1979 Robert Blendon, an American physician-researcher who joined the wave of U.S. medical professionals visiting China after the Cultural Revolution, published an article in the *New England Journal of Medicine* titled "Can China's Health Care Be Transplanted without China's Economic Policies?"[9] He concluded that improved health outcomes in China resulted from the entire context of the country's development policies. Thus, for example, policies that prohibited invest-

[6] Dean Jamison et al., *China: The Health Sector* (Washington, D.C.: World Bank, 1984).

[7] Thomas McKeown, *The Role of Medicine: Dream, Mirage, or Nemesis?* (Princeton: Princeton University Press, 1979).

[8] Abdel R. Omran, "The Epidemiologic Transition: A Theory of the Epidemiology of Population Change," *Milbank Memorial Fund Quarterly*, Vol. 49 (October 1971), pp. 509–38.

[9] Robert J. Blendon, "Can China's Health Care Be Transplanted without China's Economic Policies?" *New England Journal of Medicine*, Vol. 300 (1979), pp. 1453–58. In the late 1970s it was reported that 10 percent of all delegations to China from the United States were composed of physicians.

ment in expensive foreign technology allowed the government to put more resources into rural health care. The collective agricultural system provided the opportunity to develop a collectively funded welfare program for health and community sanitation. The anti-intellectual movements of the late 1950s and the Cultural Revolution promoted a less elitist view of training requirements for health care professionals. And the mass campaign strategies of the Chinese Communist Party, such as those it used during land reform, easily translated into health education campaigns launched to attack endemic health problems and to change individual behaviors that placed people at risk for disease.

Within this national context, at the local level and especially in rural areas there was a major effort to redistribute resources toward community welfare programs, including health insurance, clinics, and community hospitals. One of the most impressive achievements of the Maoist period was the creation of a three-tiered triage and referral system to provide integrated preventive and curative health care services in all of China's rural counties. This included hospitals at the county and township (formerly called commune) levels and village-run clinics staffed by locally recruited village paramedics (the well-known "barefoot doctors"). It also included maternal and child health (MCH) departments and public health departments that directed countywide prevention work.[10]

The result of these policies was an increase in the total number of hospitals between 1949 and 1989 from 2,600 to 61,929, including 47,523 township hospitals, established as part of the commune movement during the Great Leap Forward of 1958–61. The number of hospital beds per 1,000 persons rose from .15 beds per 1,000 persons in 1949 to 2.33 beds in 1989. Likewise, in 1949 there were no public health departments and only 9 MCH departments; but by 1989 these numbers had risen to 3,591 public health departments and 2,796 MCH departments. Although the state provided subsidies for health care through its budget allocations and through price controls, it did not implement a universal health-insurance program. Rather, following the Soviet model, health-insurance was provided for urban employees of enterprises and government workplaces, and in rural areas collective programs funded insurance for about three-fourths of the popula-

[10] Called "anti-epidemic disease stations" (*fangyi zhan*), these county-level public health departments administer disease-prevention work at the county, township, and village levels. Their departments consist of epidemiology, food hygiene and nutrition, labor and school health, education, endemic diseases, and data management. The township-level public health departments directly oversee the village doctors' immunization, infectious-disease reporting, sanitation, and health-campaign work. Public health departments also exist at the district, municipal, and provincial levels.

tion. Despite better health-care services and insurance coverage for urban residents, for the most part development efforts were aimed at rural health care. It was not until the post-Mao period that investment in urban facilities and medical schools also increased substantially.[11]

Many developing nations have experienced an initial improvement in health outcomes due to foreign-sponsored medical programs, including importation of foreign pharmaceuticals, malaria-eradication programs, and maternal and child health programs focusing on nutrition, immunization, and diarrhea prevention. Yet after an initial rapid decline in mortality, progress has often stalled, particularly with regard to infant and child mortality. In the early 1970s this pattern was described by the epidemiologist Abdel R. Omran, who asserted that in most developing countries further improvement in health outcomes would depend upon "supplementing the imported medical technology with genuine health care and social development." He proceeded to outline a list of recommendations that, coincidentally, read like a description of changes implemented in China during the 1950s and 1960s:

- Reorientation of health programs from hospital-based curative systems toward community-based total-care (both preventive and curative) systems with emphasis on primary care.
- Improved management and efficiency of health programs.
- Health education to change patterns of life that are detrimental to health.
- Improved training and motivation of health and community workers.
- Community participation in health and welfare programs.
- Environmental control and sanitation.
- A political and economic structure responsive to the health needs of the population.
- Progress in public services such as schooling and road construction.
- A rise in the standard of living.

---

[11] A study of government health expenditures between 1976 and 1983 (directly following the Maoist period) reported that the proportion of state funding for provincial hospitals almost tripled, while the proportion devoted to the commune (township) hospitals and public health departments declined by approximately one-third. See Liu Zongxiu and Yu Xiucheng, "Discussion of the Reform of Health Planning Work," *Zhongguo weisheng jingji yanjiuhui* (China Conference on Health Economics), December 1984. During the same period the percentage of hospital beds in the cities rose from 39.9 percent to 42.4 percent, and the percentage of medical personnel in the cities rose from 41.9 percent to 50.2 percent.

- Equitable access to good health care for the poor and disadvantaged, especially in rural areas.[12]

Public Health After Mao

China's public health achievements were thus closely related to the economic and political policies of the Maoist period. For that reason, during the 1980s and 1990s analyses of health in China have often been cast in terms of the changes that the reforms of the Deng era have brought to what was portrayed as the ideal health-care system of Maoist China.

As collective farming was replaced by the household responsibility system, welfare programs such as rural health insurance were affected. In 1980 almost 70 percent of villages had insurance coverage. In 1985 the figure had dropped to 5.4 percent, rising to almost 10 percent in 1987; but according to one recent article, in 1989 only 4.8 percent of all administrative villages continued to offer collective welfare insurance.[13]

Many local-level clinics were taken over by doctors themselves and operated on a fee-for-service basis. In some places the former "barefoot doctors" were able to make more money working in the new family-based economy than in health care, and their numbers began to decline. In 1975 there were 1.6 million, or one for every 400 rural inhabitants; by the late 1980s the number had declined by more than 300,000. However, the extent of privatization of clinics varied considerably by province, ranging from 2.3 percent in Shanghai to 85.5 percent in Anhui Province.[14] Furthermore, even when village doctors receive most of their income from selling medicines, they continue to be subject to supervision by township-level hospitals and public health departments.[15]

[12] Abdel R. Omran, "Epidemiologic Transition: Theory," *International Encyclopedia of Population* (New York: Collier Macmillan, 1982), pp. 174–75.

[13] *Jiankang bao* (Health Daily), February 23, 1992, p. 1. In 1992 reports in health journals and in the press indicate that the government is trying to revive the collective welfare system.

[14] See the *1989 Zhongguo weisheng tongji* (China Health Statistics Yearbook; Beijing: People's Medical Publishing House, 1989). In 1988, for example, in Shanghai, only 2.3 percent of clinics were privately run, and in Jiangsu Province, only 10.9 percent were private; but in Beijing, 45.3 percent were private; in Hunan, 53 percent; and in Guangxi and Guizhou, 62.5 percent and 69.5 percent respectively.

[15] In a recent study of health-care services in a rural Shandong county, village doctors were found to be very diligent in infectious-disease reports, health-education campaigns, and immunizations. See Gail Henderson and Scott Stroup, "Preventive Health Care in Rural Shandong" (Manuscript).

National statistics show that the shift from a collective to a family-based economy did undermine community-funded preventive medicine programs such as childhood immunizations, infectious-disease reporting, and sanitation work. This resulted in a rise in infectious and fecal-borne diseases (including schistosomiasis, dysentery, and hepatitis A) in the early 1980s. After the transition period, however, the incidence of many of these diseases stabilized. This was due in part to a major international effort to increase childhood immunizations in China in the mid-1980s and to the resilience of the rural health infrastructure.

During this post-Mao period, urban hospitals, which had previously operated with substantial subsidies from the state, were also encouraged to implement reforms in finance and management. Many have instituted better work-evaluation criteria (linked to bonuses) and more-efficient patient-management systems. State control of prices, however, has been a major roadblock to increasing economic efficiency. In the past, because health care was seen as a public good, the government subsidized many aspects of the provision of care, including setting prices for all medical and hospital charges well below actual cost. During the 1980s, despite several price increases, the provision of medical care continued to be a money-losing proposition.

In response, many hospitals (cooperating with local finance departments) instituted a system of charging higher prices for those urban government employees and enterprise workers who continued to enjoy insurance, thus encouraging the development of a bias toward provision of services to the insured. Second, because one of the few areas that did not immediately fall under the state price regulations was new medical technology, hospitals began to turn to acquisition of new profit-generating technology, including such diagnostic equipment as ultrasound machines and CAT scanners, and treatment equipment such as cardiac defibrillators or critical care units. With central planning in decline, it was difficult to promote regional efficiency and to centralize information about machine type, spare parts, and support services; hence a great number of errors were made in the purchase of new technology.[16] Furthermore, decisions about investment in new technology and criteria for patient selection were often left to the local-level physicians and hospital administrators. The

---

[16] See Gail Henderson et al., "The Rise of Technology in Chinese Hospitals," *International Technology Assessment in Health Care*, Spring 1987, and Gail Henderson, "Issues in the Modernization of Health Care in China," *Science and Technology in Post-Mao China*, ed. Denis F. Simon and Merle Goldman (Cambridge, MA: Council on East Asian Studies, Harvard University, 1989).

result of all these changes was that during the 1980s health-care expenditures were increasingly devoted to spending for hospital care, especially for technology-related diagnosis or treatment.

Western analysts writing about these changes echoed a common theme as they observed the development of familiar patterns of a market economy: "Learn from our mistakes." In 1984, just five years after the Blendon article cited above appeared, the *New England Journal of Medicine* published an article by the Harvard public health economist William C. Hsiao, in which he detailed the "transformation" of health care in the countryside and warned of the dangers of letting the market govern the distribution of health care.[17] As international agencies such as the World Health Organization (WHO), UNICEF, and the World Bank have continued to engage in health work in China, their messages have consistently reflected these concerns. Perhaps because of unrealistic expectations built from the Maoist era, the West still seems to hold China to very high standards.

Is the Chinese health-care system falling apart? It is hard to reach this conclusion when China's public health system continues to produce such impressive results. In a 1991 article titled "Chinese Grow Healthier from Cradle to Grave," *New York Times* correspondent Nicholas Kristof wrote that a baby born in Shanghai "will have better odds of survival than a baby born in New York City," and in fact the infant mortality rate (defined as the number of deaths per 1,000 live births in the first year of life) in Shanghai is 10.9, whereas New York City's rate is 13.3.[18] Kristof joined the ranks of authors who attribute this success to a government that emphasizes the "unglamorous but critical foundations of public health," such as sanitation work and prenatal care. Equally impressive are the efforts (noted above) to improve child health in rural areas through immunization programs. Kristof quotes a WHO representative in China:

> The typical Chinese mayor is far more conversant with health issues than mayors of other countries. High-level government backing has been crucial in one of the most critical initiatives, to vaccinate children against infectious diseases. About 85 percent of infants are inoculated before their first birthday against six ailments: whooping cough, diphtheria, tetanus, tuberculosis, measles, and polio.[19]

---

[17] William C. Hsiao, "Transformation of Health Care in China," *New England Journal of Medicine*, Vol. 310 (1984), pp. 932–36.

[18] *New York Times*, April 14, 1991, p. A1. Overall, the U.S. rate is below 10; however, for black Americans it is twice that of whites.

[19] *Ibid.*, p. A6.

In Chinese cities the combination of greatly increased prosperity during the past decade and the one-child family policy has produced lower infant mortality rates than found in many cities of the developed world. In fact, a recent analysis of mortality trends in China between the mid-1970s and 1990 demonstrates that age-specific mortality rates have declined or stabilized for males and females at almost all ages.[20] The greatest gains have been for children of both sexes at ages 1–4 and 5–9. In 1990 urban males reported a slight increase in life expectancy to 70.4 years and declines in mortality at all ages except 30–34 and 45–49. Urban females reported a greater gain in life expectancy than males, to 74.4 years in 1990, and reduced mortality in all age groups. In rural areas life expectancy for males was 67.1 in 1990, and for females, 70.2. Rural females reported a decline in mortality at all ages, whereas for males age-specific mortality increased slightly at ages 30–34 and 65–79.[21]

As the majority of the population in China has experienced increased economic prosperity in recent years, dietary patterns have shifted to higher consumption of fat and protein,[22] and major health problems now consist of the diseases associated with higher levels of economic development. Cancer, stroke, respiratory disease, heart disease, and accidents are now the five leading causes of death for the urban population, accounting for more than 80 percent of all reported deaths. For the rural population respiratory disease is still the number-one killer, followed by the other four.[23] Other major causes of morbidity and mortality include congenital abnormalities, infectious diseases (including tuberculosis), digestive disorders, and urinary system diseases. In addition, the incidence of sexually transmitted diseases has increased within the past decade, in contrast to the Maoist era when they were literally eradicated in China. A small number of AIDS cases have also been identified, transmitted by contaminated needles into Yunnan Province via the so-called golden triangle opium-growing region of Southeast Asia.

Risk factors related to major chronic diseases are also on the rise. These include dietary changes leading to obesity, high blood pressure, and increased cholesterol; lack of exercise; and, most promi-

---

[20] Banister, "Recent Mortality Levels."

[21] According to Banister (*ibid.*, pp. 15–17), for urban and rural males the increases (or lack of decreases) can be attributed to work-related injuries or health problems and to smoking-related deaths.

[22] See Barry Popkin et al., "The Nutrition Transition in China: A Cross-Sectional Analysis" (Paper presented at the Annual Association for Asian Studies Meeting, Washington, D.C., April 1992).

[23] *1989 Zhongguo weisheng nianjian*, p. 805.

nently, smoking. Cigarette smoking contributes more to the risk of cancer, heart disease, and chronic lung disease than all other risk factors combined. A recent World Bank study estimates that by the middle of the next century, smoking-attributable deaths in China will increase from the current annual rate of 100,000 to between 1 million and 3 million yearly. This dramatic jump will result from increases both in the number of elderly adults and in the number of people with lifelong cigarette use.[24]

The irony of many of these problems is that they are a product of China's improved living conditions and public health programs that have increased life expectancy. Given China's success in combating infectious and parasitic diseases, current health statistics very likely reflect a rise in chronic conditions and in risk factors for those conditions. International observers from countries that have already experienced some of these problems are ready with advice on cutting down the incidence or the fatality rate of preventable chronic diseases.

Another area of concern, however, is the extent to which all people in China are benefiting equally from the factors that have fostered improved health outcomes in recent years. No country is able to distribute perfectly the risk of disease and death, and in China, despite overall positive trends, the variation continues to be wide. As the data cited above demonstrate, there is a three-to-four-year gap in life expectancy between urban and rural residents. Furthermore, a persisting urban-rural gap in health status is reflected in the difference in number of deaths from respiratory diseases in cities (16 percent of all deaths) versus the countryside (25 percent of all deaths). National studies of child nutrition in China point to the disturbing trend of coexisting malnutrition and obesity.[25] International agencies in China currently focus on the "poverty counties" and highlight the fact that, as with diet, there appear to be coexisting diseases of poverty and diseases of wealth. Pockets of extreme poverty exist, and with them,

---

[24] The World Bank conducted an extensive review of the long-term consequences of a variety of chronic health problems and risk factors, including smoking. See *China: Long Term Issues in Options for the Health Sector* (Washington, D.C.: World Bank, 1989), Annex C. Recent studies on the future health effects of tobacco in China include Richard Peto, "Tobacco-Related Deaths in China," *Lancet*, Vol. 2 (1987), p. 211, and Yu Jingjie et al., "A Comparison of Smoking Patterns in the PRC with the U.S.," *American Journal of Public Health*, Vol. 264, no. 12 (1990), p. 1576.

[25] In fact, the recent analysis of dietary intake conducted by the Chinese Academy of Preventive Medicine Nutrition Institute found that "among adults in the 1989 China Health and Nutrition Survey, over 8% had inadequate body fat. Among children aged 1 to 6, one-third were stunted in stature, and about 8% had weight-for-height Z-scores so low as to indicate current acute malnutrition." Popkin et al., "Nutrition Transition," p. 12.

extreme statistics. A 1989 Ford Foundation delegation found that in a remote minority area of Yunnan Province, the infant mortality rate approached 100, meaning that 10 percent of all babies die before they reach age one.[26]

One of the most disturbing health consequences of rural poverty seems to be the misfortune associated with being born female:

> Each year in China, about 600,000 fewer girl births are reported to the authorities than there should be based on the number of boy births and the ratio that should exist between them. A large number appear to be surreptitiously given up for adoption, and many others are simply raised quietly by their parents or relatives without registering the birth. Some are also drowned at birth by a midwife who keeps a bucket by the mother's side, in case the infant proves to be an unwanted girl, but it is impossible to know how often this happens. . . . [In addition] anecdotal evidence suggests that selective abortion may be having an impact on the statistics.[27]

Apparently, under pressure from the economic reforms that place a premium on family labor power, some Chinese families are forced to do away with female babies.

> The . . . missing include females of all ages who are aborted or killed at birth, or who die because they are given less food than males, or because family members view a daughter with diarrhea as a nuisance but a son with diarrhea as a medical crisis requiring a doctor.[28]

A balanced evaluation of these reports is complicated by a deterioration in relations between China and the West after more than a decade of intense professional and political interactions. In the late 1970s Western doctors and representatives of international health agencies literally flocked to China to see with their own eyes what had been accomplished. Suddenly China became a "model" for other developing countries and even for those much richer industrialized nations still confronting difficult public health problems. Subsequent modernization efforts in biomedical science and clinical medicine were fueled by academic and professional exchange programs in which tens of

---

[26] Joan Kaufman, "Background Notes, Women's Health and Child Survival Assessment Mission, Xundian County, Qujing Prefecture, Yunnan," October 1989.

[27] Nicholas Kristof, "Stark Data on Women: 100 Million Are Missing," *New York Times*, November 5, 1991, p. B9.

[28] *Ibid.*, p. B5.

thousands of Chinese researchers and physicians studied in the United States, Europe, and Japan.

Concurrent with this heartfelt effort to help China, disturbing information about the Chinese political system gradually emerged and built a momentum of criticism that countered previous, enthusiastic assessments. In the early 1980s this centered on birth control policies that were implemented in such an aggressive fashion that an unknown number of women were reportedly forced into abortions even in their third trimesters of pregnancy. Later, stories of female infanticide surfaced that tarnished China's well-known claims to gender equality embodied in the slogan "Women hold up half the sky." The coup de grace to the Western romance with an idealized China was delivered by the Tiananmen massacre in June 1989. Suddenly Westerners were once again willing to believe even unsubstantiated negative reports and to question the validity of data coming out of China. These reactions have softened as distance from 1989 increases; nevertheless, we are still left to grapple with complex, contradictory images influencing our assessment of the health of China.

This is ironic, since it is because of the advances in the collection of health statistics and China's increased openness about sharing these data that the West has been able to learn so much about health trends in China. For example, in contrast to earlier years when death reports were summarized from nonrandom samples, mortality and morbidity data are increasingly representative of the entire population, and the monitoring of chronic conditions has been added to the earlier infectious-disease reporting system that extends to the grass-roots level in all counties. Nutrition- and disease-surveillance sites in every province have monitored health outcomes for more than a decade. The 1982 and 1990 census results, as well as selected fertility surveys in the intervening years, have been made available to foreign researchers and have contributed enormously to knowledge about birth rates, death rates, and other demographic trends. While reports of some health problems represent sensitive topics, China, in contrast to many other developing countries and to its own recent past, is increasingly forthcoming. Probably the best example of this has been its treatment of the outbreak of AIDS near the border between Yunnan and Southeast Asia. Rather than denying the problem, as so many nations have initially done, China quickly mobilized both domestic and international health personnel to launch treatment and prevention efforts.

Public Health Versus the Market in the 1990s

Because so many aspects of life, work, health, and medical care have been affected at the same time by the reforms of the Deng era, it is often impossible to disentangle cause from effect. Furthermore, as noted above, conclusions about changes since the Maoist era are difficult to reach because of noncomparability of many of the data. Nevertheless, understanding the determinants of health under China's current version of market socialism is undoubtedly the most important issue in public health for China's future—and for the future of many other countries that will turn to China as a model for dealing simultaneously with the diseases of poverty and development.

Differences in health outcomes within a given population are correlated with disparities in income, education, occupational prestige, and other factors such as living conditions—quality of housing and degree of crowding. Even in the case of China, which was able to make great headway in terms of overall national health statistics during the Maoist period, substantial within-country differences in infant mortality and life expectancy remained. For example, a World Bank analysis of mortality rates from the 1973–75 cancer survey showed that life expectancy in urban areas was 12 years higher than in average rural areas, and 17 years higher than in the poorest rural areas.[29] In a sense, what is being described by these statistics is the difference between the part of China that had already begun to resemble wealthier industrialized countries, and the remote, rural regions of the country that were still part of the developing world. Clearly the recent statistics on the urban-rural gap in life expectancy of three to four years, cited above, represent a sizable improvement in comparison with the past and indicate that most rural areas have passed through the epidemiologic transition.

Access to medical care is also related to better health; this is determined by geographic proximity of services, by the quality of services available, and by insurance for relatively costly services, such as inpatient care or use of expensive technology. Studies in all parts of the world, as well as in China, consistently demonstrate that use of medical care increases sharply in the presence of insurance coverage. As recent studies of Great Britain have shown, however, even in a developed country with a national health service, universal access to services is not sufficient to make up for the health disadvantages of poverty. In Great Britain it was shown that sizable differences in infant

[29] Nicholas Prescott and Dean T. Jamison, "The Distribution and Impact of Health Resource Availability in China," *International Journal of Health Planning and Management*, Vol. 1 (1985), pp. 45–46.

mortality and life expectancy between the lowest and the highest social classes had persisted and even increased since the 1930s.[30] The largest gap in life expectancy was seven years.[31]

In post-Mao China, income has risen; people are eating more and better-quality food; housing has improved, with better water and toilet facilities; and labor markets have diversified in rural areas as the private and collective sectors have expanded. Recent studies of the sources of income in rural and urban areas have documented that the introduction of a semimarket economy has resulted in both higher incomes and greater inequality of income distribution in rural areas.[32] In other words, rural residents are getting richer on average, but the range of incomes is much wider. At the same time, as noted above, collectively sponsored health programs in preventive medicine have been cut back, increasing the potentially negative impact of the reforms in areas that have not experienced increases in income. In the cities the narrow wage differences (partly a result of state-sector wage policies) have persisted, with the largest source of income differences derived from the government subsidies or benefits ("perks") that are linked to high-status jobs.

Health insurance is a prime example of this irrational subsidy program. There are three major types of health insurance in China: public insurance for government employees (*gongfei yiliao*), worker insurance for enterprise workers (*laodong baoxian*), and collective welfare insurance for rural village residents (*hezuo yiliao*). In contrast to the breakdown in rural insurance, the public and worker insurance programs have continued to provide medical coverage for increasingly costly, increasingly hospital-based care. The rise in chronic conditions, together with the increase in both the number and the proportion of elderly in China and a greater demand for "high-technology medicine," has already started to strain the system.[33] Articles on the need to reform the health-care financing system regularly appear in jour-

[30] See Department of Health and Social Security, *Inequalities in Health: Report of a Research Working Group* (Black Report; London, 1980).

[31] This is still considerably lower than the 10- to-15-year difference in life expectancy between China's richest cities and poorest rural areas. Thus, for example, life expectancy in Shanghai is 75.5 years, while in a minority county in Yunnan Province visited by the Ford Foundation, it was estimated to be approximately 60 years.

[32] Azizur Rahman Khan et al., "Sources of Income Inequality in Post-Reform China" (Paper presented at the annual Association for Asian Studies meeting, Washington, D.C., April 1992).

[33] In 1964 the proportion of the population 65 or older was 3.6 percent, but by 1987 it was 5.5 percent. Furthermore, the absolute number of elderly went from 24.7 million to 58.7 million.

nals and the lay press.[34] A 1989 household survey of almost 4,000 households in eight provinces in China demonstrated the extreme inequality in insurance coverage between urban and rural areas, with 70 percent and 7.3 percent coverage respectively.[35] Because in most instances insurance is a workplace benefit, it is not surprising that having insurance coverage is strongly related to occupation and to whether a person is employed in the state, the collective, or the private sector. For example, only 4 percent of farmers surveyed had insurance, compared with 50.9 percent of service workers, 67 percent of unskilled workers, and 89.2 percent of those in high-level managerial and professional occupations. Among state-run enterprises, 87.5 percent of employees had insurance, whereas 50.1 percent working in collective enterprises and only 3.8 percent in private enterprises (including farms) had health insurance coverage. Insurance coverage is also clearly related to income, with only 9.3 percent of the lowest-income third enjoying coverage, compared with 41.9 percent of the highest third. Thus the people with arguably the greatest need for health insurance are the least likely to receive this benefit.

Have the gains in income been enough to offset these trends? Or are those with the greatest health-care benefits the ones who have also enjoyed the largest increase in income? During the past decade, income differences between urban and rural areas have actually declined.[36] Many of the initial gains were, in fact, experienced by farmers and residents of small towns. In addition, although annual per capita health expenditures have increased about 500 percent in the past 20 years, they remain low in comparative terms, at about Rmb 37 per person in 1987. On the other hand, the increase in expenditures has been disproportionately borne by rural residents, with a 20 percent annual increase (equivalent to over 2 percent of annual income) for them compared with a 7 percent increase for urban residents (less than 1 percent of income).[37] This disproportionate increase may offset the income advantage recently experienced by rural areas, particularly in poorer regions. Furthermore, the government contribution to

[34] There have been many calls for reform of these insurance systems, which, like insurance in the United States until the current era, are essentially cost-reimbursement systems that pay what the doctor bills. Many worker and public insurance programs in China now include some kind of deductible or copayment intended to discourage overutilization. Their effect is questionable.

[35] Gail Henderson et al., "Gender and Welfare Benefits in China: The Distribution of Health Insurance Coverage" (Paper presented at the Conference on Engendering China, Harvard University and Wellesley College, February 1992).

[36] Khan et al., "Sources of Income Inequality."

[37] World Bank, China: *Long-Term Issues*, Annex I-10.

health expenditures has declined relative to insurance and out-of-pocket payments, and consumption of health care by insured compared with uninsured persons has increased dramatically.

Have these changes affected people's ability to get needed health care? Because comparable data from earlier time periods are not available, it is difficult to draw firm conclusions. A 1988 Ministry of Health survey found that 20 percent of rural households reported that because of economic difficulties, they were unable to seek health care when they were ill.[38] Sixteen percent reported that members of their household did not receive needed inpatient medical care because they could not afford the cost. To understand the meaning of these results, however, we need to know if these figures represent an increase or a decrease in access to health care over previous years. We also need to know what type of care is being sought, and for what kind of health problems. For example, it may be that people in rural areas did not have access to a higher level of care even during the late Maoist era.

Very different findings are reported in a 1989 study of working-age adults, based on the same eight-province survey described above. About 10 percent of the sample of 6,513 adults (aged 20–45) identified themselves as ill or injured within four weeks prior to being interviewed, and 85 percent of these people sought care for their problems. Of the reported illnesses or injuries, half were mild, one-third moderate, and about one-sixth severe. Most people used outpatient services, and the average reported costs were quite low. The median total cost for care was Rmb 11.2; the mean was Rmb 79.0 (ranging from zero to Rmb 4,450). Only three factors were found to be related to using health services: gender (women use more services than do men), employment in a state-run enterprise, and severity of illness or injury. What is even more interesting is that none of the following factors was related to using health care: urban-rural location, occupation, education, family ties with cadres, minority status, income, insurance, province, or distance to nearest services.[39]

The pattern of women using more health-care services than men (even excluding conditions related to childbearing) has been documented in many studies from developed nations. This is consistent with mortality and life expectancy figures for Chinese women compared with those for men, which are quite similar to those for women and men in developed nations. It is also not surprising that in China

---

[38] *Jiankang bao* (Health Daily), February 23, 1992, p. 1.

[39] Gail Henderson et al., "Equity and the Utilization of Health Services: Report of an Eight-Province Survey in China" (Paper presented at the annual Association for Asian Studies meeting, Washington, D.C., April 1992).

health-services use is higher among employees of state-run enterprises. These enterprises often offer convenient workplace clinics and hospitals for their employees, as well as comprehensive insurance coverage.

The results of this study suggest that China has achieved a very wide distribution of clinics and other services at the local level, and that they are extensively used by those who identify a need for them. Data from this survey indicate that it is rare to be more than half an hour away by bicycle from some form of care. The majority of services appear to be reasonably inexpensive. This broad availability contrasts with the reports that stress declining accessibility, and paints a picture of relatively equal access to health care.

On the other hand, these data are based on a community survey of illness and injury; they describe a range of mostly mild or moderate conditions for which medical treatment was available and accessible. For many of these health problems, differences in the quality of available clinic or hospital facilities would not adversely affect outcomes. For more complex and serious health conditions, however, the differences between care provided at a rural township hospital, with an average of 50 beds and staff who have received training at three-year health schools, and an urban medical center, with ten times the number of hospital beds, more sophisticated equipment, and staff with the highest level of training, could be very important. Furthermore, while insurance coverage did not influence use of health care for inexpensive problems, this was not the case for more costly care.

An examination of patients hospitalized with severe, costly conditions demonstrates that factors such as urban residence, government or worker health insurance, and cadre status are important determinants of access to the "best" care. Between 1978 and 1986, 137 patients were treated for chronic kidney failure at the First Teaching Hospital of Zhongshan (Sun Yat-sen) University of Medical Sciences in Guangzhou (Canton).[40] Long-term kidney dialysis, one of the most expensive medical treatments in China (Rmb 15,000–20,000 per year), began in Guangzhou in 1978. By 1986 there were 95 machines in 18 hospitals in the city and 300 patients in treatment. At the time of the study, there were approximately 500–1,000 potential candidates for dialysis in Guangzhou alone each year. Most were not referred, either

[40] Gail Henderson et al., "High-Technology Medicine in China: The Case of Chronic Renal Failure and Hemodialysis," *New England Journal of Medicine*, Vol. 318 (1988), pp. 1000–04.

because of lack of information about the treatment or because of the high cost.[41]

Of the 137 patients admitted to the ward at the First Teaching Hospital, men outnumbered women by 2:1 (perhaps because of differences in the incidence of kidney failure, perhaps because of gender differences in insurance coverage). Although the mean age for both men and women was 42, all physicians interviewed stated that age was not a criterion for admission. They were, however, very forthcoming about the importance of economic considerations in treatment decisions. One physician noted, "We don't have the luxury of a policy to treat or not to treat. It just depends on the physicians and the economic position of the patients."[42] On this ward, patients' occupation and type of medical insurance were very clearly related to admission and length of stay. Even for patients with insurance, it was difficult to convince work-unit leaders to pay the bill.[43] Of the 137 patients, only 11 (8 percent) were farmers, and their average number of treatment days was 57. In contrast, 47 percent of the patients were government employees and 39 percent were workers, with mean number of treatment days totaling 365 and 357, respectively. Furthermore, all patients selected for kidney transplantation were either government employees or workers.

In addition to demonstrating inequality in access to expensive, high-technology medical care, this study pointed to a second, equally troubling trend in the post-Mao period. Like health insurance in the United States and other countries with cost reimbursement programs that promised payment for "whatever the doctor ordered," China's fragmented insurance system promoted the same process of resource allocation according to ability to pay rather than according to a more centralized decision-making process. The conclusion of the dialysis study is still relevant today:

> Dialysis represents only one area of medical expenditure, but we believe it is a harbinger of challenges to come for China's system of medical care. Other new technologies introduced during the reform period, such as diagnostic radiology and radiotherapy, have also contributed to the

---

[41] In some Chinese cities, dialysis centers specifically excluded patients without insurance; in others, patients were offered dialysis only if a transplant donor could be identified. In contrast, in the United States all patients are treated under a provision of the government Medicare insurance plan, but at a cost of more than $2 billion per year.

[42] Henderson et al., "High-Technology Medicine," p. 1003.

[43] One patient said that no one in his workplace had ever incurred medical expenses of more than Rmb 1,000. His annual bill was 12 to 15 times higher than that. *Ibid.*, p. 1002.

> rising cost of care. In the absence of strong, centralized planning and a unified insurance program, such changes in medical treatment will bring increasing pressure on the system to pay for medical care.[44]

China continues to produce impressive results in public health, in mortality and life expectancy figures, and in the apparent broad availability of services at the local level. Much of this may be due to the great gains in per capita income and the improved quality of nutrition experienced in most regions, rather than to the contributions of the health-care system to individual health outcomes. In general, however, people are near health-care facilities and seem to seek care when they need it. The rural health-care infrastructure that was the foundation of the Maoist model of primary care is still functioning; and it is still able to ensure that most women receive some kind of prenatal care and most rural infants are immunized. Again, improvements in living standards, privatization of local-level clinics, and the demise of the collectively funded insurance programs appear to vary within regions and have differential effects on poor versus better-off groups.

Despite these remarkable achievements—and as many other observers have cautioned—there are significant negative trends. The reforms have fostered incentives for investment in expensive health-care services, and this is occurring in the context of weakened central decision making. Though a tradeoff between curative and preventive services is not automatic, a tendency toward such a tradeoff emerges in a system that increasingly rewards profit-generating activities. The changes in health-insurance coverage have added to the increasing inequality in access to expensive care. This is not a direct consequence of the reforms, however. The deterioration of the insurance system was exacerbated by the reforms, but even during the Maoist era there was never a national system for covering all citizens, and the insurance system that existed never was adequate to the task of providing equitable distribution of health benefits to all citizens—particularly when those benefits became very costly.

China must overcome a number of obstacles if it is to avoid the health-care dilemmas experienced by more-developed nations. First, the demand for better and more-expensive services to treat new disease conditions will not abate; hence attention must be paid to the issues of cost control and equitable distribution of limited resources. Second, prevention of some part of the rise of chronic conditions as well as control of infectious diseases must continue to be fostered by

[44] *Ibid.*, p. 1004.

the public health system. China is almost unique in the world for a health-care infrastructure that reaches from national to local levels and for its ability to mobilize grass-roots communities to combat sanitary and public health problems. Drawing upon current knowledge about risk factors for major chronic conditions, such as smoking, diet, lack of exercise, and environmental hazards, China may well be able to avert some of the problems experienced in the West. There is much to be accomplished regarding education of the population in prevention and in the application of risk management to chronic conditions. Reorganizing and reorienting the existing strong corps of public health workers to realize this objective will be China's major health-care challenge of the 21st century.

6
Chinese Cinema Enters the 1990s

Paul Clark

In both 1991 and 1992, movies by the Chinese director Zhang Yimou were nominated for an Academy Award in the foreign-language-film category. *Ju Dou* and *Raise the Red Lantern* were the first Chinese films to attract such international attention. Zhang Yimou's achievement was not a fluke, nor was it simply a product of post-Tiananmen international sympathy. These two films were products of a reworking of Chinese cinema and cultural practice in general that had begun in the early 1980s and had its roots in the Cultural Revolution. The films were also signs that the tragic events in 1989 had not killed off cultural innovation and relevance to contemporary conditions. By mid-1992 the filmmaking enterprise was beginning to overcome the impact of Tiananmen.

Since 1949 the fortunes of Chinese cinema have directly reflected changes in the cultural climate, political control, and level of economic development. Paradoxically, in the last decade, just as China's filmmakers rediscovered a distinctive voice, film's preeminence as a mass medium was challenged by the rise in ownership of television sets. Increased restrictions after the Tiananmen massacre in 1989 compounded existing financial problems for the industry. In 1992 the film industry in China faced indifferent audiences, cautious political managers, and a narrowing of choices for filmmakers. The changing relationships among party, artists, and audiences continue to ensure that a study of Chinese filmmaking can illuminate change in China's society and politics.

Film Before the 1980s

The importance of the tripartite relationship among government, filmmakers, and audiences was well established in China long before the Chinese Communist Party (CCP) victory in 1949. The first screenings were in 1896, when French shorts were shown in a tearoom in

Shanghai to mixed audiences of Chinese and Europeans. For all but a few years of the nine decades since then, imported films have dominated the Chinese film market.

By the 1920s Shanghai had become the center of Chinese filmmaking, a position the city retained until the 1980s. Chinese business leaders saw the potential profits to be made from the medium and invested in production. The specialized, complex nature of the medium, however, obliged these capitalists to depend on artists, writers, and technicians whose political views were decidedly left-wing. Communist Party organization among Shanghai film ranks began early. One of the strongest branches of the League of Left-Wing Writers, the party's cultural front organization, was among Shanghai film artists. The Kuomintang government before 1949 showed great distrust of film artists and tried to control the use of the medium, setting a pattern much refined by its communist successor.

The films produced in these studios competed in the marketplace with Hollywood and other foreign movies. Audiences until the 1950s generally came from the most westernized parts of China and Chinese society. At least until the late 1940s they had a distinctly middle-class cast. Film theaters were confined to the treaty ports and other important cities of coastal and riverine China. Peasants saw no movies unless a local missionary happened to show one. Given the interests of filmmakers and audiences, Chinese films of the 1930s were generally set in highly westernized, urban, upper-middle-class households, much like the products of the Hollywood studios. Not infrequently, however, a subtext addressed some social concerns. A handsome student, for example, might fall in love with a poor young woman from the countryside trying to make a living in Shanghai. In this way, left-wing filmmakers were able to insert social and political messages into an otherwise bland story.

The artistic achievements of Chinese filmmakers in the 1930s were properly acknowledged only some 50 years later, when film scholars abroad and in China drew attention to the work of directors like Sun Yu (1900–91), Ying Yunwei (1904–67), and Fei Mu (1906–51). Until the 1980s Chinese politicians and culture critics regarded film as a foreign art and emphasized the dependent nature of Chinese cinema before 1949, discounting the innovation that had emerged from the Shanghai studios. The 1934 film *The Goddess* (*Shennü*), directed by Wu Yonggang, for example, was perhaps the first in world cinema to examine prostitution directly and without moralistic overtones as an occupation in which women tried to make a living. Sun Yu's *The Highway* (*Dalu*, 1934) combined an unusual emphasis on physicality among the male and female characters with a disguised patriotic message directed against the Japanese.

The War of Resistance against Japan, like the Cultural Revolution 30 years later, marked a sea change in modern Chinese cultural history. Many film artists were forced out of their urban enclaves and exposed to a fuller range of society. The result in the late 1940s was a series of films that reflected more directly than anything before the reality of Chinese life. Several films, including *The Spring River Flows East* (*Yijiang chunshui xiang dong liu,* directed by Cai Chusheng and Zheng Junli, in two parts, 1947 and 1948), captured the national trauma of war and reconciliation so well that they played for months and remain much cherished by Chinese around the world. The artistic achievement of *Spring River* and other films came despite considerable efforts by the Kuomintang regime to censor what filmmakers could produce. The late 1940s were regarded, at least until the 1980s, as the "golden age" of Chinese cinema. What followed in the 1950s and beyond only served to encourage this assessment.

After 1949, filmmakers who had grown accustomed to underground existences on the fringes of respectable bourgeois society now found themselves expected to cater to a much broader and more variegated audience. The communist government saw in film an effective means to carry a new, mass culture to the farthest reaches of the country. Having nationalized the studios, however, the new authorities were as dependent as the previous owners on the specialized skills of film artists. Like their Kuomintang predecessors, the communist authorities distrusted these former denizens of the Shanghai demimonde. A proper balance between control and encouragement was difficult. Too much interference could lead to empty screens. For a while, however, audiences could be satisfied, as before 1949, with imported movies, though the Hollywood fare disappeared in the early 1950s, to be replaced by Soviet and other socialist films.

As filmmakers adjusted to the new demands that their work reach vast audiences, the films that emerged from the studios took on several general characteristics typical of "socialist realism." Films told simple, clear stories. Characters were identified as good or bad, although occasional relaxations in censorship allowed for some middling characters who might reform themselves in the course of the narrative. Messages were clearly set out and happy endings essential. Some of the most popular genres before the 1980s catered to audience expectations for escape and fantasy. Films set among the non-Han ethnic minorities, for example, catered to the fascination with exotic locations and customs that had once been served by Hollywood imports. The repertoires of Beijing and other Chinese operas were adapted to the screen, immortalizing some of the classic performers of the art. Films set in the anti-Japanese or revolutionary wars were also popular, even if action most often gave way to stilted dialogue on the importance of party leadership.

With the start of the Cultural Revolution in 1966, feature filmmaking in China stopped. Not until five years later did the studios resume production. The first films produced in the early 1970s were celluloid versions of the six modernized Beijing operas and two ballets that made up the artistic canon of the Cultural Revolution radicals led by Jiang Qing. Given the nature of the film medium, the artists who made these screen adaptations of the eight "revolutionary model performances" (*geming yangbanxi*) were the same people who a few years earlier had been condemned as unrepentant bourgeois artists. But Jiang Qing and her allies needed the skills of men like Xie Jin (1923–) and Xie Tieli (1925–) in order to make full use of the medium to take standardized versions of the model operas and ballets to audiences throughout the nation. More people saw these models for the new culture on screen than in live performance. By 1973 new feature films began to appear with stories of collective solidarity in the face of class enemies, reminiscent of the films of the early 1950s. Audiences complained privately about the stereotyping and falseness of these new works, but went to watch them anyway as not much else was offered.

With the end of the Cultural Revolution in 1976 and after several years in which the state-owned studios were put back into running order, a flurry of new works appeared that reminded critics of the films of the late 1940s. As in the war against Japan, filmmakers in the Cultural Revolution had been exposed to Chinese society in ways that enabled them to capture the spirit of the times. The post–Gang of Four "literature of the wounded" that examined the trauma of the Cultural Revolution had its screen equivalents. Several of these new films were made by artists who had waited more than ten years after graduation from film school to get a chance to direct.[1]

The Fifth-Generation Filmmakers

But real innovation came at the hands of the next generation of film artists, who burst upon Chinese and international screens with works of an originality and power unmatched by Chinese artists in any medium since at least the 1930s. The new group was made up mostly of members of the first post–Cultural Revolution degree class of the Bei-

---

1 Post-1949 filmmaking is examined in Paul Clark, *Chinese Cinema: Culture and Politics since 1949* (New York: Cambridge University Press, 1988).

jing Film Academy, China's only film school. They entered the academy in 1978 and graduated four years later. One of their teachers called them the "fifth generation" of Chinese filmmakers. The label stuck and obliged historians of Chinese film to try to identify the previous four generations. The fourth comprised those who had been at film school on the eve of the Cultural Revolution and generally had to wait until the late 1970s to direct their own films. Members of the third generation were the products of Soviet training in the 1950s; they included Xie Jin, who had in fact begun work in the Shanghai industry before 1949. The second and first generations had been the creators of the Shanghai film legacy.

The fifth-generation innovation came in both the style and the content of the new films. The first to gain international recognition was Chen Kaige's *The Yellow Earth* (*Huang tudi,* 1984). At first glance the film's wartime setting in northern Shaanxi, not far from the communist headquarters in Yan'an, seems rather orthodox. But the Eighth Route Army hero is, of all things, a folksong collector who acts alone. Billeted in a peasant home, he tells the young woman of the household about the better treatment of women in Yan'an. The peasant girl is soon trapped in an arranged marriage. Her attempt to escape to freedom in Yan'an ends with her apparent drowning. The story closes with the soldier returning to the village to discover the peasants conducting a rain-making ritual. Though the village is on the banks of the Yellow River, the fertile yellow loess soil will not yield its richness for lack of rain.

Chinese audiences who saw *The Yellow Earth* and the other new, fifth-generation films found themselves in an unaccustomed position. They were required to think about the films and in effect to help construct them. In *The Yellow Earth,* for example, the peasant girl's entrapment in marriage to a much older man is only hinted at by a gnarled hand reaching out to remove her veil on their wedding bed. Whether she drowns or not in her attempt to reach Yan'an is not made clear. The peasants in the film are taciturn, dirt-poor, and superstitious, more like real peasants than in any previous Chinese film. Characters rarely enter or exit at the edges of the screen. Rather, they appear to emerge out of the folds of the yellow hills that trap them in poverty and backwardness. *The Yellow Earth* was photographed by Zhang Yimou, a 32-year-old graduate of the Beijing Film Academy, who would soon after become one of China's most internationally acclaimed directors. Images are major elements in *The Yellow Earth* and in films like *Horse Thief* (*Daoma zei,* directed by Tian Zhuangzhuang, 1987) and *The Last Day of Winter* (*Zuihou yige dongri,* directed by Wu Ziniu, 1987). In place of the relentless dialogue and reiteration of the narrative and message typical of earlier films, the fifth-generation films let the images carry the film and its themes.

Rural misery was something with which many of the fifth-generation filmmakers were familiar. Most of these artists had been sent from high school to rural exile in the late 1960s during the Cultural Revolution. Chen Kaige, for example, was sent from Beijing to a rubber plantation in Yunnan Province. He later was recruited to play basketball in the army and returned to a factory job in Beijing. Zhang Yimou had been sent to a commune north of Xi'an and later transferred to a cotton mill in Xianyang, northwest of his hometown. Wu Ziniu spent several years pulling boats on the Dadu River in his native Sichuan Province before entering a small local arts college and joining a drama troupe. Hu Mei, director of *Far from War* (*Yuanli zhanzheng de niandai*, 1987) and one of several women directors in the new generation, left high school to become a dancer in the army. Not all "sent-down youth" in the 1970s gave much thought to their predicaments in rural exile, but some did begin to wonder why they were there. Such thinkers were the driving force behind literary, artistic, and intellectual innovation in China in the 1980s. For the fifth-generation filmmakers, film school provided the means to express their experiences and attitudes with great effectiveness.

Their cinematic innovation came from unexpected quarters. Like the CCP victory in civil war in 1949, the fifth-generation's rise represented an injection of vigor and change from the countryside. *The Yellow Earth* and *One and Eight* (*Yige he bage*, directed by Zhang Junzhao, 1984), the first films of this Chinese New Wave, were made at one of the smallest, most remote studios in China. The Guangxi film studio in Nanning was far from the huge, overstaffed studios in Shanghai, Beijing, and Changchun. But, in a new studio with fewer than 200 staff, youthful innovation was more possible.

The momentum continued through the mid-1980s in the Xi'an film studio. Xi'an was selected as the first film studio to try the factory managerial responsibility system, which placed greater authority in the hands of the enterprise managers and less in those of government and party bureaucrats. Wu Tianming, elected in late 1984 to be head of the Xi'an studio, used the powers given him in this new system to redirect the studio's efforts. Directors who had done nothing for years were asked to step aside to give younger talents an opportunity to make films. Wu was himself a fourth-generation director. He encouraged the making of "Chinese Westerns," that is, films set in the Northwest. His own *Old Well* (*Laojing*, 1987) won several awards at the Tokyo International Film Festival. Wu Tianming also invited several fifth-generation artists to make films at the Xi'an studio. Chen

Kaige made *King of the Children* (*Haizi wang*, 1987), about an educated youth in the Cultural Revolution who ends up as a village schoolteacher somewhere in the Southwest. Chen's *The Yellow Earth* had been about the impact of new ideas on a previously closed community. His *King of the Children* was a study in how a culture educates and destroys its young. In 1986 another fifth-generation talent fostered by Wu Tianming completed China's first film satire since the Hundred Flowers liberalization 30 years earlier. Huang Jianxin's *The Black-Cannon Incident* (*Heipao shijian*, 1986) follows a hapless mining engineer whose innocent telegram to retrieve a chess piece is mistaken by the party leaders in his mine as a spy message. Wu Tianming also encouraged Zhang Yimou, the cinematographer of *The Yellow Earth*, to become a director.

Zhang Yimou's debut film, *Red Sorghum* (*Hong gaoliang*, 1987), found a mass audience, unlike previous works of the Chinese "New Wave," which were not given wide domestic distribution. It was also the most successful Chinese film abroad, winning the Golden Bear at the 1988 Berlin Film Festival, the highest award ever won by a Chinese director. *Red Sorghum* combined elements of folktale and patriotism in a story that had an immense impact on the emerging youth culture in China. An off-screen narrator tells the story of "My Grandfather and My Grandmother." The former is a sedan-chair carrier in rural northern China in the 1920s. He woos and marries the widow of a sorghum distillery owner. Together they prosper, making wine from the red sorghum that grows in profusion in the area. Their free and happy life ends when the Japanese Imperial Army seizes the district. The story ends with an unsuccessful ambush of a Japanese convoy in which the grandmother is killed. Punctuating *Red Sorghum* and encapsulating its earthy masculinity are several songs done in the style of northern Shaanxi folksongs. These songs became enormous hits among young people, particularly young men in northern China. Tickets to *Red Sorghum* were sold at a premium over the usual nominal rate. Cassette tapes of the songs from the film and other so-called northern Shaanxi folksongs were big commercial successes, and the film created a youth-culture phenomenon in 1988.

The reaction of older filmmakers to the new films covered a full range. The fourth-generation director Wu Tianming actively encouraged the new talents. Wu Yigong, another fourth-generation director who became head of the Shanghai film studio soon after Wu Tianming took over in Xi'an, served as spokesperson for a distinctly Shanghai view of the New Wave. In a widely reported speech to film workers in his city in early 1988, Wu Yigong disparaged the artistic achievements of the new-style films, arguing that they appealed only to a very limited Chinese audience and to foreign film-festival viewers. Wu Yigong set these allegedly elitist films against the products of his own Shanghai studio. The latter, he suggested, were much more popular and worthy of critical attention.[2] Wu Yigong was not speaking alone: his skepticism about the New Wave films had the backing of conservatives in the top echelon of the Ministry of Radio, Film, and Television and at higher levels in the CCP.

Since the appearance of *One and Eight* and *The Yellow Earth* four years earlier, the party authorities had shown concern about the fifth-generation innovation. Some officials had criticized *The Yellow Earth* for showing the Chinese countryside as a backward place, even though the film had carefully identified its setting as the countryside of 1939. Tian Zhuangzhuang likewise had been obliged to make clear that his *Horse Thief* was set in the Tibet of 1923. However, the censors in the Film Bureau, the organ of the Ministry of Culture and (after 1986), of the Ministry of Radio, Film, and Television, charged with approving films for distribution, held an old-fashioned view of film. They regarded the written script as the basis of any submitted film, a view that had long been paramount in a culture that put such store on the written word. For innovative fifth-generation filmmakers, this attitude meant that visual and other nonverbal suggestions of a less-than-orthodox nature could often slip past the censors' gaze. *King of the Children, Horse Thief,* and *The Last Day of Winter* cannot be regarded as dissident films, but some of the implications of these respective studies of destructive acculturation, of the relationships between people, nature, and gods, and of labor reform camps in Qinghai Province could be seen as subversive from the perspective of Beijing's orthodox communists. More effective than censors' requests for deletions was the inadequate domestic distribution of fifth-generation films before *Red Sorghum.* The distribution system was not set up to handle such limited-interest films, and efforts in Shanghai, Beijing, and some other cities to set up art houses specializing in these films in 1987 and again in 1989 were short-lived.

In Search of an Audience

A fascination with the fifth-generation films should not obscure changes in the mainstream of filmmaking in the second half of the 1980s and the early 1990s. The main problem for films before and af-

---

[2] The speech is translated in Chris Berry, "Market Forces: China's Fifth Generation Faces the Bottom Line," in *Perspectives on Chinese Cinema*, ed. Chris Berry (London: British Film Institute, 1991), pp. 133–39.

ter June 4, 1989, was less political than financial. Audience numbers had dropped precipitously by mid-decade. The main cause was the rise in television ownership. In 1980 there were about 9 million television sets in China. By the end of the decade the number was over 170 million. In 1992 there was a surplus of several million unsold sets in the nation.[3] What had happened in the United States in the 1950s and Japan in the 1960s occurred in China in the 1980s—people stayed home to watch television instead of going to the movies. When they went to the cinema, they preferred an imported film from Hong Kong, Japan, or elsewhere. Television was of course not the sole cause of the drop in film audiences. With increasing prosperity, ordinary citizens had considerably wider entertainment and recreational choices. "Box office" had been a dirty term in the film enterprise before the 1980s; now officials and artists became obsessed with audience appeal.

The studios' response to wider choices for audiences was to try to attract people to cinemas by outdoing the imported films. Wu Tianming's support of Chen Kaige, Zhang Yimou, and the other fifth-generation directors was subsidized by earnings the Xi'an studio made from films like *The Magic Braid* (*Shenbian*, directed by Zhang Zi'en, 1986). A martial-arts film with a patriotic theme, *The Magic Braid* tells of a warrior who turns his hair into a weapon. His fame spreads far and he becomes involved with the Boxer Rebellion. Another big earner for Xi'an was a series of thrillers centered on imperial-grave robbers in the 1920s. Other studios experimented with detective stories, usually set in the 1930s or 1940s. In 1986 Tian Zhuangzhuang had made a facetious remark about making films for 21st-century audiences, when, supposedly, mass tastes would be more sophisticated; this reportedly prompted Deng Xiaoping to suggest that he wait until the next century to collect his wages. To show that he could make a popular film, Tian directed *Rock 'n Roll Kids* (*Yaogun qingnian*) in the summer of 1988. Break-dancing sequences in front of the Meridian Gate of the Forbidden City were among the highlights of this story of an ambitious young choreographer.

By mid-1988 the near bankruptcy of some of the 16 or so feature film studios could no longer be ignored. Intent on economic reform, the government was less willing to subsidize the studios even though the system of annual assignment to each studio of set numbers of

[3] *Far Eastern Economic Review*'s *Asia 1991 Yearbook* (Hong Kong, 1990, p. 6) put the number at 165.67 million. *China Daily Business Weekly*, May 18, 1992, p. 4, noted China had an annual production capacity of 21.25 million sets. Because of a growing stockpile, production in 1991 was limited to 10 million sets.

films, including a quota of major "national policy" films, remained in operation. Some flexibility was introduced when studios were allowed to negotiate with the central distribution apparatus the terms for at least some of their films. This increased the relatively small return studios received from the copies ordered by provincial distribution corporations by allowing the studios a percentage of box-office receipts. This greater reliance on the marketplace was fully in line with the government's reform policies.

One way the leaders of some studios sought to tackle the financial problems of the industry was to encourage so-called independent productions. In the summer of 1988 the Beijing film studio announced plans for a thriller to be filmed in Yunnan Province using investors' funds and a crew hired explicitly for that production. Wu Tianming made plans to make a film with money from a group of farmers in suburban Xi'an.[4] At the same time, Zhang Yimou wrestled for several months with a script idea about a Beijing laborer whose exercise-and-dieting regime turns him unexpectedly into a woman. The writer was Wang Shuo, perhaps the most creative of contemporary Chinese novelists, who had a big following among young people. Although that script proved unsatisfactory, Zhang felt obliged to make a film to use the money a young entrepreneur had made available to him. The result was *Code-Name 'Cougar'* (*Daihao Meizhoubao*), a rather clumsy, but in a Chinese context "politically correct," thriller about the hijacking of a Taiwan airplane diverted to the mainland. Gong Li, the popular star of *Red Sorghum*, plays a flight attendant. The film authorities seemed to approve independent productions, as long as a state studio's insignia preceded the credits. Almost immediately objections were raised at a high political level: film was too important a communication medium to be privatized in this manner. Four years later, however, individual directors, cinematographers, and others were making films under contractual arrangements with the studios. Studios and contractors provided funds and shared potential profits or losses. By 1992 de facto independent production was well established.

In late 1988 attention shifted to the production of a number of commemorative (*xianli*) films designed to celebrate the 40th anniversary of the founding of the People's Republic of China (PRC). The centerpiece was a three-part epic, *The Decisive Battles* (*Da juezhan*). Each part centered on a major campaign in the Red Army's victory in the civil war. The army's own August First Film Studio was given enormous resources to plan and complete the task, reportedly including funds

[4] Paul Clark, "Independent Film-Makers Go Panning for Cash," *Far Eastern Economic Review*, September 15, 1988, pp. 73–74.

equivalent to a good proportion of the annual budget for all other film productions. Release of the films came after the political upheaval of mid-1989, with mixed responses that will be discussed later.

On the eve of June 4, 1989, the Chinese film enterprise was in poor shape financially and needed to set priorities for its spending. In late 1988 Chen Haosu, the vice-minister in the Ministry of Radio, Film, and Television in charge of the film industry, reflected considerable realism when he said, "The prospect for Chinese cinema in the next decade or so is to emphasize these aspects: social significance, artistic quality and entertainment value. The third should be the priority when approaching the first two."[5] A few months later Teng Jinxian, the head of the Ministry's Film Bureau, was a little more cautious. Of the three categories of films Teng suggested as the focus of the film industry, two would require continued government subsidy. The first category included films on serious themes, like the series of rather unpopular "national policy" productions about reform in various enterprises, as well as children's films. This category could not survive in the marketplace without help. Teng also acknowledged that experimental or avant-garde films should be assisted, at least to win awards in international film festivals. There was a place, he implied, for a continuation of fifth-generation innovation even if domestic audiences were not impressed. The film market would be left to support the third broad category of films, entertainment movies.[6]

After Tiananmen

Given the straitened circumstances of the film enterprise as it entered 1989, it could be argued that June 4 had surprisingly little direct impact on the industry. The political restrictions placed on filmmakers in the aftermath of the Beijing massacre simply compounded their problems. The restrictions also narrowed the choices available to film audiences. As they had done in times of heightened control in the past, most film artists adjusted to the new circumstances and applied their skills to the newly approved products of the studios. More emphasis was put on the commemorative films. *The Bose Uprising* (*Baise qiyi*, directed by Chen Jialin, 1990), *The Kunlun Column* (*Weiwei Kunlun*, directed by Hao Guang and Jing Mukui, 1988), and *The Birth of New China* (*Kaiguo dadian*, directed by Li Qiankuan and Xiao Guiyun, 1989) were all released in celebration of the 40th anniversary of the PRC. The celebration did not extend much beyond the ranks of actors

[5] *China's Screen*, no. 1 (1989), p. 11.
[6] *Ibid.*, no. 3 (1989), p. 10.

who had discovered their resemblance to a dead or living CCP leader and could make a career of filmed impersonation. Audiences hardly flocked to the cinemas, although impressive ticket sales could be reported because party organizations and unions bought blocks of seats for workers in their enterprises.

The emphasis on the commemorative films continued through 1991, when, for the 70th anniversary of the founding of the CCP, the first two parts of *The Decisive Battles* were released. *The Liaoxi-Shenyang Campaign* (*Liao-Shen zhanyi*, directed by Yang Guangyuan) and *The Huaihai Campaign* (*Huaihai zhanyi*, directed by Cai Jiwei) filled theaters in August and September respectively. Ticket sales were impressive. One statistical table for 1991 has more than 188 million people watching *The Liaoxi-Shenyang Campaign* and almost 109 million seeing the second film.[7] But the biggest box-office winner in 1991 was a biography of a model party secretary who had died in 1964. *Jiao Yulu* (directed by Wang Jixing) was in the familiar mold of respectful biography and very much a throwback to the films of the 1950s and 1960s. It is set in 1962, when Lankao County in Henan Province suffered one in a series of crop failures. Party Secretary Jiao, supported by higher authorities and the local people, resolves to save the county from its backwardness and poverty. His industry and devotion work wonders, but he dies two years later from liver cancer caused by overwork. Released in March 1991, the film attracted an audience of almost 303 million.[8]

But an exercise in audience research by the staff of the Tianshan Cinema in Shanghai helps put these enormous figures into perspective. Four hundred people in the theater's neighborhood were asked to complete questionnaires, of which 338 were returned. More than 90 percent of those who claimed to have seen *Jiao Yulu* had had tickets provided by their work unit. For *The Liaoxi-Shenyang Campaign* the figure was close to 75 percent. About half of those who said they had seen *Jiao Yulu* felt it was an excellent film. Only about one in five viewers of *The Liaoxi-Shenyang Campaign* felt the same way about it. A mere 1 percent of respondents had the daring to say that they thought the highly orthodox *Jiao Yulu* was a film people "need not go out of their way to see" (*kekan ke bukan*). Four percent held that view of the war film.[9]

---

[7] *Zhongwai dianying shichang dongtai* (Chinese and Foreign Film Market Trends), no. 3–4 (1992), p. 27. The third film in the series, *The Beiping-Tianjin Campaign* (*Ping-Jin zhanyi*), was released in 1992.

[8] *Ibid.*, p. 27.

[9] *Ibid.*, pp. 4–7.

One 1991 film had commemorative qualities without being officially grouped with the other epics. *Mao Zedong and His Son* (*Mao Zedong he tade erzi,* directed by Zhang Jinbiao) by one count attracted 136 million viewers and was the second most popular film in 1991, after *Jiao Yulu.*[10] People went to watch this film, even without their work unit providing tickets, for one reason: to see Chairman Mao cry. The film shows how Mao deals with the death of his son Anying in the Korean War and with the grief of his daughter-in-law. This human portrait of Mao, combined with numerous portrayals of Mao in other epics released between 1989 and 1991, contributed to the Mao craze that emerged in 1991 and grew in 1992. By the summer of 1992 vehicles throughout China sported plastic laminated portraits of the late chairman as rearview mirror decorations.[11] In the mix of nostalgia for a simpler past, ironic comment on the present, and the search for something to believe in that the Mao craze represented, the domestication and depoliticization of Mao were important aspects. *Mao Zedong and His Son,* released in June 1991, gave impetus to this conversion of the chairman into part god and part good-luck charm.

Perhaps the most important of the commemorative films was released on National Day (October 1) in 1991. *Zhou Enlai* (directed by Ding Yinnan) had a running time just short of three hours but drew a huge audience. By the end of 1991 more than 183 million people had seen the film.[12] It dwells mostly on the Cultural Revolution, with Zhou spending his time acting as a peacemaker between different factions and all the while being undermined by Jiang Qing and her allies. Occasional brief flashbacks to pre-1949 episodes serve to explain the debts of friendship and trust that Zhou owed many of the people he helped in the 1960s and 1970s. At least to a foreign viewer, the overwhelming impression is of Zhou and the national leaders living highly choreographed existences in another world, spacious but simple, spotless, and teeming with servants. For all viewers, the impeccable impersonation of the premier by Wang Tiecheng is breathtaking. Despite the apparent success of *Zhou Enlai* in filling theaters, the box-office sales continued to decline. One report in early 1992 noted that the annual attendance for 35-mm films, meaning essentially the urban audience, had declined from roughly 7 billion in the late 1970s and early 1980s to almost half that level: in 1991, 3.8 billion seats were filled.[13]

---

[10] *Ibid.,* p. 33.

[11] See Nicholas D. Kristof, "China's Newest God: The Godless Mao," *New York Times,* June 2, 1992, pp. 1, 6.

[12] *Zhongwai dianying shichang dongtai,* no. 3–4 (1992), p. 27.

[13] *Ibid.,* p. 26.

One response to declining numbers was theater renovation to make going to the cinema a more entertaining and pleasant experience. In Shenyang and Shanghai, for example, theaters were converted into smaller-screened viewing rooms, filled with comfortable chairs for a relatively small number of people. Fold-down tray tables could hold drinks and snacks available on the premises. Elsewhere video projection rooms seated 50 to 100 people in comparative comfort. In Shanghai some travelers reportedly found it cheaper to spend all night in a theater with continuous shows than to find a hostel bed.[14] In 1991 ticket prices even for old-style theaters were raised from the few *fen* (cents) they had been fixed at since 1949. Though tickets were still cheap, audience figures continued to drop.

Given the continuing slump in overall box-office revenues and increased caution on the part of film officials, makers of experimental or art films had an even harder time filming the sorts of works that had characterized the fifth generation in the mid-1980s. After June 4, artists carefully selected settings at a suitable distance from the present in order to minimize potential problems with more conservative censors. Tian Zhuangzhuang, who had completed *Rock 'n Roll Kids* in 1988, in 1990 directed two of China's most popular actors in a historical drama, *Li Lianying, the Imperial Eunuch* (*Da taijian Li Lianying*), starring Liu Xiaoqing and Jiang Wen. Liu, who served as producer and raised much of the budget herself, plays Empress Dowager Ci Xi. Jiang Wen, who had been central to *Red Sorghum*'s mass appeal, plays the part of the empress dowager's eunuch ally with consummate skill. Neither man nor woman, he is a ruthless and yet pathetic figure. Comparisons with the Academy Award–winning *The Last Emperor*, another drama set in the imperial palace at the end of the Qing dynasty, are unavoidable. Unlike Bertolucci, director Tian is not overwhelmed by the spectacular potential of his setting. The passing of the Xianfeng emperor, the Boxer Rebellion, and the deaths of the Guangxu emperor and Ci Xi are all presented indirectly. Tian's focus is on the domestic, human side of these historical developments. Some foreign critics perceive parallels between the ruthless factionalism of the late Qing court and divisions in the chambers of the late Deng Xiaoping era. But the film was approved by the censors and did rather well at the box office.

Historical settings were the rule for film academy classmates of Tian Zhuangzhuang. Zhang Yimou, the most popular of the fifth-generation directors, chose a story from the 1920s for his third feature. *Ju Dou* was made in the autumn following Tiananmen, although

---

[14] *China's Screen*, no. 1 (1992), p. 28, and interview with Qiu Cuiding, China Film Export and Import Corporation, Beijing, May 15, 1992.

The cast of Zhang Yimou's *Ju Dou* (left to right): Zhen Ji-An, Gong Li, Zhang Yi, Li Wei, and Li Bao-Tian. *Photo courtesy of Paul Clark.*

Li Bao-Tian (left) and Gong Li star in Zhang Yimou's *Ju Dou. Photo courtesy of Paul Clark.*

Zhang had started planning for the film the year before. A young woman (Ju Dou) is bought as a bride by the elderly owner of a cloth-dye works. He has had two wives before, both of whom died in mysterious circumstances. It is soon clear how they died: Yang Jinshan is impotent and desperate for a son to continue the family line. Refusing to acknowledge his inadequacies, he tortures his new bride, as he did her predecessors. The young woman seeks sympathy from her husband's adopted nephew, Tianqing. Soon they become involved in an illicit love affair. When Ju Dou becomes pregnant, Yang Jinshan thinks the baby is his own son. The old man is crippled in an accident, which emboldens Ju Dou and Tianqing to flaunt their affair in front of him. The gothic tale ends in death for all the adults, watched by the brutish son.

Again, foreign commentators have chosen to see parallels between the dye-works owner and China's elderly leaders and between the boy who kills or watches others die and soldiers in Tiananmen Square. But Zhang Yimou's intentions are broader than simple political allegory. *Ju Dou* is a film about repression in general and patriarchy in particular. The characters are all helpless in a family system that denies or destroys natural feelings. The tale is told with visual imagery that charges the film with great eroticism. Although they seem historically authentic, the dye works were in fact an invention of the director and his art director, who wanted to use the dazzling primary colors of the dyed cloth and the mechanical thumping of the machinery to invest the story with great power.

Like a number of other directors after June 4, Zhang sought foreign funding for the *Ju Dou* project. In this way the financial risks could be spread and the film at least find an international audience. The Tokuma Group, a Japanese company with long-standing ties with China, produced *Ju Dou*. The film was never officially released in China, but in May 1990 it competed at the Cannes Film Festival. Teng Jinxian, head of the Film Bureau in Beijing, had spoken in March 1989 about the need for some Chinese films to be made for international film festivals. In late 1990 the Film Bureau submitted *Ju Dou* as China's official entry in the foreign-language category of the spring 1991 Academy Awards competition. Academy rules state that films must have been released in their domestic markets. The PRC Film Bureau determined that some limited screenings in Beijing and elsewhere fulfilled this requirement. Success came in February 1991 when *Ju Dou* was one of five nominees for best foreign-language film. This was the first time a Chinese film had been nominated for an Oscar. The previous year the Indian feature *Salaam Bombay* had been the first film from Asia outside Japan to compete in the awards.

Suddenly Chinese cultural politics intruded on a world stage when the Film Bureau informed the Academy of Motion Picture Arts and Sciences that it wished to withdraw *Ju Dou* from competition. The details of this turnaround remain murky, but it appears that conservative cultural figures in the Ministry of Radio, Film, and Television above the Film Bureau and in the party propaganda apparatus took offense at the film and the international attention it was gaining. In the United States, members of the Senate and House of Representatives and prominent filmmakers, other artists, and intellectuals, who in the past had paid scant if any attention to the plight of Chinese artists, also took offense. Petitions and resolutions insisting that *Ju Dou* remain in competition and that Zhang Yimou not be impeded from attending the Academy Award ceremonies in Los Angeles were directed at the Chinese authorities. In fact, *Ju Dou* remained in the competition, though it did not win the prize.

Most explanations of the Beijing authorities' change of heart about *Ju Dou* focused on the strong eroticism of the film. It is easy to poke fun at old men in Zhongnanhai getting upset at the comparatively explicit sexuality of Zhang Yimou's film. But *Ju Dou*'s real problem was *Red Sorghum*'s earlier success. The cultural authorities realized that *Red Sorghum* had established a potentially huge youthful audience for another film directed by Zhang Yimou and starring Gong Li, especially if it won a major international award as *Red Sorghum* had in Berlin. *Red Sorghum* had been an uplifting, optimistic song to living life to the fullest. The somber tone of *Ju Dou* was completely different. Both films directly reflected the public mood in the years of their making. The men and women who wanted *Ju Dou* out of public gaze feared what Chinese audiences would make of the contrast. Illicit videotaped copies of *Ju Dou* circulated widely in 1991–92, so that large numbers of Chinese managed to see the forbidden film despite its banning.

In 1991 Zhang Yimou completed another film about patriarchal oppression starring Gong Li. *Raise the Red Lantern* (*Dahong denglong gaogao gua*) was again an international coproduction. In this case the money came from Taiwan, from Chiu Fu-sheng, who had produced *City of Sadness* (*Beiqing chengshi*, 1990), the Taiwan director Hou Hsiao-hsien's ground-breaking historical epic about the February 28, 1947, incident in which thousands of Taiwanese were killed by Kuomintang troops. Hou Hsiao-hsien, in a gesture of friendship between creators of cinematic New Waves on both sides of the Taiwan Straits, served as executive producer on Zhang's new film. *Raise the Red Lantern*, also set in the 1920s, adds complexity to *Ju Dou*'s picture of oppression. Songlian, a 19-year-old college student, becomes the fourth wife of the master of the Chen clan. She is given her own courtyard in the sprawling family mansion and settles into the complex relationships among the four wives. Red paper lanterns are hung in the courtyard and bedroom of the wife with whom the master chooses to spend the night. The wives compete for their husband's favor. Songlian pretends she is pregnant, but soon her ruse is exposed, and the ensuing events turn her into a gibbering madwoman.

Just as *Red Sorghum* and *Ju Dou* captured the contrasting spirits of their times of production, so *Raise the Red Lantern* reflects its moment.[15] Many Chinese after the June 4 debacle had come to realize the destructiveness of an apparent Chinese capacity for internecine struggles, treachery, and concern for appearances. The wives of the Chen household collaborate in their oppression. *Raise the Red Lantern,* like *Ju Dou,* was not released in China. At the Venice Film Festival in August 1991 it won the Silver Lion and a half-dozen critics' awards. In early 1992 the film was selected as a nominee for the Academy Awards to be presented in March. But this time the Chinese film was considered a Hong Kong production, as Chiu Fu-sheng had been obliged to set up a company there to funnel the funds for the film. To compete for an Academy Award two years successively was a remarkable achievement for Zhang Yimou. In 1992 he was able to attend the awards ceremony in Los Angeles and was expected by many critics to win, but the academy members gave the prize to a lugubrious Italian comedy.

Reports from Beijing in late June 1992 that *Ju Dou* and *Raise the Red Lantern* would be released domestically in the fall were a further sign of the cultural relaxation that had begun in the spring.[16] This appeared to be part of a general reassessment of films that had previously been banned. Although no explanation was offered, falling box-office receipts may have been one motivating factor: film revenue had dropped by $13 million in the first four months of 1992, according to a report in the *Legal Daily*.

Signs of Relaxation

In 1990 and 1991 other filmmakers managed to produce works of considerable merit, despite tight ideological oversight and changes in personnel. Some of the most talented staff resigned from many of the studios, seeing opportunities elsewhere to make money and exercise

[15] Both *Red Sorghum* and *Ju Dou* are available on videotape in the United States, and *Raise the Red Lantern* is expected to be released to the home video market in 1993.

[16] On *Red Lantern*, see Sheryl WuDunn, "Leniency Preview? Censors Give Chinese Film Their O.K.," *New York Times*, June 28, 1992, p. 8.

more artistic control. Li Shaohong, a film academy classmate of Zhang Yimou, made *Bloody Dawn* (*Xuese qingchen*, 1990). She based the film on a story by the Latin American writer Gabriel García Márquez, "Chronicle of a Death Foretold," changing the setting to contemporary times in a small mountain village somewhere in northern China. The story is told through the investigator who comes to the village to conduct an inquest after the murder of the local schoolteacher. A series of flashbacks sets out events that lead to the stabbing of the seemingly popular teacher. Upon completion the film was banned from screenings in China and abroad. The film's problem was clearly its naturalistic portrayal of actual conditions in a poor village. The schoolroom is a makeshift shack, where three different grades take classes together. The village head has no hesitation in helping himself to the villagers' meager food. A prominent display of the dowry in a wedding procession makes obvious the commercial motives for the marriage. As the narration reaches its climax, the clumsiness, stupidity, and indifference of the villagers as the teacher heads for a murderous ambush are exposed with scathing clarity.

After June 4 such realism in a contemporary setting could not expect to find an audience. By mid-1992, however, Chinese artists were looking for signs that the renewed emphasis on economic reform promoted by Deng Xiaoping's remarks during winter travels in the southern provinces would be paralleled by an easing of cultural restrictions. In May *Bloody Dawn* was approved for export, a small indication of a relaxation in control. In the same month the relatively restrained commemoration of the 50th anniversary of Mao Zedong's "Talks at the Yan'an Conference on Literature and Art" that had been the font of cultural policy after 1949 was another sign of an easing of conservative control. Meanwhile, Li Shaohong followed the pattern of several of her classmates by making her next film an international coproduction. Taiwan's Chiu Fu-sheng was the producer of *A Man at Forty* (*Sishi buhuo*), which Li completed in the late summer of 1992.

There were other signs that June 4 had not killed off the innovation that had emerged in the mid-1980s. The Xi'an film studio had established a reputation for its so-called Chinese Westerns. A 1991 feature, *The Swordsman in Double-Flag Town* (*Shuangqizhen daoke*, directed by He Ping), continued the effort. Double-Flag Town sits in desert territory. Two brothers, renowned for their martial-arts skills, terrorize the place. One day a solitary young man rides out of the desert into the town. Hai Ge is fulfilling the wish of his late father by coming to fetch his fiancée, the daughter of the town butcher. When the two brothers try to rape the young woman, the young stranger reveals extraordinary skills with his swords. He kills one of the brothers. When the other returns to avenge his brother's death, Hai Ge wins his duel with him in the main street of the dusty town. At daybreak, Hai Ge and his fiancée leave Double-Flag Town for a new life together.

He Ping's film marked a reemergence of folktale-inspired narrative that *Red Sorghum* had also essayed. After June 4, fantasy like this, set in vaguely historical times, was a safe outlet for both filmmakers and their audiences. But the popularity of *The Swordsman in Double-Flag Town* and other martial-arts films that had formed the bulk of domestic entertainment film production since the mid-1980s had significant implications. The importance of individual struggle in hostile social surroundings set these films apart from the cinematic mainstream, with its general emphasis on the collective. *Red Sorghum*'s appeal in 1988 as a celebration of lives lived free and untrammeled by social restrictions could still be found in films of the early 1990s. Again, the impact of Tiananmen on film may not have been as great as might have been anticipated.

The more somber cultural climate helped account for some of the contrast between one of the most accomplished films released in 1992 and its director's debut film from 1987. Filmmakers mature in ways responsive to their political and social surroundings. Sun Zhou's *Coffee with Sugar* (*Gei kafei jia diantang*, 1987) featured a self-employed advertising executive in a rather flashy love story punctuated by disco dance sequences. Sun's 1992 feature, *Heartstrings* (*Xinxiang*), was hailed by Chinese critics for its serious exploration of human relationships. Jingjing goes to live with his maternal grandfather when his parents divorce. The grandfather is a retired Beijing opera actor who still enjoys great respect among his friends and opera lovers. Grandfather and grandson learn to appreciate each other despite their different ages and temperaments. The boy even deepens his understanding of opera. The understatement and discretion of the 1991 film are in marked contrast to the 1987 feature's dazzling superficiality. The difference between the two films indicates a maturation, at least on the part of fifth-generation directors like Sun Zhou. A fascination with the surface features of modern and imported lifestyles gives way in *Heartstrings* to a steadier contemplation of the transmission of cultural values from generation to generation. This more subtle approach to culture and change was encouraged by the somber lessons of Tiananmen.

Pronouncements by the head of the Film Bureau served as a barometer of the changing political atmosphere after June 4. Teng Jinxian in mid-1990 had reflected a hard line, citing "harmful trends" in recent films. These included deemphasis of politics, excessive westernization, humanism, "art for art's sake," and commercialism.[17] His tone in an interview published in 1992 was somewhat more temperate. Teng suggested simply that the main problem was "a tendency of directors to cut themselves off from life, reality, and above all else, the masses."[18] A superficial reading of his statement might call to mind similar comments from Teng's counterparts in the 1950s or 1970s. The cultural authorities after 1949 made careers of accusing film artists of sins of which they themselves were just as guilty. But in the 1990s party definitions of reality and life have become somewhat broader than they were before the reform era. The rise of the market economy has its parallels in cultural practice. In the 1990s cultural officials have become more "realistic" in their demands on artists and in their understanding of audiences.

In mid-1992 Zhang Yimou, the most accomplished Chinese filmmaker of his generation, completed a new project that gave realism in Chinese cinema a new standard. *Qiu Ju Goes to Court* (*Qiu Ju da guansi*) again starred Gong Li, but this time she played an ordinary peasant in contemporary Shaanxi Province. Qiu Ju seeks legal redress against a local official who has abused her husband. Determined to get justice, Qiu Ju journeys from her village to town and on to the city protesting her husband's innocence. The stylistic formalism of *Ju Dou* and *Raise the Red Lantern* is not evident in the 1992 film, produced by a left-wing Hong Kong film company. Three-fifths of *Qiu Ju Goes to Court* was shot in secret, with a hidden camera and crew on the streets of several towns in northern Shaanxi. Except for a few actors and other people playing themselves, the participants were unaware they were being filmed. Synchronized sound recording with microphones hidden on the actors enhances the exceptional naturalism of the scenes. No other Chinese filmmaker has attempted to incorporate real life into a feature film to this extent. In late August domestic approval of the film was indicated when Zhang won the top award at the Changchun International Film Festival. In mid-September *Qiu Ju Goes to Court* received the Golden Lion at the Venice Film Festival and Gong Li won the award for best actress.[19]

Qiu Ju Goes to Court has a significance beyond its stylistic innovation. With its contemporary setting, the film marks the end of the fifth-generation experiment that peaked between 1984 and 1987, but

---

[17] *China's Screen*, no. 3 (1990), p. 2.

[18] *Ibid.*, no. 1 (1992), p. 2.

[19] On Changchun, see *Los Angeles Times*, August 31, 1992, p. F2. For a review of *Qiu Ju Goes to Court* (The Story of Qiu Ju), see Janet Maslin, *New York Times*, October 2, 1992, p. C12.

which now seems to many observers to reflect a somewhat old-fashioned obsession with China's culture and history on the part of the Cultural Revolution generation. But the fifth generation has had a lasting impact on China's filmmakers, cultural managers, and audiences. In the 1990s the empty stereotyping and falseness that had been typical of most films before the New Wave no longer satisfy anyone in the tripartite relationship. Film audiences have declined in numbers but have raised their expectations and demands for what appears in theaters. Filmmakers of all generations can respond to changing times or become irrelevant. The political authorities are finding it harder to insist on their primacy in shaping cultural change, while the changing fortunes of the Chinese film industry continue to reflect the uneasy and evolving relationship between the leaders, the general public, and the intellectuals caught in between.

Chronology

Nancy R. Hearst

July 1991

1 The 70th anniversary of the founding of the Chinese Communist Party (CCP). General Secretary Jiang Zemin vows that China will remain a socialist country under communist rule. Jiang calls for open talks with Taiwan.

The U.S. Department of State warns that China faces new sanctions if missiles sold to Pakistan exceed guidelines.

3 Taiwan eases the ban on return of exiled dissidents.

4 Britain and China reach an agreement on the building of a new Hong Kong airport on the condition that China gain more influence in Hong Kong affairs.

5 China bans the sale of T-shirts with slogans expressing discontent or anti-government attitudes.

10 The U.S. House of Representatives votes 313 to 112 to renew China's most-favored-nation (MFN) status for one year, but to impose stiff conditions on further renewal if the human rights situation there does not improve.

11 Floods in Anhui and Jiangsu provinces leave 1,700 people dead and millions homeless; China issues an appeal for $200 million in international humanitarian aid for victims.

13 A *Renmin ribao* (People's Daily) article warns that the China market will be closed to the United States if MFN is suspended.

14 The first foreign delegation to examine human rights conditions in China arrives from Australia.

15 Talks begin in Beijing between Premier Hun Sen of Cambodia and three Cambodian opposition groups to reach an agreement to end 12 years of Cambodian civil war.

23 The U.S. Senate votes 55 to 44 to restrict MFN status, 11 votes short of the two-thirds majority needed to override a presidential veto.

27 Xu Shijie, former party chief of Hainan, dies of stomach cancer.

Asia Watch reports the arrest of nationalist dissidents and the suppression of two dissident organizations in Inner Mongolia.

28 China releases three student activists, including Zheng Xuguang of the Aeronautical College, whose name was included on a list of the 21-most-wanted Tiananmen pro-democracy demonstrators.

30 Dissident Shanghai journalist Zhang Weiguo is rearrested.

August 1991

2 Hou Xiaotian appeals to foreign journalists to improve prison conditions for her ailing husband, prominent pro-democracy activist Wang Juntao.

10 In the first visit to China by a leader of an industrialized country since Tiananmen, Prime Minister Toshiki Kaifu begins a three-day visit to normalize ties.

Three days of talks with visiting Vice-Foreign Minister Nguyen Duy Nien of Vietnam end with a joint statement aimed at future consultations on formal ties.

Premier Li Peng announces that China has decided "in principle" to sign the Nuclear Nonproliferation Treaty.

14 Chen Ziming, imprisoned "black-hand" leader of the 1989 protests, begins a prison hunger strike to support his jailed colleagues' demands for better treatment.

17 The PRC Justice Ministry denies that Wang Juntao is seriously ill with hepatitis in prison.

20 The Chinese government issues a statement giving tacit support to the anti-Gorbachev Soviet coup.

22 Two Americans and one Canadian are expelled from China for supporting dissidents and pressing for improved prison conditions.

Zhang Weiguo is released into "residential surveillance" after three weeks of interrogation regarding underground dissident movements.

Renmin ribao carries a brief report on Gorbachev's return to power.

Deng Xiaoping turns 87 years old.

23 A Washington news conference announces that there has been no substantial progress in four days of Sino-American trade talks and warns of sanctions if no gains are made by the end of the year.

Chinese Red Cross officials, the first PRC representatives to visit Taiwan since 1949, end a four-day visit.

24 *Renmin ribao* quotes General Secretary Jiang Zemin as saying no one should interfere with China's socialist system.

China rejects a U.N. resolution expressing concern over human rights violations in Tibet.

26 Vice-President Wang Zhen stresses that the CCP will not tolerate any challenge to its rule.

28 Responding to the failure of the Soviet coup, the PRC Foreign Ministry issues a formal statement saying it respects the will of the Soviet people.

The Xinhua News Agency reports that China will move ahead on plans for the controversial Three Gorges dam.

September 1991

1 The Xinhua News Agency issues a brief report on prison conditions and confirms the hunger strike of Wang Juntao and Chen Ziming.

On the first day of the academic year, *Renmin ribao* publishes a call for vigilance against renewed democracy protests.

A televised interview quotes Premier Li Peng as saying China will continue "walking the socialist road."

The political commissar of Nanjing Military Region reports that China's armed forces have been put on alert along the Soviet border.

2 A front-page *Renmin ribao* commentary emphasizes continuing economic reforms that increase prosperity in order to guarantee socialism's survival.

British Prime Minister John Major arrives in Beijing for talks with President Yang Shangkun, General Secretary Jiang Zemin, and Premier Li Peng and to sign a formal agreement for the building of the new Hong Kong airport.

Chinese police halt U.S. legislators who hold up a banner and attempt to lay flowers in Tiananmen Square in honor of the pro-democracy demonstrators of 1989.

Prime Minister John Major arrives in Hong Kong and announces the release of Hong Kong businessman Lo Haixing, imprisoned in China for trying to help pro-democracy activists escape in June 1989.

An outlawed Taiwanese pro-independence group holds a rally in Taipei in defiance of government warnings of possible arrest on charges of sedition.

The Standing Committee of the National People's Congress (NPC) passes a tough anti-prostitution law that mandates labor-camp sentences for prostitutes and their customers.

5 Prime Minister Major delivers a message to try to reassure Hong Kong residents of Britain's commitment to the colony.

The PRC Foreign Ministry accuses members of the U.S. Congress of breaking Chinese law by attempting to lay flowers in Tiananmen Square.

A visiting U.S. delegation reports that China will cut off aid to the Khmer Rouge after a Cambodian peace plan goes into effect.

7 Based on advice from Deng Xiaoping, the Chinese Communist Party circulates confidential Central Committee Document No. 4, which blames the collapse of socialism in the Soviet Union on the poor choice of successors by the Soviet communist leadership.

China announces its recognition of Estonia, Latvia, and Lithuania.

8 China protests the raid on 23 Chinese-linked companies in the United States in an investigation of illegal trade practices.

In Taipei, police clash with 15,000 protestors demanding a referendum on whether Taiwan should seek U.N. membership as an independent state.

9 An internal essay, reportedly sponsored by PRC neoconservative "crown princes" (the adult children of a number of senior party officials), titled "Realistic Responses and Strategic Choices for

China after the Soviet Upheaval" and circulated among high party leaders, urges the CCP to reform Marxism or "be destroyed by its own hand."

Vietnamese Foreign Minister Nguyen Manh Cam arrives in Beijing to negotiate the first normalization agreements since the 1979 border war.

15 A Beijing-based correspondent of the British newspaper *Independent* is expelled from China for having reported in June 1991 on a confidential document about secret arrests in Inner Mongolia.

Landslide liberal victory (16 out of 18 seats) by the United Democrats of Hong Kong over candidates backed by the PRC for seats in the Hong Kong Legislative Council.

John King Fairbank, dean of American China scholars, dies in Cambridge, Massachusetts, at the age of 84.

20 Cambodian government and resistance leaders announce in Beijing that they have reached agreement on all major issues.

22 "Sixty Minutes" televises a segment on the export of Chinese prison-made goods. U.S. House Subcommittee on International Economic Policy and Trade begins hearings on Chinese prison labor.

A secret CCP "study and reference document" vows hard-line attack on Gorbachev and the West and declares that China will "hold fast to the leadership of the Communist Party and never allow a multiparty system."

29 The PRC Foreign Ministry praises the U.S. plan that Washington and Moscow eliminate more nuclear weapons.

30 On the eve of National Day, Premier Li Peng's speech urges Chinese to "win new victories" in building socialism, proclaiming, "The road is tortuous, but the future is bright."

October 1991

1 The 42nd anniversary of the founding of the People's Republic of China.

4 U.S. Customs orders inspection of shipments of Chinese goods suspected of being produced by prison labor.

5 General Secretary Jiang Zemin is quoted as telling visiting North Korean President Kim Il-sung that the two communist powers will stand by each other.

6 The Chinese government announces on national television news that it will pay peasants more for their wheat crop beginning in January 1992.

9 President Yang Shangkun, in a speech marking the 80th anniversary of the Nationalist revolution that overthrew the imperial system, ranks economic development as the top priority.

Speaking at Yale University, the Dalai Lama appeals for international pressure on the Chinese government to allow his return to China.

10 China bans export of prison-made goods.

The Bush administration orders a wide-ranging investigation into Chinese import barriers.

11 The PRC Ministry of Foreign Economic Relations and Trade expresses "strong dissatisfaction" over the U.S. probe of Chinese trade barriers to American products.

13 At its national congress, the Democratic Progressive Party in Taiwan approves a resolution renouncing claims to sovereignty over China.

19 The PRC Foreign Ministry denies involvement in developing Iran's nuclear weapons program.

22 The Beijing Intermediate Court rejects libel suit of former culture minister Wang Men, who had sued the Chinese paper *Wenyi bao* for claiming he had made a veiled attack on Deng Xiaoping in one of his short stories.

25 Internal CCP document, "The Struggle Between Peaceful Evolution and Counter-Peaceful Evolution Is a Class Struggle in the World Arena," accuses President George Bush and the U.S. Congress of attempting to bring about the collapse of communism.

November 1991

1 The China State Council issues a "white paper" defending China's human rights situation.

3 U.S. Secretary of State James Baker announces his forthcoming visit to China, ending one of the last U.S. sanctions imposed after the 1989 Chinese government crackdown.

4 Israeli Defense Minister Moshe Arens secretly visits Beijing.

China admits selling nuclear equipment to Iran, but only for peaceful purposes.

5 China and Vietnam normalize diplomatic relations after 13 years of hostility. Vietnamese Communist Party chief Do Muoi and Prime Minister Vo Van Kiet arrive in Beijing.

11 China denies nuclear cooperation with Iraq.

12 General Secretary Jiang Zemin, in a meeting with former U.S. secretary of state Alexander Haig, says U.S.-China relations can be salvaged if both sides take a long-term view.

15 U.S. Secretary of State James A. Baker III arrives in Beijing.

Ten jailed Chinese political activists are reported to begin a prison hunger strike to coincide with Secretary Baker's arrival.

16 Dissident Dai Qing and Hou Xiaotian, wife of imprisoned activist Wang Juntao, are detained to prevent their meeting with Secretary Baker.

17 Secretary Baker's meetings with Chinese leaders end, with no breakthroughs on China's arms exports or human rights policies.

19 A U.S. House Foreign Affairs Committee resolution calls on Beijing to detail publicly the steps it has taken to enforce its ban of prison-made exports.

27 U.S. Trade Representative Carla Hills proposes $1.5 billion in tariffs on Chinese imports by January 16, 1992, after failure of patent and copyright negotiations.

29 China releases Wang Youcai, a former graduate student in physics at Beijing University, and Han Dongfang, a railway worker accused of organizing an independent labor union during the 1989 protests.

Five-day CCP plenum adjourns, issuing a communiqué stressing rural development, stepped-up party building, and socialist education in rural areas, and urging the 50 million party members to rally around the leadership.

30 The Xinhua News Agency reports Premier Li Peng's message to the Palestinians, stating that Israel's security should be guaranteed.

December 1991

6 A Beijing University student leader, Li Minqi, detained on June 4, 1990, for giving a commemorative speech on the first anniversary of the Tiananmen crackdown, goes on trial.

12 Li Peng, in the first visit to India by a Chinese premier in 31 years, arrives in New Delhi for six days of talks aimed at improving relations.

16 PRC Foreign Minister Qian Qichen, in a *Renmin ribao* article, stresses that Beijing will not alter its foreign policy "no matter how the world situation changes."

18 Qinshan, China's first nuclear power plant, begins trial operation in Zhejiang Province.

19 Dissident journalist Dai Qing receives permission to go to the United States.

20 In order to control the budget deficit, Finance Minister Wang Bingqian proposes cutting food subsidies and closing tax loopholes, in an article in *China Daily*.

22 The Kuomintang wins 71 percent and the Democratic Progressive Party wins 24 percent of the votes in the first full elections in four decades for seats in the National Assembly in Taiwan.

24 The PRC Foreign Ministry confirms a visit by Vice–Foreign Minister Yang Fuchang to Israel to discuss establishing diplomatic relations.

25 The Xinhua News Agency blames Gorbachev for the collapse of the Soviet Union.

27 China recognizes Russia and the independence of the other republics of the new Commonwealth of Independent States.

28 A Chinese rocket misfires and fails to put a satellite in its proper orbit.

29 The Standing Committee of the National People's Congress votes to approve the signing of the Nuclear Nonproliferation Treaty to limit transfers of nuclear materials.

30 At a news conference, government spokesman Yuan Mu reports that China's economy grew by 7 percent in 1991.

Britain announces that Sir David Wilson will retire as governor of Hong Kong within 12 months.

31 China announces that it will export a 300-megawatt nuclear power plant to Pakistan.

January 1992

7 China expels three members of the Canadian parliament in retaliation for their investigation of human rights abuses in China.

10 At the closing of a five-day national conference on economic reform, Premier Li Peng announces plans to speed up market-oriented reforms.

13 Bao Tong, adviser to ousted CCP chief Zhao Ziyang, is charged with subversion in connection with the 1989 protests.

16 The United States and China reach an agreement on protection of U.S. copyrights and patents by the deadline to avert imposition of tariffs of up to 100 percent on a range of Chinese exports to the United States.

Zhu Senlin is appointed governor of Guangdong Province.

19 Deng Xiaoping arrives in the Shenzhen Special Economic Zone.

21 Deng Xiaoping makes a rare public appearance in Shenzhen to rally the country behind a new round of economic reforms.

22 David Levy, foreign minister of Israel, visits Beijing.

24 Sino-Israeli relations are established in a ceremony in Beijing.

Deng Xiaoping, in Shenzhen, is quoted as saying that Hong Kong will stay capitalist for the next 100 years.

26 Premier Li Peng is greeted by hundreds of protesters as he arrives in Rome on a tour intended to boost his image.

28 Bowing to foreign pressure, Beijing releases a Roman Catholic bishop and two priests arrested in July 1990 for having remained loyal to the Vatican.

30 U.S. intelligence reports that China is continuing to sell missile technology to Syria and Pakistan.

31 The U.S. Department of State issues its annual human rights report, citing Chinese abuses and assailing "repressive" practices.

Premier Li Peng arrives in New York to attend the U.N. Security Council meetings with other world leaders; Li meets with President Bush.

February 1992

1 The PRC Foreign Ministry denounces the U.S. Department of State report critical of China's human rights practices.

Li Peng meets with U.S. business leaders in New York.

A bipartisan group of 17 U.S. senators sends a classified letter to Secretary of State James Baker complaining about recent Chinese arms sales.

4 Deng Xiaoping is shown on national television at a lunar New Year's party in Shanghai.

13 China selects 40 conservatives from Hong Kong to advise it on the territory's affairs.

21 China welcomes foreigners to participate in the Shanghai stock market for the first time since 1949.

The Bush administration lifts sanctions on the sale of U.S. high-technology equipment to China, in exchange for the Chinese abiding by the international agreement restricting sale of missiles and missile technology.

23 In a front-page article titled "Opening Up to the World and Using Capitalism," *Renmin ribao* attacks the hard-line attitudes of the last two years and calls for bolder economic reforms.

25 Ten dissident activists, including a former *Renmin ribao* editor, Wu Xuecan, are convicted for opposing communist rule.

The U.S. Senate votes 59 to 39 to attach stringent conditions to renewal of MFN status, but fails to obtain the two-thirds majority necessary to override an expected presidential veto.

28 Zhang Zhongji of the State Statistical Bureau estimates a record budget deficit for 1991.

After years of official silence about Kuomintang troops gunning down protesters in Taiwan, a memorial service is held in Taipei to commemorate the 45th anniversary of the February 28, 1947, uprising against harsh KMT rule.

March 1992

2 President Bush vetoes legislation requiring China to improve human rights policies and curb exports of nuclear and missile technology if it wants renewal of MFN in July.

4 The U.N. Human Rights Commission in Geneva votes to take no action on a resolution censuring China for violating human rights in Tibet.

7 Acting hard-line minister of culture He Jingzhi is reported to have offered his resignation in a power struggle with senior leaders.

8 A government leader in the Xinjiang Autonomous Region announces a crackdown on subversive secessionist activities.

China and Vietnam sign four agreements for direct rail, air, postal, and shipping links.

10 Major newspapers nationwide announce plans to reform the civil service by 1995 and to reinvigorate economic reforms.

11 The U.S. House of Representatives votes 357 to 61 to override President Bush's veto of conditional renewal of MFN.

12 A CCP Politburo meeting endorses aggressive liberalization of the economy and calls for 100 years of market-oriented reforms. The call is headlined in every state newspaper and on government TV.

14 The English-language PRC newspaper, *China Daily*, quotes Personnel Minister Zhao Dongwan as saying the government will fight the brain drain with bonuses for scholars.

14–15 One hundred leading economic reformers launch an open attack on conservative attempts to roll back market reforms, in a forum sponsored by the progressive *Gaige* magazine.

16 Wang Renzhong, 75, former deputy premier, dies of a heart attack.

18 The government announces higher prices for rice, flour, corn, and other grains, moving a step closer to eliminating costly subsidies.

The U.S. Senate votes 60 to 38 in favor of overriding President Bush's veto of conditions attached to renewal of MFN, falling six votes short of the needed two-thirds majority.

19 Labor activist Han Dongfang reports that the government refuses to accept his application to hold a demonstration.

20 In a speech to the fourth session of the Seventh National People's Congress, Li Peng vows deepened economic reforms, but warns that political change that undermines CCP rule will not be tolerated.

The National Assembly convenes in Taiwan in a two-month session to reform the constitution of the Republic of China.

21 Guangdong Governor Zhu Senlin announces drastic price reforms for the province, including the eventual removal of grain subsidies.

PRC Finance Minister Wang Bingqian, in a speech to the National People's Congress, reveals a projected $3.8 billion budget deficit for 1992 and announces a 13.8 percent increase in the military budget.

24 Procurator-general Liu Fuzhi announces that Bao Tong, aide to ousted party general secretary Zhao Ziyang, will be tried on charges of leaking state secrets and "counterrevolutionary propaganda."

29 Dissident Wei Jingsheng completes his 13th year of a 15-year sentence for counterrevolutionary activities.

31 The Chinese media launch an offensive praising Deng Xiaoping's call for faster economic reforms, with lengthy comments on his January visit to Shenzhen.

April 1992

1 PRC urban residents begin paying the same price for their grain rations as the state pays to peasants, thus ending long-standing government subsidies.

3 The National People's Congress approves construction of the Three Gorges–Yangtze River dam.

The presidium of the NPC makes changes in the final version of Li Peng's state-of-nation report by adding a call to counter leftism.

The NPC adjourns.

7 The U.S. Department of State reports that two senators who had been outspoken about human rights in China have been denied visas to visit the PRC.

10 CCP leader Jiang Zemin ends a five-day visit to Japan during which he received only a few promises for financial assistance; the Japanese ignore his request that Emperor Akihito visit China in 1992.

14 Government spokesman Yuan Mu revives a call for combating "bourgeois liberalism," in a front-page *Renmin ribao* article.

20 The Democratic Progressive Party in Taiwan launches a three-day series of demonstrations to press for a constitutional amendment to provide for direct presidential elections.

22 Bao Tong is expelled from the CCP.

23 The world's largest McDonald's opens in Beijing.

Kang Keqing, 80, veteran of the Long March and widow of the military leader Zhu De, dies in Beijing.

24 Christopher Patten, former Conservative member of the British Parliament and close associate of Prime Minister John Major, is named governor of Hong Kong.

May 1992

1 Hard-liner Chen Yun backs reform, telling leaders in Shanghai "to accelerate the pace of reform and

opening to the outside world and [to] concentrate on developing the economy."

6 Arnold Kanter, U.S. undersecretary of state for political affairs, arrives in Beijing for talks on human rights, arms proliferation, and other bilateral issues.

14 Nie Rongzhen, 93, a major military figure of the communist revolution, dies.

15 Labor activist Han Dongfang reports being kicked and beaten with an electric prod by court officials who had summoned him to discuss a housing dispute.

17 Security agents search the office of *Washington Post* Beijing correspondent Lena Sun and seize files.

19 Beijing conducts underground nuclear testing, equivalent to one million tons of TNT, at Lop Nur in Xinjiang Province.

22 Deng Xiaoping tours the Capital Iron and Steel Corp. in Beijing, seeking to advance his efforts to shake up inefficient state-run industries.

25 Taiwan lifts the ban on student exchanges with China.

27 Dissident writer Wang Ruowang is told by Shanghai officials that he can apply for a passport to visit the United States.

28 China rejects U.N. sanctions on the Federal Republic of Yugoslavia.

30 Dissident Dai Qing is refused entry into China from Hong Kong after his visit to the United States.

June 1992

1 Xu Jiatun, the highest ranking CCP official to defect to the West, breaks a two-year silence and pub-

lishes a 10,000-word essay in Hong Kong, urging the Chinese Communist Party to abandon Marxism and defending the pro-democracy movement.

2 President Bush tells Congress that he will extend MFN for one more year.

3 Chinese police beat and detain foreign television reporters trying to cover the third anniversary of the Tiananmen crackdown. One protester is arrested in Tiananmen Square.

4 To mark the third anniversary of the Tiananmen massacre, 30,000 demonstrators hold vigil in Victoria Park in Hong Kong.

7 Dai Qing is allowed to return to Beijing.

13 *China Daily* reports that more than one million workers have been laid off thus far in 1992 as part of the government campaign to turn around money-losing factories.

14 One hundred liberal PRC scholars hold an unofficial forum to condemn the still powerful hard-liners.

17 China publishes a strict law banning all public demonstrations that do not have official permission.

18 The president of a U.S. oil company announces that China has signed a contract for oil exploration in the disputed South China Sea.

19 The U.S. Department of State confirms a draft agreement prohibiting Chinese prison-labor exports to the United States. U.S. officials are to be allowed to inspect prisons, camps, and companies employing prison laborers.

21 Li Xiannian, 82, former president of China, dies.

27 Pro-China forces in Hong Kong's Legislative Council defeat (25 to 23) a motion to add direct voting in the colony.

Ministry of Radio, Film, and Television approves domestic release of Oscar nominee *Raise the Red Lantern*.

29 China places a $1 billion order for 40 McDonnell-Douglas jets.

Glossary

Common Abbreviations

CAC: Central Advisory Commission
CCP: Chinese Communist Party
CMC: Central Military Commission
CPPCC: Chinese People's Political Consultative Congress
KMT: Kuomingtang
MFN: Most Favored Nation
NPC: National People's Congress
PLA: People's Liberation Army
PRC: People's Republic of China
PSB: Public Security Bureau
ROC: Republic of China
SEZ: Special Economic Zone
TVE: Township Village Enterprise

Boxer Rebellion. The anti-foreign populist movement that exploded in 1900 throughout much of northern China. The rebellion was a response to both internal and external crises facing China at the turn of the century, including the corruption and ineffectiveness of the Qing dynasty and the increasing encroachments of foreign powers on Chinese sovereignty. The movement was put down by an international military force, but only after great loss of life and destruction of property. The name "Boxer" derives from the fact that many of the adherents of the movement practiced martial arts that they believed would make them invulnerable.

Cadre. Any person in a position of official authority or responsibility in the PRC. Top-ranking officials are cadres, as are local grass-roots leaders. Not all cadres are party members, nor are all party members cadres. There are estimated to be 50–60 million cadres in China.

Central Advisory Commission (CAC). A commission of the CCP established in 1982 to serve as a consulting body to the Central

Committee. Members must have at least 40 years of service to the party. The CAC was designed to encourage party elders to retire from their active posts by offering them a position on a body with some prestige and privileges, but with little real power. In fact, the CAC has become quite influential in Chinese politics.

Central Committee. The organization that directs party affairs when the National Party Congress is not in session. However, the large size (about 300) and relatively infrequent meetings (one per year) of the full Central Committee mean that real power is vested in smaller top-level party organizations like the Politburo. The general secretary of the Central Committee is now considered to be the formal leader of the party since the abolition of the position of chairman in 1982.

Central Military Commission (CMC). There are, in theory, two separate Central Military Commissions, a state CMC and a party CMC. According to the PRC constitution, the state CMC commands the nation's armed forces and is responsible to the National People's Congress. In practice, the state CMC is firmly under CCP control. Although the precise relationship between the two CMCs is ambiguous, they have complete personnel and functional overlap.

Central Secretariat. The organization responsible for administering the day-to-day affairs of the CCP and for supervising government agencies to make certain that they are working in accordance with party policy.

Chen Yun (b. 1905). Chairman of the Central Advisory Commission. Active in the CCP since the 1920s, Chen was an architect of the PRC's First Five Year Plan (1953–57) and was influential in restoring order to the economy after the Great Leap Forward (1958–60). Although a close associate of Deng Xiaoping, he has been a critic of radical economic reform and political liberalization.

Chinese Communist Party (CCP). The ruling party of the People's Republic of China. The CCP was founded in 1921 and won national power in 1949 after defeating the Kuomintang in a civil war that lasted more than two decades. The party currently has about 50 million members.

Chinese People's Political Consultative Congress (CPPCC). Established by the CCP in September 1949, just prior to the founding of the PRC, as a mechanism for incorporating the views of other political parties and groups in the running of the new state. Until

1954, when its principal functions were taken over by the National People's Congress, the CPPCC was the PRC's highest legislative body—though always operating under party control. Since 1954 the CPPCC has been a forum for consultation between the CCP and minor noncommunist political parties, although it is principally used to generate support for CCP policies.

Ci Xi (1835–1908). China's "Empress Dowager," who exercised enormous power from behind the throne for much of the late 19th and early 20th centuries. She made her way from imperial concubine to the pinnacles of power through intrigue, conspiracy, and political skill. Among her most notorious acts was squandering the funds allocated for the modernization of China's navy on the reconstruction of the Summer Palace, including the building of a stationary marble boat on one of the palace's lakes. Her last act before her death was to engineer the accession of her three-year-old grand nephew to the recently vacated throne, where he served as China's "Last Emperor."

Cultural Revolution. A decade of political turmoil initiated by Mao Zedong in 1966 and terminated by the arrest of the Gang of Four in 1976. Mao launched the Cultural Revolution to stop what he considered to be China's drift away from socialism and towards capitalism. The first stage of the Cultural Revolution (1966–69) was marked by the radicalism of the Red Guards, millions of high school and university students who took it as their mission to purge China of all ideologically impure influences. The latter phases of the Cultural Revolution focused mostly on intense intraparty struggle between rival CCP leaders and factions.

Dalai Lama. The title of the spiritual and temporal leader of Tibetan Buddhism. The current Dalai Lama—the 14th in a line traced back to the 16th century—fled Tibet after the Chinese invasion in 1959. He lives in exile in India.

Deng Xiaoping (b. 1904). China's senior leader, who won international respect for introducing market-oriented reforms after the end of the Cultural Revolution. An old-time revolutionary, Deng was himself purged, first in 1966 and again in 1976, but returned to power in the 1980s. He retired in November 1989 from his last formal post as chairman of the party's Central Military Commission. However, Deng clearly remains China's most powerful leader, although his reputation and popularity have been severely tarnished by his role in the suppression of the 1989 democracy movement.

Dual-Track Pricing System. A mixed pricing system in which certain goods are sold at two different prices: one a fixed price set by the state, the other determined by the market. Also called the "two-tier" pricing system.

Forbidden City. The inner ring of the "northern capital" (Beijing), established by the third emperor of the Ming dynasty in the early 15th century. The walled city of about 250 acres contained audience halls and the palaces of the imperial family. Destroyed and rebuilt several times, the Forbidden City flourished under the Qing dynasty but was occupied and looted by armies from Japan and the West during the Boxer Rebellion. It is now a public park and museum complex. On the western perimeter of the Forbidden City is a complex of lakeside pavilions called Zhongnanhai that serves as the residential headquarters of the CCP leadership.

Four Cardinal Principles. Principles enunciated most fully by Deng Xiaoping in a major speech in 1979 that have become a cornerstone of CCP rule in the post-Mao era. The four principles are: keeping to the socialist road; upholding the dictatorship of the proletariat; upholding the leadership of the Communist Party; and upholding Marxism-Leninism-Mao Zedong Thought. These principles define the limits of the permissible in China; the party retains the right to suppress any opinion or opposition that it deems to have violated the "four cardinal principles."

Gang of Four. The ultra-left faction accused of exploiting power in the Cultural Revolution. In constant struggle with Deng Xiaoping and his reform-oriented supporters, the gang was arrested and purged after Mao's death in 1976. The four are Jiang Qing (Mao Zedong's widow), Wang Hongwen, Zhang Chunqiao, and Yao Wenyuan. In 1981 they were all sentenced to long prison terms. Jiang Qing committed suicide in May 1991; Wang Hongwen died of liver disease in August 1992.

Great Leap Forward. A utopian campaign, begun in 1958, to promote rapid economic development and to bring China from socialism into the more egalitarian stage of communism. The Great Leap was premised on a strategy of mass mobilization and ideological incentives that represented a profound break with the more conservative Soviet model of socialist development. By the time the Leap was halted in 1960, it had led to economic disaster for China and contributed to a famine that claimed millions of lives.

Hong Kong. A British colony that borders China's Guangdong Province. Britain initially gained control of parts of Hong Kong in the mid-19th century through treaties forced upon the Chinese in the aftermath of the Opium Wars. Part of Hong Kong (the New Territories) was leased by China to Britain in 1898 for 99 years. The anticipated expiration of that lease set in motion Sino-British negotiations that culminated in the agreement to return all of Hong Kong to Chinese sovereignty on July 1, 1997. After that time, Hong Kong will become a "Special Administrative Region" of the PRC.

Hua Guofeng (b. 1920). Rose to prominence in the cataclysmic power struggles of 1976. Hua emerged from relative political obscurity as a compromise choice for premier to replace Zhou Enlai, who died in January 1976. In October of that year (a month after Mao's death), he ordered the arrest of the radical Gang of Four. Shortly thereafter Hua was named chairman of the CCP, claiming that Mao had specifically designated him as his successor. In 1977 Hua allowed the political rehabilitation of Deng Xiaoping; over the next few years, Deng outmaneuvered Hua, and he was replaced as premier (by Zhao Ziyang) in 1980 and as party chairman (by Hu Yaobang) in 1981.

Hu Qili (b. 1929). CCP Politburo member from 1985 and Standing Committee member since the Thirteenth Party Congress in October 1987. He was in charge of party propaganda until 1989, when he was dismissed for showing sympathy toward the student democracy movement. Hu was rehabilitated and appointed to a vice-ministerial post in June 1991.

Hu Yaobang (1915–89). General secretary of the CCP from 1981 to 1987. He was forced to resign in the wake of widespread student demonstrations demanding greater democratic freedoms. However, Hu was able to retain his seat in the Politburo. His death on April 15 sparked the demonstrations that eventually led to the June 1989 crackdown.

Hundred Flowers Movement. In May 1956, with the slogan "Let a hundred flowers bloom, let a hundred schools of thought contend," Mao Zedong called on China's intellectuals to offer constructive criticism to the party. Mao felt that such criticism was necessary to shake up the party and overcome its growing tendency towards conservatism and bureaucratism. Mao and other party leaders were stung by the virulence of the criticism and launched the Anti-Rightist Campaign in mid-1957 in order to silence the critics.

Jiang Qing (1914–91). Wife of Mao Zedong from 1938 until his death in 1976. A stage and screen actress when she joined the CCP in 1933, Jiang met and married Mao in the communist base area of Yanan. She did not become politically active until the 1960s, when she emerged as one of the most radical leaders of the Cultural Revolution with a special interest in revolutionizing the arts. She was one of the Gang of Four arrested shortly after Mao's death. In 1981, Jiang was sentenced to life imprisonment for "counterrevolutionary crimes"; she committed suicide in 1991, reportedly while living under house arrest in a government villa.

Jiang Zemin (b. 1926). Former mayor and party secretary of Shanghai who replaced Zhao Ziyang as general secretary of the CCP in June 1989 in the aftermath of Tiananmen. In November 1989 he succeeded Deng Xiaoping as chairman of the party's Central Military Commission.

Kuomintang (Guomindang, Nationalist Party, KMT). The governing party in Taiwan. Organized in 1912 by Sun Yat-sen, the KMT became a major political force in China during the first half of the 20th century. In 1928 Chiang Kai-shek became chairman of the KMT and head of the ROC government in Nanjing, and he remained the leader throughout the civil war. In 1949 the KMT government on the mainland collapsed; Chiang and his followers retreated to Taiwan.

Lei Feng. A rank-and-file PLA soldier whose diary, found after his death in 1962, displayed qualities of loyalty and self-sacrifice. During the 1960s and again in the aftermath of Tiananmen, Lei Feng was held up as a model of the true "communist spirit" to be emulated by the army and the nation.

Li Peng (b. 1928). China's premier and member of the Standing Committee of the CCP's Politburo. Li became premier in 1988, succeeding Zhao Ziyang. He is a hydroelectric engineer by training and studied at the Moscow Power Institute in the 1950s. Considered to be among China's most conservative leaders, Li played a major role in the suppression of the Tiananmen democracy movement.

Li Ruihuan (b. 1934). Former carpenter and mayor of Tianjin, now a member of the Standing Committee of the Politburo. He is considered a moderate in the Chinese political spectrum.

Li Xiannian (1909–92). Former president of the PRC and high-ranking CCP official, Li was, in his last years, one of China's most conservative leaders. He was a veteran revolutionary who joined the CCP in 1927, participated in the epic Long March, and occupied many important positions after the founding of the PRC, including those of vice-premier and minister of finance. His last active position was as chairman of the Chinese People's Political Consultative Congress.

Mao Zedong (1893–1976). Paramount leader of the Chinese Communist Party for nearly four decades until his death in September 1976. Mao led the CCP to victory against the Kuomintang in the Chinese civil war that culminated in the founding of the PRC in October 1949. In addition to his position as chairman of the CCP (which he held until his death), Mao also served as president of the PRC from 1949 until 1959.

Most-favored nation (MFN). An agreement in which two countries promise to extend to each other the same trading terms that either of them grants to any other countries: that is, each nation that is party to the agreement will be treated in the same way as the nation "most favored" by the other party. The United States extended MFN status to China in 1980, which had the effect of greatly reducing the tariffs imposed on Chinese goods exported to the U.S. (especially textiles). In the aftermath of Tiananmen, the U.S. Congress and President George Bush have become locked in an annual battle over whether China's MFN status should be renewed; many members of Congress believe that human rights abuses by the PRC warrant revocation, while the president argues that change in China is best promoted by maintaining trade and other kinds of Sino-American interchange. As of 1992, the president has prevailed in each of these battles.

National People's Congress (NPC). The supreme state legislative body in the PRC. The NPC consists of 2,700 delegates nominated by senior party leaders and elected for five-year terms by local people's congresses. It elects the president and vice-president of the PRC, the State Council, Central Military Commission, and Supreme People's Court. The NPC is firmly under CCP control and therefore serves largely as a "rubber stamp" for party decisions.

1911 Revolution. The revolution that overthrew the Qing dynasty and ended the Chinese imperial system. Beginning as a series of localized mutinies against the Qing dynasty, the revolt snowballed and culminated in the founding of the Republic of China on January 1, 1912, and the abdication of the emperor the following February. The anniversary of the revolution is celebrated each year on October 10th ("Double Ten"), which commemorates the date of the uprising at Wuchang in 1911 that sparked the rebellion.

Open policy. A development strategy adopted in 1978 by the Chinese government based on active participation in the world market. Under this policy, the government has sought to increase technology transfer and foreign direct investment, become more active in international organizations, and encourage study and training abroad.

Party congress. In theory, the supreme authority in the Chinese Communist Party. But according to the party constitution, the National Party Congress is—under normal circumstances—held only once every five years and attended by more than 1,500 delegates. Thus its actual functions are largely limited to ratifying decisions taken by more elite party organizations and listening to reports by top party leaders. The 1st Party Congress marked the party's formal founding in 1921. The 13th Party Congress met in October–November 1987. The 14th Party Congress is scheduled to meet in October 1992.

People's Daily (Renmin ribao). The official newspaper of the Central Committee of the Chinese Communist Party. It is distributed nationally and has a circulation of over 5 million. Articles in the *People's Daily* reflect official party policy, and editorials and commentaries are often used to publicize authoritative pronouncements of the party leadership.

People's Liberation Army (PLA). The armed forces of the People's Republic of China, including the army, the navy, and the air force. The size of the PLA is estimated to be over 3,000,000, not including reserves.

People's Republic of China (PRC). Founded by the CCP under the leadership of Mao Zedong on October 1, 1949, following the communist victory over the Kuomintang in the Chinese civil war.

Politburo. Elected by the Central Committee, the Politburo (or Political Bureau) handles the daily running of the CCP and makes the party's major policy decisions. Greatest power resides in its six-member Standing Committee.

Procuracy. The nationwide system of state organizations charged with overseeing the administration of justice in the Chinese legal system. The procuracy has a wide range of functions, including investigating criminal cases, issuing indictments, and serving in the courts as both public prosecutor and public defender. It also acts as a legal check on bureaucratic corruption and police abuse. It is guaranteed independence from outside interference in the PRC constitution, but, like all state organs, is ultimately under the control of the CCP.

Public Security Bureau (PSB). The principal law enforcement organization of the PRC. The PSB is a national police agency with branches throughout China. It is responsible for the maintenance of law and order, the investigation of crimes, and the surveillance of Chinese citizens and foreigners in the PRC suspected of being threats to state security. It maintains its own system of labor reform camps.

Qiao Shi (b. 1924). Member of the Politburo Standing Committee since 1987. He has been a full member of the Central Committee since 1985 and was appointed vice-premier of the State Council in 1986. In this capacity he oversaw the Departments of Public and State Security, Justice, and Civil Affairs. Qiao has a history of work in security matters and rarely lets his political views be known.

Renminbi (Rmb). Literally, "people's currency." The standard monetary unit in the PRC. Also called "yuan." In mid-1992, one U.S. dollar was worth approximately Rmb 5.4.

Renmin ribao. *See* People's Daily.

Republic of China (ROC). The government established by Sun Yatsen in 1912 after the overthrow of the Qing dynasty and the imperial system. The government of the ROC and its ruling party, the Kuomintang, moved to Taiwan in 1949 following the communist victory in the Chinese civil war. The ROC was recognized as the official government of China by the United States until January 1, 1979, when diplomatic recognition was switched to the PRC.

Special Economic Zones (SEZs). Areas designated by the PRC government to attract foreign capital by offering overseas investors a variety of economic incentives, including reduced tariffs, tax breaks, modern facilities, and flexible labor policies. The largest of China's five SEZs is Shenzhen, which borders Hong Kong. The bold experimentation with market reforms and related social problems in the SEZs is often a target of criticism by hard-line party leaders. The spread of "open development zones"—smaller-scale variations of the SEZ model—in many areas of China in the early 1990s was part of Deng Xiaoping's strategy to revitalize economic reform in the PRC.

State Council. The executive arm of the PRC government, headed by the premier and composed of numerous ministries, commissions, and subordinate organizations.

Tiananmen. Literally "Gate of Heavenly Peace," it forms the principal entry to the imperial palace (the Forbidden City) that was home to China's emperors for more than five centuries before the fall of the imperial system in 1911. Tiananmen Square, to the south of the palace, is the largest (100 acres) public square in the world. Mao Zedong declared the founding of the People's Republic on October 1, 1949, from a rostrum on the gate. During the Cultural Revolution, millions of Red Guards gathered in the square to be greeted by Chairman Mao. In 1976 it was the site of mass protests against the radical Gang of Four and the huge memorial meeting held after Mao's death. In the spring of 1989 the square was the focal point for pro-democracy demonstrations that culminated in the bloody repression of June 4–5.

Township and Village Enterprises (TVEs). Nonagricultural businesses owned and run at the township and village levels that are outside the realm of central planning and operate largely according to market forces.

Wang Zhen (b. 1909). Vice-president of the PRC. A career military officer, Wang is among China's most hard-line leaders.

Xinhua (New China News Agency). The PRC's official domestic and international news agency.

Yang Baibing (b. 1920). Director of the General Political Department of the People's Liberation Army and secretary general of the party's Central Military Commission. Yang Baibing is President Yang Shangkun's younger half-brother. He gained considerable influence after the Tiananmen massacre and has been in charge of carrying out political campaigns within the PLA.

Yang Shangkun (b. 1907). President of the PRC, first vice-chairman of the party's Central Military Commission, and member of the CCP Politburo. A professional military man, Yang has devoted much time to reform of the armed forces and the modernization of China's national defense. Among China's most conservative leaders, he strongly supported the suppression of the 1989 democracy movement. However, he endorsed Deng Xiaoping's call for renewed economic reform in 1992.

Yao Yilin (b. 1917). Member of the Standing Committee of the Politburo and a vice-premier of the PRC. Regarded as a competent technocrat and economist, Yao is credited with having implemented a number of significant economic reforms aimed at increasing efficiency of individual enterprises and stimulating new technological development. However, he is still considered to favor central planning.

Zhao Ziyang (b. 1919). Premier of the State Council from 1980 until his appointment in 1987 as general secretary of the CCP. A trusted colleague and protégé of Deng Xiaoping, Zhao built a reputation at home and abroad as a capable technocratic leader and a chief architect of the post-Mao reform program. He fell from power during the pro-democracy demonstrations in the spring of 1989 for being too sympathetic to the students and opposing the use of force to suppress the protests.

Zhou Enlai (1898–1976). One of the most important figures in the history of the CCP and the PRC. Zhou was premier of the PRC from 1949 until his death in January 1976. For a number of years he also served concurrently as foreign minister and became China's best-known diplomat. In his later years, he became a fierce opponent of the radical Gang of Four and a strong supporter of Deng Xiaoping and his plans for modernizing China.

Zhu Rongji (b. 1928). A vice-premier of the PRC. A former mayor of Shanghai who has been given great credit for presiding over that city's economic revitalization, Zhu was promoted to vice-premier in April 1991. He is an ally of Deng Xiaoping and a strong proponent of economic reform. Zhu is widely considered to be a leading candidate to succeed Li Peng as premier.

Suggestions for Further Reading

Peaceful Evolution with Chinese Characteristics

Amnesty International. *China: Punishment without Crime: Administrative Detention* (London: Amnesty International, 1991).

Bachman, David. *The Fourteenth Congress of the Chinese Communist Party* (New York: The Asia Society, 1992).

Baum, Richard, ed. *Reform and Reaction in Post-Mao China: The Road to Tiananmen* (New York: Routledge, 1991).

Goodman, David S. G., and Gerald Segal, eds. *China in the Nineties: Crisis Management and Beyond* (Oxford: Clarendon Press, 1991).

Saich, Tony. "The Reform Decade in China: The Limits to Revolution from Above," in *The Reform Decade in China: From Hope to Dismay*, ed. Marta Dassu and Tony Saich (London: Kegan Paul International, 1992).

Wasserstrom, Jeffrey N., and Elizabeth J. Perry, eds. *Popular Protest and Political Culture in Modern China: Learning from 1989* (Boulder: Westview Press, 1992).

The Chinese Economy: Moving Forward

Byrd, William. *The Market Mechanism and Economic Reforms in China* (Armonk, NY: M. E. Sharpe, 1991).

Chen, Kang, G. H. Jefferson, and I. J. Singh. "Lessons from China's Economic Reform," *Journal of Comparative Economics*, Vol. 16 (1992), pp. 201–25.

McMillan, John, and Barry Naughton. "How to Reform a Planned Economy: Lessons from China," *Oxford Review of Economic Policy*, Vol. 8, no. 1 (Spring 1992).

Putterman, Louis, ed. "Symposium: Institutional Boundaries, Structural Change, and Economic Reform in China" (Part 1), *Modern China*, Vol. 18, no. 1 (January 1992).

U.S. Congress, Joint Economic Committee. *China's Economic Dilemmas in the 1990s: The Problems of Reform, Modernization, Independence*, Vol. 1 (Washington, D.C.: U.S. Government Printing Office, 1991), pp. 234–51.

China and the New World Order

China Quarterly, no. 124 (December 1990). Special issue entitled "China and Japan: History, Trends, Prospects."

Garver, John W. *Foreign Relations of the People's Republic of China* (New York: Prentice Hall, forthcoming).

Harding, Harry. *A Fragile Relationship: The United States and China since 1972* (Washington, D.C.: Brookings Institution, 1992).

Macchiarola, Frank J., and Robert B. Oxnam, eds. *The China Challenge: American Policies in East Asia* (New York: Academy of Political Science and The Asia Society, 1991).

Ross, Robert S. "National Security, Human Rights, and Domestic Politics: The Bush Administration and China," in *Eagle in a New World, American Grand Strategy in the Post–Cold War Era*, ed. Kenneth A. Oye, Robert J. Lieber, and Donald Rothchild (New York: Harper Collins, 1992), pp. 233–313.

U.S.-Japan Policy Dialogue on China: Political Issues (New York: The Asia Society and Japan Institute of International Affairs, 1992).

Whiting, Allen S., ed. *The Annals of the American Academy of Political and Social Science*, Vol. 519 (January 1992). Special issue entitled "China's Foreign Relations."

Courts, Justice, and Human Rights

Alford, William. "Building a Goddess of Democracy from Loose Sand: Observations on Human Rights in China," in *Cross Cultural Perspectives on Human Rights*, ed. A. An-Naiem (Philadelphia: University of Pennsylvania Press, 1992).

Cohen, Jerome. "Tiananmen and the Rule of Law," in *The Broken Mirror: China After Tiananmen Square*, ed. George Hicks (Chicago: St. James Press, 1990).

Edwards, R. Randle, Louis Henkel, and Andrew Nathan. *Human Rights in Contemporary China* (New York: Columbia University Press, 1986).

Lee, Wei-chin. "Heaven Can Wait? Rethinking the Chinese Notion of Human Rights," *Asian Thought and Society*, Vol. 16, no. 46 (January–April 1991), p. 28.

Leng, Shao-chuan, and Hungdah Chiu. *Criminal Justice in Post-Mao China* (Albany: State University of New York Press, 1985).

Sypnowich, Christine. *The Concept of Socialist Law* (Oxford: Clarendon Press, 1990).

Public Health in China

Banister, Judith. *China's Changing Population* (Stanford: Stanford University Press, 1987).

Henderson, Gail. "Increased Inequality in Health Care," in *Chinese Society on the Eve of Tiananmen: The Impact of Reform*, ed. Deborah Davis and Ezra Vogel (Cambridge and London: Council on East Asian Studies, Harvard University, 1990).

Hsiao, William C. "Transformation of Health Care in China," *New England Journal of Medicine* Vol. 310 (1984), pp. 932–35.

Jamison, Dean, et al. *China: The Health Sector* (Washington, D.C.: World Bank, 1984).

Chinese Cinema Enters the 1990s

Berry, Chris, ed. *Perspectives on Chinese Cinema* (London: British Film Institute, 1991).

Clark, Paul. *Chinese Cinema: Culture and Politics since 1949* (New York: Cambridge University Press, 1988).

Kaige, Chen, and Tony Rayns. *King of the Children and the New Chinese Cinema* (London: Faber & Faber, 1989).

McDougall, Bonnie S. *The Yellow Earth: A Film by Chen Kaige* (Hong Kong: Chinese University Press, 1991).

About the Contributors

Paul Clark is Research Associate at the Institute of Culture and Communication of the East-West Center in Honolulu, where he also leads an international research effort on youth popular culture in the Asia-Pacific region. He is the author of books on Chinese cinema and New Zealand Maori history. Dr. Clark is currently completing a book-length study of China's fifth-generation filmmakers.

John W. Garver teaches in the School of International Affairs of the Georgia Institute of Technology. He is the author of *China's Decision for Rapprochement with the United States, 1968–1971* (1982) and *Chinese-Soviet Relations, 1937–1945: The Diplomacy of Chinese Nationalism* (1988). His most recent book, *Foreign Relations of the People's Republic of China,* will be published in 1993. Professor Garver is currently working on studies of the U.S.-Nationalist alliance and the geopolitics of Sino-Indian relations.

Nancy R. Hearst is Librarian at the Fairbank Center for East Asian Research, Harvard University, and Associate Editor of the *CCP Research Newsletter.*

Gail Henderson is on the faculty of the Department of Social Medicine at the University of North Carolina School of Medicine. She received her Ph.D. in sociology from the University of Michigan, where she later held a Mellon postdoctoral fellowship in public health. She is the author (with M. S. Cohen) of *The Chinese Hospital: A Socialist Work Unit* (1984) and of a number of articles addressing issues in the modernization of medicine in China. Professor Henderson is currently involved in several research projects in China, including a study of health, nutrition, and economic change, in collaboration with the Chinese Academy of Preventive Medicine.

Gary H. Jefferson is Associate Professor of Economics at Brandeis University and Research Coordinator for the World Bank Project for

Industrial Reforms and Productivity in Chinese Enterprises. He has collaborated with various Chinese research and policy institutes and has published numerous articles on the impact of China's industrial reform program on the conduct and performance of Chinese enterprises. Professor Jefferson is currently preparing a book on Chinese enterprise reform.

William A. Joseph is Associate Professor of Political Science at Wellesley College, where he has also served as codirector of the Chinese Studies program, and Associate in Research at the Fairbank Center for East Asian Research at Harvard University. He is the author of *The Critique of Ultra-Leftism in China, 1958–1981* (1984) and coeditor of *New Perspectives on the Cultural Revolution* (1991).

Tony Saich is Professor of Contemporary Chinese Politics and Administration at the Sinologisch Instituut, Leiden University, and Senior Research Fellow at the International Institute of National History, Amsterdam. He has published widely on politics in contemporary China and the history of the Chinese Communist Party. His most recent publication is *The Reform Decade in China: From Hope to Dismay* (1992), and he has just finished work (with David E. Apter) on a monograph entitled *Discourse and Power: The Revolutionary Process in Mao's Republic*. He is currently the International Studies and Overseas Program Visiting Fellow at the University of California at Los Angeles.

Margaret Y. K. Woo is Associate Professor at Northeastern University School of Law and Associate in Research at the Fairbank Center for East Asian Research at Harvard University. She also holds a visiting professorship at the South Central Institute of Politics and Law in the People's Republic of China. Her published work includes articles on Chinese legal institutions and criminal procedure. In 1990 she was a Fellow at the Bunting Institute of Radcliffe College, where she conducted comparative research on issues affecting women and work in the United States. Professor Woo's current research focuses on the concept of "legal culture" in the Chinese legal system.

About the Book

With the dissolution of the Soviet Union, international attention has focused on China as the only remaining communist giant. This latest volume in the China Briefing series explores the external and internal forces now shaping the country, with essays by prominent scholars tracing political, economic, military, social, and cultural trends in the People's Republic of China.

Index